BACK TO SCHOOL
A COLLEGE GUIDE FOR ADULTS
by DR. LaVERNE L. LUDDEN

Park Avenue

An imprint of JIST Works, Inc.

Back to School
A College Guide for Adults
© 1996 by LaVerne L. Ludden

Published by Park Avenue Productions
An imprint of JIST Works, Inc.
720 N. Park Avenue
Indianapolis, IN 46202-3431
Phone: **317-264-3720** Fax: **317-264-3709** E-mail: JISTWorks@AOL.com

Cover Design by Bill Anderson

Ludden, LaVerne, 1949-
    Back to school : a college guide for adults / by LaVerne L. Ludden.
        p.   cm.
    ISBN 1-57112-070-X
    1. Adult education—United States. 2. Continuing education—United States.
    3. College student orientation—United States. 4. Student aid—United States.
    I. Title.
    LC5251.L84   1996
    374' .973—dc20   95-48391
                                                                        CIP

Printed in the United States of America

99 98 97 96   5 4 3 2 1

We have been careful to provide accurate information throughout this book, but it is possible that errors and omissions have been introduced. Please consider this in making any career plans or other important decisions. Trust your own judgment above all else and in all things.

ISBN: 1-57112-070-X

Dedication

This book is dedicated to my father, Richard Ludden, who started work on a bachelor's degree at 27 and completed a Master of Divinity degree when he was 43. His example inspired my own educational endeavors. The book is dedicated also to my mother, Bonnie, who made it possible for my father to pursue his dream.

Acknowledgments

Several people have made significant contributions to this book. I gratefully acknowledge their assistance and thank them for their time and efforts.

Marsha Ludden, my wife, has been a major collaborator on the book. She helped research many topics and, more importantly, wrote significant portions of Chapters 4, 5, 7, and 8. Without her contributions, this book would not have been finished on time and would not have been so complete. Marsha's perspective and experience as an educator and author added significantly to the quality of the book. Her assistance is even more amazing and appreciated because she accomplished this while completing a book of her own.

Linda Fitzhugh is Assistant Dean for Graduate and Adult Studies at LeTourneau University in Longview, Texas. One of her responsibilities is to manage the assessment of prior learning experience for the LeTourneau Education for Adults Program (LEAP). Linda is an expert in evaluating transfer credits, credits by exam, and learning portfolios. This made her a valuable resource in reviewing and critiquing Chapter 4, "Speeding Up The Process." Her cheerful, helpful suggestions made the chapter much better and assured me that the advice given was accurate. I also appreciate the time she took with me as a colleague to teach me most of what I know about these subjects, and I value her friendship.

Kent McGowen is Director of Financial Aid at Colorado Christian University. Prior to that he managed the financial aid program for adult students at LeTourneau University. Kent has assisted thousands of adult students in planning their financial aid programs for college. Because of his expertise, it was only natural for me to ask him to review Chapter 5, "Getting Over the Financial Hurdle." He made many critical changes that reflected his knowledge and expertise regarding the ever-changing financial aid regulations. Without his advice, the chapter would not have been complete. I'd also like to thank Kent for the hours he spent with me at LeTourneau University explaining the fine points of financial aid issues related to adult students. He is a true professional and a good friend.

The many case studies that appear throughout the book were compiled from studies submitted by students in the graduate adult education program at Ball State University. During the past year, these students were in two courses on Adult Learning that I taught and were kind enough to include interviews with college students as a part of their course work. The only enticement I offered was an inclusion in the acknowledgment section of this book. So here is their reward: Thanks to Joan Anderson, Jim Baily, Robert Becker, Robert Bennett, Juanita Brand, Wanda Braun, Donald Brown, Jennifer Caruso, Pete Formica, Karen Miller Ferris, Denise Haggerty, Peggy Hanes, Rose Hauser, Marsha Hearn-Lindsey, Lana Kocher, Mary Krull, Roseann Landolfi, L'Jean McCaleb, Elizabeth Maxey, Richard Moser, Stephen Morrow, Kelli Overmyer, Drew Peterson, Sandra Pickard, Patrick Reiter, and Patricia Ryan. The insights and written case studies these individuals provided from interviews with more than 100 adult learners furnished a strong pool from which to choose the case studies included in this book.

Finally, thanks to our sons, Chris, Matt, and Tim, who worked hard to send out surveys to colleges. In addition, Chris and Matt did the data entry to compile the information collected from the colleges. Their efforts truly made this book a family effort.

Contents

Chapter 3 College Education—The New and the Old

Chapter 4 Speeding Up the Process 97

Chapter 5 Getting Over the Financial Hurdle

Chapter 6 Selecting the Right College

Chapter 7 Making It Work for You

Chapter 8 Succeeding in College

College and University Guide

Introduction

College and university campuses look different today than they did 30 years ago, and the feature that has changed the most is the student body. As you walk through most campuses, you will see a large number of adult students. In fact, it is difficult to distinguish many students from faculty and staff. Higher education has traditionally served college students who go directly from high school to college, are under 22 years of age, attend classes full-time, and reside on campus.

Many students attending college now do not fit this traditional pattern. The following statistics demonstrate how much the student body of most campuses has changed. These are national statistics based on information from the Census Bureau and the Department of Education, covering the years 1990-1994.

- Forty percent of all college students are over 25 years old.

- Sixty-eight percent of full-time graduate students and 90 percent of part-time graduate students are 25 and older. Even more dramatic is the fact that 17 percent of graduate students are 40 and older.

- The average age of students at many colleges and universities is near 30 years.

- Over 70 percent of all part-time students are 25 and older.

- It is projected that sometime during the 1990s, over 50 percent of all college students will be 25 or older.

- Only 20 percent of all college students finish a degree in four years, and about 50 percent finish within six years.

- The percentage of part-time students continues to increase and is expected to stand at 50 percent by the end of the 1990s.

- Approximately 80 percent of college students are commuters.

As we enter the 21st Century, experts predict that only 16 percent of college students will fit the pattern of traditional students. The majority of students at most institutions of higher education will be working adults who attend college part-time.

This book is written for those working adults who are considering returning to school to get a college degree—associate, bachelor's, master's, or doctor's. Many people have not achieved their career goals and recognize that a college degree can provide a powerful tool to help them reach these goals. Many organizations no longer promote employees to supervisory and management positions unless they have college degrees. In cases of corporate downsizing, supervisory and management personnel without college degrees are frequently the first to lose their jobs. Many studies show that the more education a person completes, the more earning potential increases and unemployment decreases. This knowledge encourages people to obtain a degree or a higher-level degree than they currently possess.

Other individuals feel a need to reach a college goal in order to fulfill a void that exists in their life. In their new book *Going To Plan B* (Simon & Schuster, 1996), Nancy K. Schlossberg and Susan P. Robinson present a concept called *the nonevent*. People often experience nonevents in their lives. These nonevents are unfulfilled dreams and goals that leave psychological gaps in a person's life. For many adults, the unfulfilled goal of getting a college degree is such a nonevent. In fact, the failure to get a degree may be a disappointment to parents and others, which in turn creates feelings of guilt in the individual.

The fact that you're reading this book indicates you have an interest in returning to college. *Back to School: A College Guide for Adults* is a valuable resource if you're thinking about getting a college degree. It provides information you can use in making this important career decision and getting started in college. It also contains a valuable guide to 240 colleges and universities that offer degree programs designed to meet the needs of working adults.

The first section of the book contains useful information and advice about getting a college degree. Chapter 1 examines doubts that are common to adults contemplating a return to school. It helps readers identify doubts that might restrain them from going to college and demonstrates how these doubts can be overcome.

Chapter 2 explains how the decision to get a college degree relates to your career. A career model is presented and guides you in making important decisions about your career goals. Worksheets help you identify values, skills, and needs related to achieving that goal. This chapter also shows you how to relate your career needs with the choice of a college.

In Chapter 3, you will learn about concepts and terms that are important in understanding how colleges are organized and run. Accreditation, degrees, and majors are explored. The traditional process for earning a college degree is described. The most important items in this chapter are the descriptions of nontraditional college degree programs that open up possibilities you may not realize exist for completing a college degree.

For many adults, the thought of getting a degree is quickly dismissed when they think about the length of time it takes to complete the task. Chapter 4 explains several strategies for shortening the time required to complete a degree. These include credit through exams, transfer of previously earned college credits, military and corporate training, and prior learning assessment. The process of getting credit for life and work experience is explained.

Financial issues are examined in Chapter 5. You will discover how to get scholarships, loans, and grants. This chapter also explores the option of using employer assistance to finance a degree program. Other options are described that can be used by most adults to finance a college education.

Choosing a college is an important step in the process of getting a degree. Chapter 6 examines the issues you need to consider when selecting a college. The chapter also explains how to evaluate a college and make sure it matches your personal needs. A worksheet for comparing the most relevant features of colleges—based on the needs of adult students—is included.

A smooth adjustment to college can make the difference between success and failure in earning a degree. Chapter 7 reviews the many changes that occur when you begin studying for a college degree. It presents tips and advice that can be used to adjust successfully to the many changes that occur with your family, work, and social activities.

Your ability to succeed at college can be enhanced if you use effective strategies for studying and fulfilling course assignments. Chapter 8 provides tips and techniques for completing college course work. This chapter helps prepare readers to meet the expectations of instructors, perform well in the classroom, prepare assignments, and work effectively with classmates.

Two useful resources are included throughout the first section of the book. In each chapter, there is a description of a college and the degree programs it offers adult students. These colleges were selected in an effort to provide readers with an understanding of the many innovative degree programs available for adult students. Several of the colleges offer degrees that can be obtained by students regardless of where they live and work. The following icon marks each of these descriptions.

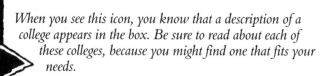

When you see this icon, you know that a description of a college appears in the box. Be sure to read about each of these colleges, because you might find one that fits your needs.

The second resource that appears throughout the first section are case studies of adult college students. There are two case studies in each chapter. One reason for including these is to demonstrate how other adults, with situations and issues common to many readers, have successfully returned to school—providing encouragement and inspiration. Another is to illustrate practical strategies used by adult students to complete a degree program. The following icon signals each of these case studies.

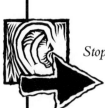

*Stop and read the case studies with this icon. Look for
similarities between yourself and the students described.*

Section 2, the Appendix, is a valuable and unique resource. It
contains a guide to 240 colleges and universities. These institutions
offer a total of almost 1,000 degree programs that have been designed
for adult students. There are colleges with classrooms located in 47
states. However, in this modern age of technology, location is often
irrelevant. You can earn degrees through televised classes or online
classes accessed by computers. Innovative programs deliver courses
through guided study from experts in your community, video tapes,
audio tapes, and correspondence courses. Adults anywhere in the
United States have dozens of colleges and universities to choose from
when they decide to pursue a degree. This directory is one of the most
comprehensive listings of accredited colleges that offer degree programs for adult students.

Pursuing your degree as an adult is an exciting but difficult
adventure, and success is far from assured. You can increase the probability of success by reading this book and applying the advice that it
provides. Good luck in your pursuit of an education and a more
fulfilled life!

Chapter 1

The Overwhelming Obstacle

You're thinking about going to college, but you have some doubts. It may be several years since you attended school, and you're not sure you can study, take tests, write papers, learn a foreign language, or remember enough math to complete a college course—let alone a degree. Maybe you didn't get good grades when you were in high school. Or maybe you went to college before and didn't do well, and you're afraid you won't be successful this time. You might feel better knowing that most adults contemplating a return to school have similar concerns. However, thousands of adults have earned college degrees, and you can too. This chapter explores some of the typical doubts adults have about returning to school and offers advice on how to resolve them. You may find yourself confronting one or more of these doubts—in which case this chapter should be quite useful—but even if you don't, you can get a good overview of the challenges that college presents and identify strategies to overcome them.

Doubt 1 — College isn't for adults.

Our high school system does a good job of preparing most students for college. Part of this preparation includes building a mindset that says you should begin college as soon as you complete high school. However, this strategy isn't successful for all high school graduates. Many recent high school graduates aren't mature enough to live on their own, and they may lack the discipline for greater self-direction and more independence required for college. Sometimes younger students find that social distractions keep them from concentrating on their academic work. Another challenge faced by younger students is an inability to apply what they learn to real-life situations. As a result, their learning is more theoretical than practical, making it difficult to successfully adapt to their first professional job. These are just a few of the difficulties younger college students experience, but they illustrate that it can be difficult for younger students to succeed at college. Most adults have a different set of concerns as they contemplate attending college. As we explore these concerns, you will discover that they aren't any more insurmountable than those faced by traditional students.

As people age, they are more likely to believe that they can't learn. But research shows this isn't true. Adults lose little of their ability to learn—or what some people call intelligence—as they age. In fact, some experts believe that adults simply use a different approach to learning. There appears to be some loss in an adult's ability to perform rote memorization and take timed tests. But this is balanced by an increase in judgment and application of knowledge. Most college instructors aren't interested in testing rote memorization, so adults don't need to fear this aspect of college.

Adults are problem-centered and attempt to apply what they have learned to their work, hobbies, leisure, family relationships, and other aspects of their lives. This focus of adult learners is different from that of younger students and often results in more successful learning experiences. Adults are more independent in their learning, a characteristic that is needed for the successful completion of college courses. Adults are also more practical about learning at college. They are paying the expenses and therefore expect more from themselves and from their professors. In fact, a survey of college professors and students found that adult students are perceived as more capable, confident, serious, and focused than traditional students. Basically, adult college students can expect to perform as well as or better than they might have done—or than they did—as traditional students.

Another reservation adults have about attending college is that they will be out of place. The statistics in the Introduction of this book should dispel this concern. The growth in enrollment of adult students will increase by 16 percent during the 1990s. By the end of this decade, 50 percent or more of all students will be over 25, and much of this growth will come from students who are 35 and older. These statistics reflect enrollment for adults at both the undergraduate and graduate levels. Participation by adult students is even greater when you consider continuing education activities. There are adults of all ages attending most colleges and universities. You will find many other adults in the college classes you attend. This news should be encouraging to adults for two reasons. One is that you can develop social relationships with these students that will provide support, encouragement, and assistance in your college endeavors. Another positive aspect of attending classes with adults is that a higher level of maturity and wisdom influences class discussions.

An interesting story from the University of Louisville illustrates how well adult students are now accepted on university campuses. The university has almost 22,000 students, about 60 percent of them over 22. In an effort to bolster school spirit among adult students and respect for nontraditional students, Mona Cohn, age 45, decided to run for homecoming queen in 1994. Ms. Cohn is studying justice administration and hopes to attend law school after completing her bachelor's degree. She was elected homecoming queen, and she is representative of the women over 35 who make up 16 percent of all female college students.

Adults sometimes are reluctant to attend college because colleges have been structured to accommodate the needs of traditional students. Typically classes have been offered during the day, when most adults are working. Administrative offices usually are open during these same hours, making it difficult for adults to use their services. The curriculum was designed without any thought to work and life experiences adults bring to the classroom. These factors are changing on many campuses.

There are now degree programs at many private and public colleges and universities designed to meet the needs of adult students. Courses can be taken on evenings and weekends. Classes for adults are held at convenient locations, including malls, churches, and even the workplace. Students can take courses by correspondence, video, television, and computer. They can register by mail, phone, or fax and pay for tuition by check or charge card. These changes often make it unnecessary for adult students to leave work or home responsibilities to attend courses on campus. Many campus bookstores have expanded their hours so that they are open in the evenings and on weekends. All of these changes have made it much easier for adults to attend college.

Some colleges and universities have even established offices to assist adult students with their college experience. This assistance may be geared toward women returning to college because of transitional points in their lives, such as divorce or children leaving home. Other campuses have established offices to help adult students who have experienced job loss or who are attempting to achieve independence from government-financed programs like welfare. At many colleges today, you will find administrators and faculty who understand the needs of adults and can provide guidance and address the problems and concerns of adult students.

The greatest fear many adults have about enrolling in a degree program is having to meet math and language requirements. Most adults have not had to use algebra or geometry for years, and have forgotten most of what they learned in high school. For many adults this fear is compounded because they struggled to get good grades in math during high school. Foreign language requirements create similar fears. Many adults are reluctant to take foreign language courses because of the rote memorization required to learn a new vocabulary. In addition, many adults returning to college did not take a foreign language in high school.

Many colleges and universities are aware of the concerns adult students have about these courses—actually these courses are also dreaded by many traditional students—and have made changes to help students, including providing remedial math courses in preparation for collage algebra. Some schools provide free tutoring for students taking math courses. And there are many majors that require only one or two courses in college-level math.

If you are concerned about taking a foreign language, it is possible to identify majors that don't require learning one. However, with the growth of the global economy, you may find that mastering a foreign language can be valuable to your career. Many corporations are promoting foreign language skills in their employees to help them better understand customers from other countries.

As you've discovered, a college education today is definitely for adults. Adults of all ages have an ability to learn and may perform better than younger students in course work. The composition of the student body has changed and contains a large percentage of adults. Colleges have changed their administrative structures and procedures to accommodate adults. Today, you can find a college or university that meets your needs and creates a positive environment in which you can earn a degree.

Doubt 2 — I wasn't very good in school.

Usually two types of people are concerned about failing in college. One is the person who finished high school but never went on to college because success did not seem possible. The other is the person who attended college but didn't do well and dropped out. When you are trying to decide whether college is an appropriate match for your educational needs, you should consider a number of things.

Colleges differ in their focus or purpose, and this can have a direct relationship to how successful you will be as a student. Large research universities appeal to students who want a specialized degree and who work well with little attention from faculty members. Small liberal arts institutions appeal to students who want more personal interaction with faculty, smaller classes, and challenging opportunities that are open to most members of the student body. Community colleges appeal to students who want a less expensive education, a more vocationally oriented degree program, and one designed to help students who have experienced academic problems in the past.

It is important for you to match your own needs with a college that has a compatible focus. A student who dropped out of large university might find that a small liberal arts college is a more appropriate fit. Likewise, a student who left community college might find a more appealing degree program at a major university. The type of college you select will have a direct relationship to your success. Failure at one type of college doesn't mean that you'll fail at another.

It is possible that a student's past lack of success was due to immature behavior, and that this changed as he or she became an adult. Frequently younger students place a higher priority on social activities than on their studies. As a result, they receive poor grades—not because they can't perform well in school but because they don't give enough time and attention to school. It's also possible that some students didn't do well in school because they lacked the discipline and focus needed to complete their work, allowing a variety of distractions to pull them away from studying. Some students in high school find it difficult to adjust to teachers who treat them like children instead of adults. There are many other reasons that students fail to do well in high school or college.

If you doubt your ability to perform successfully in college, you need to assess why. The following exercise is designed to help you make this assessment and determine whether you could now do well in college.

Exercise Worksheet
Assessment of College Potential

1. List courses that you enjoyed in high school and college.

    _____

    _____

    _____

    _____

    _____

2. Did you make good grades—A's and B's—in these courses? ❑ Yes ❑ No

3. What are the reasons that you did well in these courses?
    (Check all that apply.)

    ❑ Read course assignments   ❑ Completed course assignments
    ❑ Got along well with teacher   ❑ Took part in class discussions
    ❑ Studied the subject outside class ❑ Required little work
    ❑ Other students tutored me   ❑ Teacher took extra time with me
    ❑ Remembered the material easily   ❑ Took good notes
    ❑ _____   ❑ _____

4. What courses did you have the most difficulty with in high school and college?

    _____

    _____

    _____

    _____

    _____

5. Did you get poor grades—D's and F's—in these courses? ❏ Yes ❏ No

6. What are the reasons that you didn't do well in these courses?
   (Check all that apply.)

   ❏ Teacher expected too much   ❏ Subject was uninteresting

   ❏ Teacher didn't explain material   ❏ Teacher wouldn't help me

   ❏ Didn't complete assignments   ❏ Didn't do course reading

   ❏ Couldn't understand material   ❏ Didn't take good notes

   ❏ _____   ❏ _____

7. What are the general reasons for not getting good grades in most of your
   courses? (Check all that apply.)

   ❏ Spent too much time socializing   ❏ Spent too much time in
                                           extracurricular activities

   ❏ Spent too much time working   ❏ Didn't spend enough time studying

   ❏ Had difficulty taking timed tests ❏ Didn't discuss in class

   ❏ Found writing assignments hard   ❏ Didn't attend class regularly

   ❏ Found material hard to   ❏ Lacked organization
     understand

   ❏ Lacked self-discipline   ❏ _____

   ❏ _____   ❏ _____

8. Do you now do tasks at work that would help you do course work at the
   college level? Rate yourself on each applicable activity with a 1 as an excellent
   and a 5 as poor. (Rate all that apply.)

   ❏ Speak to groups   ❏ Write reports and other documents

   ❏ Read reports and other material   ❏ Participate in group discussions

   ❏ Take notes at meetings   ❏ Study problems and research solutions

   ❏ Organize your own work   ❏ Work independently to achieve goals

   ❏ Participate in training activities ❏ Gather and analyze information

   ❏ _____   ❏ _____

To understand how your answers to these questions can help you evaluate your potential for successfully completing college work, read the following guidelines.

Guideline 1 — It's a good sign if you were able to list courses in which you were successful. This means that you have potential for succeeding in an educational environment. You probably did well in these courses because your interest motivated you to follow good study habits. Look at your responses to *Item 3* to determine if you followed good study habits. Are there reasons given in *Item 3* that help you better understand what motivated you and interested you in the course? The answers will help you understand how you might succeed in college. For example, if you were successful in a course because you received lots of attention from a teacher, it's possible that you would be more successful at a college where classes are smaller and you get more personal attention from instructors.

Guideline 2 — Look at the courses that you didn't do well in. Review the reasons you checked in *Items 6* and *7* for not doing well in school. Ask yourself whether the reasons for failure then are likely to persist should you return to college. It could be that the reasons are more reflective of the situations you faced at that time in your life rather than the result of personal deficiencies that will inhibit success in future academic course work. The reasons also might relate to a lack of maturity—maturity that you probably now possess. Reviewing the responses in *Items 6* and *7* will help you make this assessment.

Guideline 3 — Most working adults develop and apply at the workplace skills that are transferable to postsecondary education. *Item 8* contains a checklist of transferable skills you might use regularly in your job. The skills contained in the list are ones that are required for a successful college experience. Any items you checked are personal skills that will help you succeed in college. The more items you checked, the more likely it is that you can get a college degree. For example, writing reports and documents at work develops writing skills that are critical for success in college.

Doubt 3 — I'm not sure that college will really help me.

The investments of time and money required for a college degree always raise doubts about its value. However, there are many monetary benefits as well as many intangible benefits. Perhaps the most significant is the sense of increased self-worth experienced by most adults on obtaining a degree. Attend a graduation ceremony where adult students are getting their first college degrees and you will see a glow of accomplishment on the faces of the graduates, their spouses, children, parents, relatives, and friends. Talk with the graduates and you will hear stories about how they had felt incomplete because they had not achieved their goal of completing college. Hear them describe how proud they are to now realize their dream. This increased sense of self-worth and personal value is worth a great deal; however, there are even more tangible outcomes that result from getting a college degree.

CLINTON, a 41-year-old, upper-middle-class African American, is a full-time student and full-time systems accountant. At the end of this year, Clinton will earn a bachelor's degree in accounting. He believes that having a diploma will make his current position more secure. It will allow him to climb the career ladder to a better-paying job. Before starting to work on the degree, Clinton often lacked confidence on the job. He has more confidence in himself since he began attending classes.

Clinton admits that he "wants to be the leader of the band," and he enjoys the self-fulfillment that attending classes has brought him. He is a real competitor. He sets goals for himself and achieves them. Before working on his degree, Clinton attended computer classes at his workplace. He taught himself to play golf. He continues to improve his golf game by playing only with someone who will help him learn more about the game. Clinton has found his adult education classes to be broadening experiences. He has become more open to opinions that differ from his own. He values other individuals' opinions. He isn't as critical of his professors and fellow students as he used to be.

Studying is not always easy. Good weather makes golfing more attractive than spending time in library research. Family commitments sometimes interfere with studying lecture notes and preparing for exams. However, Clinton has found that his good memory has helped him retain much of his learning. Enthusiastic professors continue to help Clinton strive for that diploma. Now, with his senior year starting, that goal is just around the corner.

Jobs in today's economy require a higher level of education than was needed in the '70s and '80s. Some studies suggest that by the year 2000, the average job will require almost two years of education beyond high school. The increase of technology, complexity of business operations, and global competition are behind the rising demand for highly educated employees. Newly created jobs, such as computer network administrator, illustrate this trend. Many experts predict that future occupations will require even more education. Jobs that are being eliminated in our economy are those that require only a high school education or less. People without education beyond high school find that when they lose a job in the current economy, they qualify only for low-paying, unskilled jobs. The new jobs with higher pay require advanced education. It is wise to consider a college education as a guard against your skills becoming obsolete. For those who have a degree, it may be necessary to return to college to pursue a more advanced degree to remain competitive in the labor market.

Anyone who reads newspapers, listens to radio news, or watches television news is aware of the trend in the past few years to eliminate white-collar positions in many businesses in an effort to control costs. This trend has two implications. One is that managers in most businesses, when deciding which workers to retain, will keep those employees with the highest level of skills who have the greatest potential for making significant contributions to the organization. A college degree is consistently valued as an important asset. When two employees are competing for a remaining position and have equal qualifications and experience, the typical management decision is to keep the employee with a college degree.

Another implication is the effect a college degree has on hiring and promotions. Despite cutbacks in management at many large corporations, executive, management, and administrative jobs were the fastest growing sector of the labor force in 1994. There are many good jobs for management and professional workers in the U.S. economy. However, these jobs most frequently go to those with the highest levels of education when other qualifications are similar.

A college degree provides a definite financial advantage. Reports from the Department of Labor consistently demonstrate higher levels of earnings for people with college degrees. Table 1 shows data from 1992.

Table 1

Educational Level	Average Annual Earnings	Premium over High School Graduates
Professional	$67,131	216%
Ph.D.	$52,402	147%
Master's	$40,666	91%
Bachelor's	$34,385	62%
High School	$21,241	

The time and money you spend obtaining a college degree can have a high rate of financial return. Even returning to college late in your career can be profitable. For every five years in the workforce, a college graduate will earn an average of $65,000 more than a high school graduate. *The Chronicle of Higher Education Fall 1994 Almanac* reported that the average annual cost for full-time, nonresidential students at public institutions was $6,809, and the comparable cost for private institutions was $15,200. The cost of a degree at either a public or private institution could be recovered in increased earnings within five years. Earning potential varies greatly from one college major to another, so you will need to examine the specific earning potential for your career choice.

JEANNE is a 49-year-old computer worker at a large business. She is nearing completion of an associate degree in the computer program of a local university. Although her company finances the classes, Jeanne must attend them on her own time. She believes they will make her "more marketable."

Jeanne's adult learning experience has made her more confident. Although she is happy to be nearing the end of her degree goal, she definitely feels that she is more knowledgeable for having this learning experience.

The increased earning potential is magnified by another significant factor. The January 1991 issue of *Employment and Earnings* from the Department of Labor reports that unemployment for college graduates is significantly lower than for other workers. Figure 1 illustrates this point: Unemployment for high school graduates without college is almost three times greater than that for college graduates. Even one to three years of college improves the unemployment rate for workers.

Figure 1
Education and Unemployment Rates

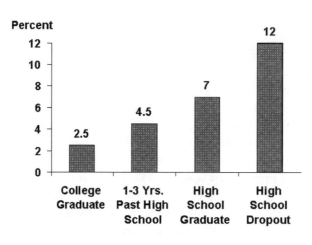

Level of Education & Unemployment Rates

Evidence of the financial benefits of a college degree will always be circumstantial. You probably know people who have a college degree who are unemployed. It is also possible that you are earning more than some college graduates you know. You may be supervising college graduates even though you don't have a degree. Many people who don't have college degrees are quite successful. The statistics just cited are averages and will vary from one part of the country to another and from one person to another. But for many people, a college degree will lead to a more satisfying life both personally and financially. You must decide for yourself whether a college degree would help you achieve a higher level of satisfaction, income, and career advancement.

Doubt 4 — Won't it take me a long time to get a degree?

Many adults avoid going back to college because they think it will take them too long to complete a degree. In fact, some students I've taught have taken as many as 12 years to complete a bachelor's degree; but other adult students I've taught have completed their degree in less than 3 years. Everyone is different, and you need to evaluate your own situation.

There are several perspectives to consider if you are concerned about the time it will take to complete a degree. One way to look at the issue is that, no matter how long it takes, you will still be better off when the work is done. Another perspective is that you can delay getting a degree, but in a few years you still won't have the benefits of a degree, and you still won't have made any progress on the degree. Putting off going to college just increases the time it takes before you finally obtain a degree. Getting started is one way to finish a degree more quickly, but there are other useful tips that you'll read about in this book.

There are colleges and universities that offer courses in a nontraditional time frame. They don't require the traditional 15- to 18-week semester to complete a course—an approach that takes a great deal of persistence. Rather, the courses are accelerated. This approach typically requires the same amount of study as a traditional course, but the work is accomplished in a shorter time span. The programs often require a more intense and disciplined effort than is needed for a traditional college program. Many colleges that use a nontraditional approach have excellent degree programs and are recognized by regional accrediting bodies and the appropriate government agencies. It is possible to find accelerated degree programs in almost every area of the United States and many that are available from anywhere in the country.

Many colleges and universities provide opportunities to demonstrate mastery of a subject through tests. The most popular of these tests is the College Level Examination Program (CLEP). This program allows you to take exams on a variety of college subjects. Successful completion of these exams qualifies you for credit at many colleges. It is possible to earn as many as 30 semester hours, which is equivalent to a year of college. Other testing programs make it possible to obtain college credit without attending classes. You should check with a college to find out what possibilities exist to earn credits through testing programs.

Another way to accumulate credits toward a degree is through prior learning assessment. This procedure involves evaluating work-related training, professional and volunteer experiences, special activities, and other relevant experience. For example, someone who has had extensive training from an employer in computer technology might be able to get credit for a course like Introduction to Computers. There are fewer colleges willing to give credit for prior learning experience than those that offer testing procedures.

An adult with experience and knowledge has a number of options to move rapidly through a degree program. You should not think in terms of how long it will take to complete a degree but, rather, how quickly it can be done. Chapter 3 provides more information about opportunities for speeding up the process.

REGENTS COLLEGE was established by the New York State Board of Regents to provide adult students with a flexible and accessible college program. The college's philosophy emphasizes the affirmation of student knowledge and abilities, regardless of the manner in which the knowledge was gained. This means that students are given an opportunity to demonstrate a mastery of subjects based on work experience, military experience, or general acquisition of knowledge through learning portfolios and exams. Courses taken through correspondence or at colleges and universities are readily accepted in transfer. The college graduates almost 4,000 students annually.

The college has no campus. Students can enroll at any time and are admitted based on self-selection—meaning that you feel the degree program is appropriate for your learning needs. Degree programs are available in the liberal arts and sciences, nursing, business, and technology. Students earn credits through exams, approved training programs in business and industry, and courses taken from regionally accredited colleges. This program is ideal for the adult who has accumulated a great deal of knowl-edge through life experience.

Regents offers a service called The Regents Credit Bank, which evaluates and consolidates an adult's learning experiences into a college transcript. The resulting transcript can be used with

> *employers and academic institutions to verify educational accomplishments.*
>
> *Regents College is an excellent example of innovative and enlightened approaches to adult higher education. It encourages adult students to view learning as a total life experience not confined to a college classroom.*

Chapter 4 demonstrates a number of practical ways an adult can earn a degree more quickly. In addition, it provides information on the resources available to help you to accomplish this.

Doubt 5 — How can I balance work, family, and college?

It is difficult to balance the demands in a busy adult's life. Family, work, volunteer work, community activities, church, a social life, and household management are typical of an adult's many responsibilities. Going back to college won't be easy, but it's not impossible to manage. This is obviously the case, or the number of adults attending college wouldn't be so high. Returning to college requires a reexamination of your priorities and successful time management. Let's examine how you can minimize the impact of college on your lifestyle.

The most important step in deciding to return to school is to solicit the support of key people in your life. Your employer's support is important for several reasons. It is easier to pursue a degree when you have some flexibility in your work schedule. An employer's cooperation can also make it possible to complete many course assignments in conjunction with your normal work activities. Knowing that an employer supports your efforts and is willing to reward you with promotions or salary increases can help motivate you during difficult times in your educational program. Ask your employer for this support and to clarify what a degree will mean to your career in the organization.

Support from family members is also important. You will not have as much time to spend on family activities. Help from your spouse in assuming more household chores can make college work much easier. Children need to be aware of your need for privacy while studying. Children also must understand that there will be limits on your participation in family activities. It is surprising how supportive even young children can be when the importance of getting a college degree is explained. When the family understands the many benefits a college degree will bring, its members will often provide a supportive environment. Your family's support also helps them identify with this important accomplishment in your life. It always excites me to hear a shout during graduation ceremonies—"Way to go, Mom!" or "Way to go, Dad!" Most children, husbands, and wives feel that they have achieved a major goal through their cooperation and support of the college graduate. Incidentally, you'll find that the example you set for your children develops a great deal of respect for college and motivates them to achieve the same accomplishment.

Because of the practical limits on your time, you will need to examine your priorities and determine what activities can be eliminated. During your college career, you may have to reduce or eliminate volunteer activities. You may have to reduce the time you spend on social and recreational activities. You may need to pass up new work assignments or promotions until your degree is complete, but this is all temporary. You must decide if these sacrifices are worthwhile.

Contemporary alternatives to a traditional college program can help you reduce the impact of college activities on your lifestyle. Look for colleges that accommodate the needs of adults. You should also consider a degree program that allows you the greatest flexibility in completing courses and course requirements. If your job requires a lot of travel, you might consider a degree from some of the more innovative programs that don't require classroom attendance.

Pursuit of a college degree will change your lifestyle. However, all good things come through some type of sacrifice. You can tolerate some losses when you know that they won't last forever. Set a timeframe for completing a degree and work hard toward reaching your goal. It will make balancing family, work, and education easier.

Doubt 6 — I don't think college is affordable.

College education is expensive, particularly in some parts of the country. We examined the financial benefits of a degree earlier in this chapter. The cost of a college degree should be balanced against the potential increase in income. It is one of the safest investments you can make today. The cost of a four-year college education at most public institutions is less than that of a new car—a purchase many families make every five to ten years. However, the value of a car depreciates every year, while the value of your college education should increase over time. You can postpone the purchase of a large item like a car in order to finance your education. A college degree is a costly purchase, but one that is quite worthwhile. And there are many strategies you can pursue to reduce the cost.

Consider the possibility of getting a two-year degree from a community college. You achieve two results by following this strategy. First, community college tuition is usually lower than tuition at a four-year college, so the first two years toward a bachelor's degree will cost less. Second, a two-year associate degree makes you more valuable in the workplace. You might experience an increase in income before completing a bachelor's degree. (The same result occurs when you work toward an associate degree at a four-year college.)

Adults are eligible for financial aid. It is not necessary to be a full-time student to qualify for financial aid or loans. Also, some colleges make it easier for students to achieve full-time status by redefining both the number of credits that must be taken and the time span in which courses are taken. For example, some colleges structure courses so that it is possible to take one at a time, but still complete three courses in a semester. This type of format usually requires a student to attend classes one or two nights a week with three to four hours per class. A schedule like this is difficult for a working adult, but not impossible. It is also possible at many colleges for adults to qualify for scholarships.

An important and often overlooked source of college financing for adults is employers. Tuition assistance is a common enough benefit that some employers in nearly every community provide it to their employees. If your employer doesn't provide this benefit, you may find it advantageous to find an employer who does while you pursue your degree. It can even be financially wise to take a small pay cut to work for an employer with this benefit when you know that you'll be taking advantage of it. A secondary gain that comes from working for an employer that offers this benefit is that a college degree is valued by the company and may result in better promotional opportunities.

Other methods are available to adults to finance a college degree. A working adult often has assets not possessed by traditional students. For instance, a house provides an asset that can be used to obtain a home equity loan. Adults can often qualify for short-term loans without providing the lender with any collateral. The loan can be repaid before the start of a new term. The credit limits on many credit cards are high enough that tuition and books for a semester can be charged.

These examples illustrate that purchasing an education is like other consumer purchases. If you really want to get an education, you can plan for it in the same way you plan for other purchases. Chapter 5 has more specific ideas and information about strategies for financing your college education.

Doubt 7 - There isn't a college nearby that has a program for adults.

You may be surprised at the number and location of colleges that have degree programs targeted at adults. The college guide at the end of this book lists 240 colleges and universities throughout the country that have adult degree programs. This list is not exhaustive, and further exploration on your part might turn up some surprising opportunities near your home. As more students have come from the adult population, colleges have realized that they must do more to recruit adults. Competition has both increased and improved the choice of colleges for many adults. Many nontraditional degree programs offer additional options to choose from.

Many colleges have established satellite locations. These sites may be located at a business office, industrial plant, public school building, community center—almost any facility imaginable. Typically, faculty members commute from the main campus to teach the courses. In addition, the college may hire qualified individuals from the local community to teach some courses. Sometimes, the courses are taught through interactive television. This allows students to see the instructor live in a classroom at the main campus. The instructor is able to hear and possibly see the students in remote locations. This type of program is part of the generic classification of programs called "distance learning" or "distance education." Ball State University, in Indiana, is in the process of identifying several facilities where interactive television will reach hundreds of students throughout the state. The state of Iowa is developing a high-tech fiber optic network linking all colleges in the state so that residents can go to the nearest site and take courses from any college that is a part of the network.

Another form of distance education that has existed from the early part of this century is correspondence degrees. Many public universities have correspondence degree programs, which result in lower tuition for state residents. An example is the University of

Nebraska. Correspondence programs have the advantage of being available to anyone, regardless of location. A further benefit is that correspondence programs give the student control and flexibility over course work.

Technology has improved on the basic concept of correspondence degree programs. It is now possible to use television, videotapes, and computers to complete a college degree. Mind Extension University (MEU) occupies a channel on all Jones Cable companies. Several well-known universities offer degree programs through MEU. You can obtain the courses through videotapes if you don't have access to a Jones Cable company. Other colleges, like Liberty University, also offer degrees through videotape delivery programs. It is also possible to obtain a degree through a computer-delivered format. A student dials into the college's computer system with a personal computer and modem. The student can read assignments from the instructor, interact with the instructor and other students in a discussion forum, send and receive messages to and from the instructor, and get information from the college's library. The University of Phoenix has established degree programs using computer technology.

The diversity of programs makes it possible for anyone in any part of the United States to earn a college degree. This not only is useful for students who live in remote locations, but also opens up the possibility of obtaining a degree for those adults who must travel extensively. Expect more exciting opportunities to appear as educators develop more creative and innovative applications of these and other technologies.

Doubt 8 — I'm not sure how to get started.

Many colleges and universities recognize the special needs and concerns of adults contemplating a return to school. The admissions officers at these colleges are interested in answering your questions and will address your concerns and doubts. Market forces have made the recruitment of adults important. As a result, most admissions officers are experienced in working with adults and helping them fit college into their career plans.

Talk with friends and business acquaintances about their experiences in returning to school. Get their advice on the information and people they found most helpful. Find out what problems they encountered and the solutions they developed. Ask about specific colleges and degree programs you're interested in. Collect as much guidance from these experienced adult students as you can.

You've already begun the process of discovering how to get started by purchasing this book. Now it's time to begin an active planning process to determine whether college fits your career plans. Reading this book is good preparation for deciding whether you should go back to school.

This book provides detailed help to adults who want to return to college. Each of the doubts described in this chapter is addressed in detail in following chapters. This book is designed to make it easier to start a college degree program, answering many of the questions posed by adult students. You will discover how to establish a career plan and evaluate the need for a college degree to reach your goals. A description of creative college degree programs is provided, along with practical advice on speeding up the process, financing your education, selecting a college, and balancing family and work. The appendix of colleges with adult programs provides a wide selection of schools that can meet your career and educational needs. Good luck with your new adventure in learning!

Chapter 2

Your Career Plans and College

A college degree can provide you with many financial benefits and career opportunities. However, people often observe that it is possible to earn a great deal of money and be highly successful without a college degree—Bill Gates is an excellent example of this success. It is also true that many people are able to find satisfying careers without college degrees. A college degree may not be a good career decision for you, but it might be the best career move that you will ever make. Understanding stages in adult development and principles of career planning can help you make better decisions about the appropriateness of a college degree.

In this chapter we will look at the process of adult development and how this affects many career decisions. This will help you understand how to apply basic principles of career planning when making the decision to attend college. The chapter also examines how to select a college major that provides the greatest opportunity for career success and describes how you can use a college degree to advance your career.

Adult Development and Career Planning

Psychologists refer to *development* as the process of growth and maturation in a person's life. At one time, psychologists didn't spend much time studying adult development. The focus was on the development of children and adolescents because the growth and changes that take place during this part of life are so dramatic. In comparison, *adult development* is much more gradual. Nevertheless, significant changes can and do take place in the psychological development of adults. You might find that some of your motivations for reading this book and considering a return to college are explained by theories about adult development.

Experts in adult development typically have one of two basic viewpoints about the way adults develop. One assumption is that adults develop through a series of stages or phases, and most go through these stages at approximately the same times in life. A second dominant view is that adults develop through significant events in life such as marriage, the birth of children, and job loss. We will examine both of these outlooks to help you understand how they affect your life and key decisions you make.

There are several models of adult development based on the idea of stages. One that has been used as the basis for many books and articles on adult and career development was first advanced by a psychologist named Daniel Levinson. He proposes that adults go through stages of development separated by periods of transition. Figure 1 illustrates these stages and transition periods. It should be noted that Levinson's original research was done on men only. However, later research by Levinson and his associates and by other psychologists supports this model as representative of both genders.

Figure 1
*Daniel
Levinson's Model
of Adult
Development*

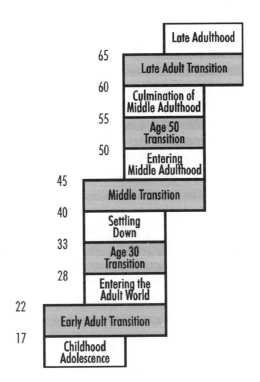

According to Levinson, each stage in an adult's life is focused on accomplishing certain tasks. For example, the first stage is "Entering the Adult World"—ages 22 to 28—and consists of two major tasks. The first is to investigate the opportunities and risks that adult life offers. The second is to establish a secure life—a contrast to the first task. The practical actions that usually result are testing career possibilities, entering into significant relationships that often result in marriage, and possibly starting a family. This first stage of adult development is followed by a transition period. Levinson found that during transition periods a person evaluates the tasks that have been accomplished and makes adjustments necessary to achieve past or new goals.

Not every person will experience the exact sequence of developmental steps shown in Levinson's model, but the sequence is typical of many adults. While experts may argue over some of the stages, and the ages at which they occur, many agree that transition periods are common occurrences in adult development. *Transition periods* involve activity designed to improve the person or position of the person to accomplish more satisfying results in life. They involve a search for meaning and integrating these thoughts and feelings into a person's current life situation.

As Figure 1 illustrates, there are several transition periods in an adult's development. Probably the most significant is the *mid-life transition*. This is a time of intense review, evaluation, and introspection because of an accompanying shift in an adult's life perspective. Until this point, a person has measured life by "how long I have lived," but now the perspective shifts to "how long I have to live." The adult thus begins to value limits on time and how they relate to accomplishing life goals. In some cases, goals, expectations, and experiences not achieved are valued highly enough to significantly alter a person's lifestyle. Just as likely, the person may realize that a goal, expectation, or experience really isn't important in contrast with current life goals. This mid-life transition has been popularized as "mid-life crisis." In fact, only a small number of people experience it as a crisis.

Transition periods are times when growth and learning are likely to occur. Adults are more likely to change a career, job, community, or lifestyle during a transition period. As you face a transition period, it is possible that you will attempt to reach new goals you've set for yourself. It is also quite possible that you'll decide to seek a college education during such a transition period. You might find it comforting to realize that this desire to change and improve is not at all unusual. Be open to new possibilities and consider how a college education can help you achieve these possibilities.

The second view of adult development is the idea that adults develop in response to significant events in life. The fact that many of these events are common to most adults in our society accounts for the appearance of stages. However, according to this idea there are not particular ages at which these events occur. To understand how this view differs from that of the life stages concept, consider a common task and then compare how the two views would explain it. Starting a new career involves locating job leads, interviewing for the position, getting hired, making a good first impression on the job, working hard, and positioning yourself for advancement. According to experts who believe in the life stages concept, this typically happens when a person is 22 to 28 years old. From the point of view of social scientists who believe in the life events scheme, this may occur at any time in life. The tasks and resulting developmental process connected with an event have the same impact whether you're 22 or 42.

Events that affect adults may be personal or cultural. Some important personal include a new job, marriage, childbirth, loss of friends and relatives because of death, and retirement. Examples of cultural events are movements—for example, the civil rights movement—wars, assassination of leaders, and natural disasters. Adult development results as adaptive strategies are implemented to cope with these life events. Personal life events frequently reported by adults returning to college are job loss, reentry into the workforce, and career change. Cultural events frequently cited include development of new technology, economic recessions, and a desire to help others.

The most important point is that growth and change in adults are normal. Understanding this should help you better understand thoughts and emotions you experience throughout life. Furthermore, these ideas prepare you for a better understanding of the career development process.

Career Development

Just as there are differing perspectives of adult development, psychologists have differing ideas about *career development*. A popular theory is that a career develops in stages—a concept similar to the life stages concept among adult development experts. Career development experts like Miller, Form, Schein, Hall, Nougaim, and Greenhouse have proposed models based on career stages.

Donald Super is one of the best-known career development experts using the idea of career stages, and his model of career development is representative of this school of thought. Super proposes five stages in the career development process. The first is physical and psychological *growth* necessary to prepare for work; this occurs from birth to age 14. The second stage occurs from the age of 15 to 24, when a person *explores* career opportunities. Next comes the *establishment* of one's career, ages 25 to 44. The fourth stage, from age 45 to 65, involves the *maintenance* of one's career. The last stage is known as career *decline;* this occurs from age 65 on.

There are two limitations to this and other stage models in explaining adult careers. First, they don't adequately explain the multitude of career and job changes most adults experience. Statistics from the Department of Labor indicate that the average individual changes careers five to seven times in his or her life. Further, people between the ages of 17 and 34 change jobs an average of once every 18 months; and after the age of 35, people on average change jobs every three years. A second limitation to the models is that they were developed before rapid advances in technology and a competitive world economy created many job disruptions now common in the workforce.

M.J. Gravis proposes a model based on four patterns of career development. One proposed pattern is a *linear* path of continuous upward development through promotions and job changes. A person following this pattern may perform a variety of jobs. An example is a person who starts work as a salesclerk with a large discount chain, moves into a department manager's position, works as an assistant store manager at a large department store, later moves into a position as store manager, and finally becomes a regional director for a large chain of franchised mall operations. A second pattern is termed the *steady state* career, in which a person pursues one career with minimal change. A person following this pattern might work as a clerk for a law firm, become a junior partner, take a position as chief of legal affairs for a large corporation, and finally assume a judgeship in a federal district court. The *spiral* pattern is typified by a person who moves from one career to another with a sense of purpose or advancement—usually every five to seven years. This pattern is illustrated by the career of a person who starts out with a position in social work, becomes a public administrator, starts a consulting firm, becomes a college professor, moves into a dean's position, and then manages software development for a medium-sized business. Finally, there is the *transitory* pattern, in which a person moves from one job to another and doesn't advance or move purposefully in pursuit of a career. Typically, the jobs are not held for a long time and are low-paying. The Gravis model seems to be a more realistic representation of careers in the general population. The usefulness of the model becomes apparent when you attempt to classify people you know. It is likely that most people you know can be associated with one of these four patterns.

These models of career development help put into context the process of career planning and management. Whether the career development process you use is stage-orientated—as Super's model suggests—or more varied—as Gravis proposes—there are some valuable concepts that can help you take control of your career and more effectively manage it. Most experts agree that career development is an important aspect of adult life and development. You can manage and control this process, and the next section of the book is designed to help you accomplish this.

Planning Your Career

As an adult, you've already embarked on a career. After reading the previous sections on adult and career development, you can probably pinpoint where you fit in the process of both. Recognize that planning your career is affected by a number of factors. Figure 2 contains a model for career planning developed by Bonnie Maitlen and LaVerne Ludden. We'll use this model to help you better understand the career planning process.

Figure 2
*Ludden &
Maitlen
Employability
Model*

According to this model, an individual's career is affected by the interaction between the person and the environment. The environment is represented by the triangle, and the person by the three circles. For the purpose of career planning, the three most important elements in a person's environment are social and cultural context, labor market, and work setting. Three critical factors an individual brings to the career planning process are personal characteristics, work skills and abilities, and career awareness and management skills. By exploring this model further, you will gain insight into how you can plan and manage your career more effectively.

The Individual

Individuals interact with environmental factors to shape a career. It is important to understand your environment, but it is just as important that you understand yourself in order to take control of your career. Each person brings three primary attributes to the career planning process. These include personal characteristics, career awareness and management skills, and work skills and abilities. A career development model proposed by Ludden and Maitlen—illustrated in Figure 3—provides a practical structure for assessing these personal characteristics and using the information to plan a successful career. The model is presented as a hierarchy because a person would typically progress from a lower level in the career development process to a higher level after first addressing matters associated with the lower level. For example, a person isn't going to be interested in career planning (fourth level) until he or she has a proper work orientation (third level). Each level will be discussed in more detail to help you understand how this model can be used to plan career decisions.

Figure 3
*Ludden &
Maitlen Career
Development
Model*

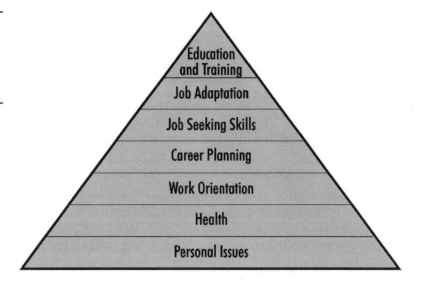

Education and Training
Job Adaptation
Job Seeking Skills
Career Planning
Work Orientation
Health
Personal Issues

*At 39, **Don** is married, with two school-age children, and is a veteran police officer. He has a bachelor's degree in Criminal Justice. He earned this degree by attending classes part-time for nine years. He refers to his first college experience as "a long haul while working full-time."*

Don has attended several "in-service training workshops" over the years. But Don has also initiated other learning activities for his own personal reasons. He paid for a nine-week polygraph school in an out-of-state location. He owns his own polygraph instrument. In the past Don has worked for another police department, and he owned a consulting business for three years. The business involved polygraph and accident work.

In addition to his standard duties as a deputy sheriff, Don is an accident reconstructionist. This means he investigates accidents in which a fatality or near fatality occurs or in which a departmental vehicle is involved. Don is responsible for providing detailed formulations, diagrams, speed estimates, and evidence about the accidents. The courts, law enforcement agencies, lawyers, and insurance companies use the information Don gathers.

To obtain this information, Don uses components of math, engineering, physics, drafting, logic, and detailed observation. He must have an ability to interpret the physical evidence to learn how the accident occurred. He is considered an expert witness in court.

Because Don believes that he needs additional knowledge to maintain his status as an expert, he has decided to obtain a degree in mechanical engineering technology. Once again he is attending classes part-time. His first goal is obtaining an associate degree within four years. He plans to reevaluate his plans at that time to decide if he wants to pursue a bachelor's degree.

Don has chosen to attend a branch campus of a major university. He believes that the school "caters to my kind of student—people with full-time jobs and pursuing degrees." Most of the classes are offered in the evening and are learner-centered, with both lectures and a hands-on approach to teaching. Don is currently a freshman, having completed 14 credit hours in two semesters. His GPA is 3.6. He finds that he has a greater commitment to learning than when he was working on his first degree in the early 1980s. He is getting better grades.

Personal Issues

Personal issues include items like intelligence and aptitudes. They also encompass an individual's status and related characteristics, such as citizenship, income, gender, and ethnicity. Personal issues should not be viewed as inherent advantages or disadvantages. Instead, you must realistically assess them and establish a strategy that builds on your strengths and overcomes what others might perceive as obstacles.

One personal issue that must be addressed is the potential for discrimination, which is typically based on gender, race or ethnicity, age, and disability. These are all characteristics you can't change. Therefore, you must plan a strategy for persuading employers to hire and promote you regardless of their prejudices. Emphasizing skills and accomplishments is the most effective way to overcome discrimination. So when planning your career, don't buy into stereotypes about occupations and make career decisions based on those stereotypes. For example, if you are a woman and interested in engineering, don't be deterred simply because there are few women in engineering positions. Determination, hard work, and employers who don't discriminate will provide you with many opportunities in any occupation that you choose.

Income level is another factor that can affect career decisions. Some people find it difficult to pursue a particular career because they lack the financial resources to get the needed education. Chapter 5 provides guidance about financial aid, as well as strategies for reducing the cost of an education. Put a priority on getting the education you need and it will become a reality. Even if you have to work a second job to save the money you need, or go to a less expensive school, there are ways to get the education.

Another personal issue is intelligence and aptitudes. There is a great deal of debate on intelligence and its relationship to educational attainment. Some people who perform poorly on intelligence tests are quite successful in pursuing a higher education. However, some people definitely have an easier time learning some subjects than others. You should identify those subjects that are the easiest for you to learn. Match these subjects with those that are required for certain occupations. For example, if biology and science are difficult for you, then it probably is not appropriate for you to become a nurse or physician. On the other hand, if you are good in English and literature, you would probably find writing, journalism, or editing to be a good career choice.

Another important personal issue is values. Values are the priorities you place on ideas, beliefs, and material things. Values are usually shaped at a young age, but they can and do change as you age. Your satisfaction with a career choice often depends on how well it satisfies your values. Values sometimes contrast with one another and create tension. For example, you might value working with people, but your need for career advancement forces you to consider a job that requires more involvement in data analysis. You must then decide which value—working with people or desire for advancement—will take the highest priority. Identifying values that are important to you is a first step in career planning. Making a list of values and ranking them can help you make sound career decisions.

Health

Health issues affect a person's career in a variety of ways. Restricted physical mobility will affect the career decisions a person makes. Chronic illnesses and subsequent absences can keep a person from succeeding at some jobs. Addictions also significantly affect a person's career. The Americans with Disabilities Act (ADA) has established laws and regulations governing how employers can respond to people with physical problems. An employer must reasonably accommodate a person with physical limitations. However, there will always be some employers and occupations that can accommodate physically restricted individuals more easily than others. Realistically assess any physical limits that you have and then identify those occupations and employers that will provide you with the greatest opportunities for success.

A person's vigor and stamina in pursuing a career are often dependent on an awareness of personal health. You should keep in mind the following points—suggested by wellness experts—when planning and managing your career.

Maintain good eating habits, including eating on a regular schedule and eating low-fat (or no-fat) foods. Exercise daily with an aerobic activity. Even walking daily improves your health. Be aware that your lifestyle affects work and academic performance. Establish a regular sleep schedule and get the number of hours of sleep—normally six to eight—that are appropriate for you each night. Effectively manage job-related stress by engaging in social and recreational activities that allow you to unwind. Also, learn some common stress-reduction techniques. Obtain regular physical and dental exams to prevent serious health problems.

Likewise, seek medical assistance when a physical problem arises. Finally, recognize that minimizing alcohol and tobacco use and avoiding drug abuse can significantly improve your health and physical performance.

Work Orientation

The term *work orientation* might also be called motivation to work or a strong work ethic. You need a strong work orientation to perform well in your choice of jobs. This includes several of the following attributes. You need a strong desire to work. Economic progress depends on hard work. To achieve the material goals that you want in life, you must work hard. Be enthusiastic about your work. This can be accomplished by focusing on the ultimate needs that are satisfied by your job, including the material benefits that come from the money you earn.

People who are most successful in their careers display two key abilities. First, they have the ability to take control of their life; they do this through personal discipline. This requires that you establish goals for yourself, develop a strategy for reaching those goals, and implement the strategy. Second, successful people concentrate on continuous self-improvement. They look for lessons to be learned in all work-related activities. In addition, they become lifelong learners through formal learning activities or self-directed learning projects. Self-examination and consequent actions to improve yourself are keys to the mastery of life. Your decision to read this book is a strong indication that you have this attribute and are looking for a strategy to improve yourself.

The more you enjoy your work, the stronger your work orientation becomes. This is just one of many reasons why it is important to select a career that is fulfilling. Satisfying experiences in the workplace reinforce your desire to achieve a high level of performance. This, in turn, motivates you to take pride in your work—a desire that is identified by employers as important in decisions to retain and promote workers.

Career Planning Skills

How often have you wondered why two people with seemingly the same skills and abilities have such differing levels of success in their careers? Frequently, the successful person has attained a particular level of achievement because of well-developed career planning skills. There are several skills that must be mastered to plan and manage your career capably, including skills that are specific to advancing on the job.

First, we'll explore basic career planning skills. Of prime importance is understanding yourself and the values, interests, and capabilities you have. Identifying occupations that match your personal attributes is another important skill. You need to know how to set goals and establish a plan that meets the goals. This includes the ability to understand how education relates to and is used to achieve career goals. Finally, you must know how to make decisions by identifying alternatives, evaluating them, establishing priorities, and making an informed choice. This chapter will aid you in acquiring these skills.

There are also skills that are important when you want to develop your career with a specific organization in mind. The ability to identify skills that are important to your employer and use them to advance on the job is foundational. You also need to know how to network within the organization to identify job opportunities and focus on the opportunities that provide the best fit with your skills. It is important to find a mentor or someone to advise you about a career path that would be most appropriate for you within the organization. You need to set career goals for yourself within the organization. Then actively pursue the education, experience, and skills needed to apply for positions that open within your established career path. Finally, you need to be capable of assessing when movement outside the organization is the best alternative because internal advancement is not realistic.

Whether you are managing a career move to another organization or trying to advance within your own organization, career planning skills are essential. It is important to spend time developing these skills in the same way that you spend time developing job-related skills.

Job Seeking Skills

Planning your career is the first step in reaching your goals. Career planning skills must be combined with job seeking skills. It is not possible to explain these skills in detail here. For an excellent book on the subject, read *The Very Quick Job Search* by Mike Farr. However, in this section we will review the job search skills that you must acquire and practice. First, a job search begins with a job objective, which is a natural outcome of the career planning process. Next, you must prepare the tools you need for the job search: resume, cover letter, thank you notes, and personal information (JIST) card. Identifying job leads is an important skill and includes networking with family, friends, and acquaintances; telephone surveying; and more conventional methods. Developing effective verbal skills that you will use in telephone calls and interviews is vital. Effective communication skills require practice, which can be done with family and friends. Finally, you must be able to negotiate a job offer to get the best salary, fringe benefits, and working conditions.

Job Adaptation Skills

You need good job adaptation skills to be accepted by coworkers and managers and to advance within an organization. These are the skills employers most frequently cite in surveys as basic requirements for the people they hire, retain, and promote. They include dependability in attendance, punctuality, fulfilling assigned responsibilities, and time management. A lack of these skills is the most frequently stated reason for firing employees.

Interpersonal skills have become very important as the economy has become dominated by service and information companies rather than manufacturers. These skills include an ability to work in a team with others and the ability to lead the team when the situation demands. Communicating well with all kinds of people, including customers, coworkers, and managers, is vital. Working well with management is fundamental to success and includes following instructions, contributing suggestions, and providing feedback about assigned work.

Adaptability skills are frequently named by executives as basic for employee success because the economy, world politics, and technology require constant adaptation by businesses to be competitive. Flexibility is the number one adaptation skill, and means that you make positive adjustments in goals, structure, policies, resources, and assignments. Encouraging other employees to remain positive and look for ways to adjust to changes is also a necessary skill.

Modern businesses also need workers who are problem solvers. This includes knowing how to identify problems, collect data about the problem, analyze the data, develop alternative solutions, and identify the best solution. Knowing how to do this in conjunction with coworkers and managers is also important. Being able to set new goals and strategies and implement them is another key to problem-solving skills. A college education helps improve these skills.

Organizational effectiveness is a basic requirement to successful job adaptation. You must understand the organization's structure and purpose. An awareness of organizational goals, objectives, policies, and expectations helps you focus your work efforts to the greatest advantage. Another key to organizational effectiveness is knowing how people within the organization can act as resources and being able to enlist their assistance.

A final element of successful job adaptability is ethical conduct. This includes following government laws and regulations and pursuing organizational policies. It is important to respect the organization's resources, such as time, supplies, telephone, and copy machine, by not employing them for personal reasons. Providing accurate information and keeping information confidential are also important from an employer's viewpoint.

Education and Training

Using education and training to constantly improve your career is the final step in the career development hierarchy. Some people might perceive it as a level lower than the other skills in the hierarchy. The reason for having it at the summit is the role it plays in helping people adapt to the constantly changing world of work. Experts from a wide range of fields, such as John Naisbitt, Peter Senge, Peter Drucker, and Malcom Knowles, have recognized the need for lifelong learning. You can obtain and keep employment without education, but it is not possible to advance on the job and reach the highest levels of your career potential without lifelong learning.

The first step in lifelong learning is learning how to learn. This requires you to identify skills deficiency, set a learning goal, develop a plan to meet the goal, explore resources for getting the needed skills, select the resource that best matches your learning style, implement a learning strategy, and evaluate your progress in achieving your learning goal. You must possess good mathematics, reading, and writing skills. It is important to know how to learn from experiences on the job. Think about what happens to you on the job and what you can learn from those experiences. Constantly looking for training opportunities is important, particularly being able to match the training with career opportunities.

College education can and does play an important role in the lifelong learning activities of many adults. The advanced training necessary for many modern job tasks often can be obtained only from colleges. Higher-level thinking skills needed in the workplace are effectively developed through a college education. Further, colleges and universities frequently provide the quickest approach for acquiring new knowledge and skills. Colleges are an important resource in the lifelong learning process.

Personal Needs and Skills Identification

Before examining the environment and its impact on your career, you must identify the needs and skills you currently possess. This exercise helps you understand how to match your personal attributes with factors in the environment to make informed career decisions.

Personal Needs Worksheet

1. Are there career issues related to discrimination that I might face?

   _____

   _____

2. What strategies will be most effective in helping me overcome discrimination?

   _____

   _____

3. What income can be used to help advance my career?

   _____

   _____

4. What subjects have I enjoyed studying?

   _____

   _____

5. List the values that are most important to you in pursuing a career. Rank them in order of importance. (You may need an extra page of paper to complete this exercise.)

_____

_____

6. Are there health issues that need to be considered in your career planning? List them.

_____

_____

7. Are there wellness issues that, if implemented, could improve your personal performance?

_____

_____

8. Describe your work orientation. Do you have a strong work ethic? Are you motivated to implement your career and do well? What would help improve your work orientation?

_____

_____

9. Write down three personal goals that, if met, will improve your career success.

a. _____

b. _____

c. _____

10. Are there career planning skills that you need to acquire? List them and describe a strategy you'll use to acquire the skills.

_____

_____

_____

_____

11. Are there job search skills you need to acquire? List them and describe a strategy to acquire them.

_____

_____

_____

_____

12. Are there job retention skills you need to acquire? List them and describe a strategy to acquire them.

_____

_____

_____

_____

Skills Assessment Worksheet

It is important that you assess your skills as a part of the career planning process. This exercise is also critical in selecting a college major that will fit your attributes and match labor market needs.

	Degree of Proficiency					
	No Skill				Mastery	
Communication Skills						
Corresponding	0	1	2	3	4	5
Editing	0	1	2	3	4	5
Writing	0	1	2	3	4	5
Drawing	0	1	2	3	4	5
Interviewing	0	1	2	3	4	5
Listening	0	1	2	3	4	5
Relating to customers	0	1	2	3	4	5
Presenting ideas	0	1	2	3	4	5
Public speaking	0	1	2	3	4	5
Coordinating Skills						
Facilitating	0	1	2	3	4	5
Managing conflicts	0	1	2	3	4	5
Mediating	0	1	2	3	4	5
Negotiating	0	1	2	3	4	5
Human Resource Skills						
Coaching	0	1	2	3	4	5
Counseling	0	1	2	3	4	5
Teaching	0	1	2	3	4	5
Developing others	0	1	2	3	4	5
Helping others	0	1	2	3	4	5

	Degree of Proficiency					
	No Skill				Mastery	
Motivating	0	1	2	3	4	5
Team building	0	1	2	3	4	5
Training	0	1	2	3	4	5
Assessing performance	0	1	2	3	4	5
Scheduling	0	1	2	3	4	5
Following up	0	1	2	3	4	5
Reporting	0	1	2	3	4	5
Recording	0	1	2	3	4	5
Cataloging	0	1	2	3	4	5
Correcting	0	1	2	3	4	5

Data Management Skills

Assessing quality	0	1	2	3	4	5
Using a computer	0	1	2	3	4	5
Measuring	0	1	2	3	4	5
Setting standards	0	1	2	3	4	5
Taking inventory	0	1	2	3	4	5
Managing information	0	1	2	3	4	5
Gathering data	0	1	2	3	4	5

General Management Skills

Advising	0	1	2	3	4	5
Approving	0	1	2	3	4	5
Making decisions	0	1	2	3	4	5
Developing procedures	0	1	2	3	4	5
Developing systems	0	1	2	3	4	5
Directing	0	1	2	3	4	5
Delegating	0	1	2	3	4	5
Implementing	0	1	2	3	4	5
Instructing	0	1	2	3	4	5
Interpreting policy	0	1	2	3	4	5
Managing details	0	1	2	3	4	5
Managing people	0	1	2	3	4	5
Managing tasks	0	1	2	3	4	5
Problem solving	0	1	2	3	4	5
Project managing	0	1	2	3	4	5
Serving as change agent	0	1	2	3	4	5

Financial Management Skills

Analyzing budgets	0	1	2	3	4	5
Analyzing finances	0	1	2	3	4	5

	Degree of Proficiency					
	No Skill				Mastery	
Researching and analyzing economics	0	1	2	3	4	5
Auditing	0	1	2	3	4	5
Budgeting	0	1	2	3	4	5
Cost accounting	0	1	2	3	4	5
Managing finances	0	1	2	3	4	5
Financial planning	0	1	2	3	4	5
Fund-raising	0	1	2	3	4	5
Planning Skills						
Analyzing	0	1	2	3	4	5
Conceptualizing	0	1	2	3	4	5
Designing	0	1	2	3	4	5
Developing strategies	0	1	2	3	4	5
Developing policies and procedures	0	1	2	3	4	5
Researching	0	1	2	3	4	5
Reviewing	0	1	2	3	4	5
Surveying	0	1	2	3	4	5
Sales and Marketing Skills						
Selling	0	1	2	3	4	5
Marketing	0	1	2	3	4	5
Writing proposals	0	1	2	3	4	5
Pricing	0	1	2	3	4	5
Analyzing markets	0	1	2	3	4	5
Forecasting	0	1	2	3	4	5
Advertising	0	1	2	3	4	5
Promoting	0	1	2	3	4	5
Managing sales	0	1	2	3	4	5
Relating to clients	0	1	2	3	4	5
Customer Service Skills						
Serving customers	0	1	2	3	4	5
Responding promptly	0	1	2	3	4	5
Building relations	0	1	2	3	4	5
Handling complaints	0	1	2	3	4	5
Technical Production Skills						
Engineering	0	1	2	3	4	5
Programming	0	1	2	3	4	5
Tooling	0	1	2	3	4	5
Inventing	0	1	2	3	4	5

	Degree of Proficiency					
	No Skill				Mastery	
Manufacturing	0	1	2	3	4	5
Designing systems	0	1	2	3	4	5
Developing products	0	1	2	3	4	5

Organizational Skills

Administering	0	1	2	3	4	5
Categorizing	0	1	2	3	4	5
Developing work plans	0	1	2	3	4	5
Setting priorities	0	1	2	3	4	5
Assigning	0	1	2	3	4	5
Clarifying vision and mission	0	1	2	3	4	5

Technical Office Skills

Arm/disarm alarm system	0	1	2	3	4	5
Use multifeature phone system	0	1	2	3	4	5
Copy documents using multiple features	0	1	2	3	4	5
Prepare mail with postage scale and meter	0	1	2	3	4	5
Operate cash register	0	1	2	3	4	5
Operate scanning unit	0	1	2	3	4	5
Operate IBM-compatible computer	0	1	2	3	4	5
Operate Macintosh computer	0	1	2	3	4	5
Create documents with word processing	0	1	2	3	4	5
Use financial/statistical software	0	1	2	3	4	5
Create reports with spreadsheet software	0	1	2	3	4	5
Use presentation graphics software	0	1	2	3	4	5
Use database software	0	1	2	3	4	5
Create, send, and read e-mail	0	1	2	3	4	5
Create overhead transparencies	0	1	2	3	4	5
Send and receive fax messages	0	1	2	3	4	5
Use a dot-matrix printer	0	1	2	3	4	5
Use a laser printer	0	1	2	3	4	5
Use a dictation machine	0	1	2	3	4	5
Bind documents	0	1	2	3	4	5
Operate a VCR unit	0	1	2	3	4	5
Use a cellular telephone	0	1	2	3	4	5
Use an online information service	0	1	2	3	4	5

Specialized Skills

Specify the job skills that you have developed and indicate your degree of proficiency.

Degree of Proficiency					
No Skill					Mastery
0	1	2	3	4	5
0	1	2	3	4	5
0	1	2	3	4	5
0	1	2	3	4	5
0	1	2	3	4	5

Identifying Your Strongest Skills

Go back through the lists of skills and identify those you rated the highest. Write these skills on a piece of paper and then rank them from the strongest to weakest. Write the top six skills in the following spaces.

1. _____
2. _____
3. _____
4. _____
5. _____
6. _____

Identifying Your Most Important Skills for Success

Which skills stand out as ones that you need to develop to succeed in reaching you career goals? Write these skills in the following spaces.

1. _____
2. _____
3. _____
4. _____
5. _____
6. _____

Environmental Factors

The environment both influences and frames the career choices you make. It influences you through family, friends, teachers, fellow students, coworkers, and supervisors. These people affect your self-concept, self-esteem, knowledge base, personal development, world view, and skills. The environment also frames the world in terms of factors over which you have no direct control. Instead you must develop strategies that allow you to fulfill your personal goals within the context set by the environment. Factors that frame your environment are community institutions, business establishments, government (local, state, and federal), economic conditions, and labor market requirements. Personal satisfaction results when you achieve a harmony between the environment and your personal needs, goals, and values. This section explores the three elements that most affect your career decisions: the social and cultural context, labor market, and work setting. It is designed to help you create the best match between personal issues and environmental factors.

JEANETTE, a 43-year-old Caucasian, grew up expecting to go to college. Both of her parents were college graduates. Many members of her extended family were doctors, lawyers, or dentists. When she graduated from high school, Jeanette and her twin sister were admitted to West Point Military Academy. Although her parents had money saved for her college tuition, Jeanette found West Point's free tuition attractive.

After graduation, Jeanette began her 20-year career in the U.S. Army. While in the army, she began working on a degree in computer science; but before it was completed, she was reassigned. Yet her learning continued. She was able to earn a master's degree in Business Administration. During a five-year assignment with the NATO forces in northern Germany, Jeanette and her husband informally studied German with the mayor of the town. Classes offered by the army were another source of formal education. Jeanette was motivated to take these classes to advance in her military career.

After spending five years in Germany, Jeanette was reassigned to the States and resumed her computer science studies. Jeanette discovered that technology had changed rapidly. Many of the courses she had taken five years before were now lower-level classes. Several programming languages were no longer in use. Jeanette had to learn new computer languages to continue her degree.

After 20 years in military service, Jeanette retired and began a new profession. She now teaches computer science full-time in a two-year technical school. Yet she still continues her education. Recently Jeanette was accepted into the doctoral program in computer science at a leading university.

Jeanette believes in continuing education. She is happiest when she is learning. She is highly motivated and firmly believes that staying current in technological areas requires continuous education. She is an example of the process of effective career planning.

Social and Cultural Context

Every person is affected by many social and cultural factors, but we'll examine those that are most important to the career planning process. The most immediate factor is your relationships with significant others in your life—your family and friends. Decisions about your career are affected by significant others. Some people are most affected by relationships with friends. Others are more affected by their spouse and children. The Family and Friends Worksheet asks questions related to your family and friends that you need to answer when planning your career. Complete the worksheet to help focus on issues that affect your career plans and interaction with family and friends.

Family and Friends Worksheet

1. How much time do I want to spend with my family and friends, and what type of work schedule will best meet my needs?

   _____

   _____

2. What level of income do I need for myself and my family to achieve the lifestyle that we want?

_____

_____

3. Are there geographical restrictions that limit my career choices because of family? What are these restrictions, such as same city or same state?

_____

_____

4. Do I want to limit geographical moves so that I can remain close to friends? What are the limits that I need to set?

_____

_____

5. Will my family and friends support the career choice I make? If not, do I think that I can succeed without their support?

_____

_____

6. Will my career choice negatively affect my relationship with family and friends? If so, am I willing to adjust to the new relationship?

_____

_____

7. Does the career provide the time, flexibility, or money needed to provide care for children or other dependents? In what ways does it meet these needs?

_____

_____

Research has shown that the impact of career choices on relationships with family and friends affects the outcome of career decisions. In many cases, a person will alter a career decision rather than experience a continued decline in a relationship. You will be a happier person if you consider family and friends in career decisions.

Going back to school is usually a temporary situation in terms of the impact it has on family and friends. It should you find a career that allows you to meet the conditions you set on the Family and Friends Worksheet. Pursuit of a college degree may require you to temporarily suspend some obligations to family and friends. But think of it as a temporary situation designed to help you better fulfill those obligations in the future. Chapter 7 explores how you can balance the demands of college with the demands of family and friends.

Labor Market

Economic conditions are often behind the decision to change careers. When the economy is in a recession, there are several effects. First, many businesses find it necessary to downsize during recessions. Further, researchers report that many larger businesses plan to use downsizing—regardless of economic conditions—as a routine strategy to remain competitive in the global economy. Second, even businesses that can avoid layoffs in a recession usually do not expand, and this limits internal opportunities for promotion. Third, it is usually more difficult to move from one organization to another during recessions unless you have highly desirable skills that are in short supply. As a result of these dynamics, many people turn to education to improve their skills and become more competitive.

Economic troubles do not mean you should put your career on hold. If you are the victim of downsizing, you may find that pursuing a college education is a viable alternative to taking another job. However, it is important to recognize that, even when the economy is on a downward trend, there are still hundreds of thousands of jobs available. One strategy is to take a job that you consider temporary while pursuing a college degree. You can explain to future employers that the reason for taking a position considered a downward move was to allow you to improve your education and skills. Most employers find this a perfectly acceptable explanation and don't hold it against you. You can use a period of limited opportunities within your organization as a time to position yourself for future potential advancement. Pursuing a college degree can be used as a reason for a lull in your career advancement within the organization.

The labor market makes other adjustments that are more long range in their ramifications. Businesses will pursue a variety of strategies to remain competitive. For example, many organizations are relying heavily on temporary workers and outside vendors as a way to control personnel expenses. These strategies affect everyone from front-line workers to executives. It is just as likely that a business will employ temporary accountants and computer specialists as clerks and secretaries. Many management experts predict that this approach will become a permanent scheme among businesses in their attempts to remain competitive.

Technological changes also affect the labor market. The impact of the computer is the most dramatic illustration of such changes. Millions of workers have found their skills obsolete and have had to become educated in the use of personal computers and software such as spreadsheets, database management, and word processing. Sales personnel have had to learn to use computers in multimedia presentations. Many occupations have not only changed but also declined in number—such as secretarial positions—while others have been created—such as the position of network administrator.

A knowledge of the labor market is important when you choose a career. The Labor Market Worksheet contains several questions to identify conditions you should consider when planning your career.

Labor Market Worksheet

1. Is the loss of my job likely to occur because I lack a college degree?

   _____

   _____

2. Will a college degree significantly improve opportunities for promotions with my employer?

   _____

   _____

3. Will opportunities for getting a new job be greatly increased if I return to college and get a degree?

   _____

   _____

4. Do job opportunities exist for a person with my skills even when there is a downturn in the economy?

_____

_____

5. Are there alternative career paths in my organization that can be pursued if I return to college?

_____

_____

6. Are there training opportunities or other job experiences that can help me achieve my career goals without returning to college?

_____

_____

7. What occupations provide the most promise for growth and economic success? Which of these am I interested in?

Occupations	Am I Interested?	
_____	☐ Yes	☐ No
_____	☐ Yes	☐ No
_____	☐ Yes	☐ No
_____	☐ Yes	☐ No
_____	☐ Yes	☐ No
_____	☐ Yes	☐ No

The United States is large, and its economy is quite complicated. There are many regional and local variations from the national economy. It is possible that you can continue to advance your career by moving to a location that provides more opportunities for someone with your skills. You will need to balance out the effects of such a move with the costs to obtain additional education.

Another labor market issue you should consider in planning your career is the variation in job potential among various occupations. Economic growth doesn't have a universal impact on all occupations.

Advances in technology, competitive adjustments by organizations, demographic changes, and many other factors can cause a particular occupation to experience an increase or decrease in job openings. Knowledge about occupational projections can help you identify jobs where growth will occur. The employment outlook and earning potential for an occupation must be balanced against requirements and personal satisfaction that the occupation will provide. These characteristics can include skills, aptitudes, education, experience, temperament, physical demands, and working conditions. It is important to research occupations to develop an informed career plan.

Two excellent publications that provide occupational information are the *Occupational Outlook Handbook* and *Occupational Outlook Quarterly,* both produced by the U.S. Department of Labor. The *Occupational Outlook Handbook* is published every two years and contains information on 250 occupations that will provide most employment opportunities. In fact, typically 85 to 87 percent of people in the U.S. workforce are employed in these 250 occupations. The *Occupational Outlook Quarterly* is published every three months and contains the most up-to-date information on careers and occupational projections. There are books from a variety of publishers that also provide information on occupations. Almost all of them use information from the *Occupational Outlook Quarterly* or data from the U.S. Department of Labor. Other sources of information on occupations can be obtained from career counselors, state employment services, college career centers, and people working in occupations in which you're interested. You should include the following questions when you collect information about occupations.

Occupational Choice Worksheet

1. What are the skills required for the occupation, and what experience and education are needed to acquire these skills?

   _____

   _____

2. What skills do I have related to this job?

   _____

   _____

Do I enjoy practicing these skills?   ❏ Yes   ❏ No

Do I enjoy studying subjects needed to develop the
skills?   ❏ Yes   ❏ No

3. Are the working conditions suitable to me?   ❏ Yes   ❏ No

4. What is the earning potential?

_____

5. Will it provide me the lifestyle I want?   ❏ Yes   ❏ No

6. What is the level of competition for jobs in this occupational field?

_____

7. What are the opportunities and requirements for advancement?

_____

_____

8. Is it likely that pursuit of this career field will require
   me to locate to another part of the country?   ❏ Yes   ❏ No

9. Is this desirable?   ❏ Yes   ❏ No

10. Does my current organization hire workers in
    this occupational area?   ❏ Yes   ❏ No

11. Is it possible for me to compete successfully for the
    jobs offered by my employer when I obtain the
    education and experience needed?   ❏ Yes   ❏ No

12. What employers in the area offer jobs in this career field.

_____

_____

13. Am I interested in working for these employers?   ❏ Yes   ❏ No

You can use the following chart when you collect data about
occupations. Information needed to complete the chart can be found in
the *Occupational Outlook Handbook* and *Dictionary of Occupational Titles,*

both published by the U.S. Department of Labor. In addition, there are three books published by JIST Works, Inc., that provide useful information about occupations. These books are *The Complete Guide for Occupational Exploration, The Enhanced Guide for Occupational Exploration,* and *The Worker Traits Data Book.* Many of these books can be found at libraries or career counseling centers.

Use the Occupational Comparison Worksheet to compare different occupations that interest you. Look up information for each occupation. Rate from 1 to 3 (1 is high and 3 is low) each characteristic of an occupation in terms of its desirability. Then discuss the occupation with a friend or acquaintance who can tell you more about it. It may be necessary to network through friends to find someone working in an occupation. Ask that person to confirm or expand on the information you've collected.

Occupational Comparison Worksheet			
Job Description	**Occupation 1**	**Occupation 2**	**Occupation 3**
Job Title			
Education required			
Experience required			
Temperament needed			
Aptitudes			
Physical requirements			
Skills			
Working conditions			
Earning potential			
Employment outlook			
Outlook for current employer			

Work Setting

Another environmental factor that affects career planning is the work setting, or the type of organization in which you'll work. A particular industry often has its own characteristics. These can be researched through popular business magazines such as *Business Week* or *Fortune.* An excellent reference for information on industries is the *Career Guide to Industry,* which is produced by the Department of Commerce. It provides information about major industries, including economic outlook and working conditions. Another useful resource for investigating an industry is the *Standard Industrial Classification Manual,* which classifies all businesses and institutions and provides a brief description about each.

It is important to know about an industry, but you should also investigate particular businesses you're interested in working for. Popular business magazines are again a valuable resource if the organization is large enough to be covered by the national press. The business section of the local newspaper is also a good source of information, and many larger communities have business journals or city magazines that feature local businesses.

Computers allow you to search through a vast array of information to identify articles about a particular business. Many libraries now have CD-ROM systems that contain information about businesses. Ask a reference librarian at your local library to help you learn to conduct searches and locate the information you want. You can also use electronic information services like *America Online, CompuServe, Delphi,* and *Prodigy,* which offer an enormous amount of information about businesses in this country. Further, there are forums where you can pose questions about a business to other system users and accumulate firsthand information. Of course, the Internet provides access to thousands of resources and millions of people.

And don't forget that good, old-fashioned personal networking with friends and acquaintances can uncover a lot of information about an organization. You should examine a number of items to determine whether an organization provides a work setting that is suitable to your needs and desires. Look for answers to the following questions.

Work Setting Worksheet

1. Does the job require working with people?   ❑ Yes   ❑ No

2. What type of people skills are needed?

   _____

   _____

3. Does the job require working with data?   ❑ Yes   ❑ No

4. What type of data skills are needed?

   _____

   _____

5. Does the job require working with things?   ❑ Yes   ❑ No

6. What skills are required to manipulate these things?

   _____

   _____

7. What is the economic outlook for this industry?

   _____

   Does it look good for the short term?

   _____

   What about the long-term outlook?

   _____

8. Is the industry highly competitive?   ❑ Yes   ❑ No

9. Do I enjoy this level of competition?   ❑ Yes   ❑ No

10. Does the future look bright for the business or
    institution?   ❑ Yes   ❑ No

11. Is the management style of the business authoritative or participative?

    _____

12. Which style am I most comfortable working with?

_____

13. Does the leadership promote employee growth and development?   ❑ Yes   ❑ No

14. Will I have an opportunity to continue my training and skills development?   ❑ Yes   ❑ No

15. Is the work facility comfortable?   ❑ Yes   ❑ No

16. Is it convenient to my residence?   ❑ Yes   ❑ No

17. Will it require relocation or a difficult commute?   ❑ Yes   ❑ No

18. Will management accommodate my interest in working at home?   ❑ Yes   ❑ No

19. Will the business provide the autonomy or direction that I want?   ❑ Yes   ❑ No

20. Does the organization promote from within?

_____

What will be my opportunities for advancement?

_____

_____

21. What are the travel requirements for most jobs in the organization?

_____

_____

22. Do these requirements fit my needs?   ❑ Yes   ❑ No

23. Are managers and coworkers people I feel comfortable working with?   ❑ Yes   ❑ No

24. Are the salary and fringe benefits consistent with my expectations.   ❑ Yes   ❑ No

25. Are they competitive with similar organizations in the industry?   ❑ Yes   ❑ No

You may want answers to a number of other questions about the work setting. Keep in mind that your satisfaction with a career choice depends on how well an organization matches your needs and desires. While research about the work setting takes a lot of time, it is worth your time because it helps avoid conflicts later on.

Deciding on College

This section is designed to help you translate the career planning guidelines discussed in this chapter into a decision about a college education. It is important to recognize that while a college education has certain economic advantages, it is not the best career choice for everyone. Completing the *College Decision Worksheet* should help you determine whether it is the best choice for you.

College Decision Worksheet

Answer these questions and then review your response. If you find more affirmative responses than negative responses, a college degree may be the best choice for you.

1. Do the occupations I'm interested in require a college degree?   ☐ Yes   ☐ No

2. Are the skills I need for my career obtained best through a college degree?   ☐ Yes   ☐ No

3. Will a college degree help me advance at my current employer?   ☐ Yes   ☐ No

4. Will a college degree help me get with another employer a job that meets my personal goals and needs?   ☐ Yes   ☐ No

5. Do I have the resources and support I need to pursue a college degree?   ☐ Yes   ☐ No

6. Do I have the motivation and self-discipline needed for a college degree?   ☐ Yes   ☐ No

7. Will the college degree of my choice require me to start at an entry level that will pay less than I currently earn?	❑ Yes ❑ No
8. Am I willing to earn less temporarily in order to change careers?	❑ Yes ❑ No

Making the Decision

The final decision to pursue a degree is an important one for your future. A college degree requires a significant investment of time and money. Take time to consider your options carefully. Completing the exercises in this chapter is a start in making this important decision. It is a good idea to get advice about a career move as significant as this. Talk with key managers at your place of employment to get their advice. Seek out former teachers whom you still know and respect. Find coworkers who have returned to college and ask their opinions. Talk with professional career counselors, including advisors at a local college. Most importantly, discuss the matter with your family and friends.

Once you've taken these steps and decided to pursue a degree, follow through with the decision. Don't procrastinate, because the longer you wait, the harder it will be to disrupt your current career. After you start, there will be problems, but don't let them discourage you. Look back at the decision you made and remain confident in the results of that decision. However, you will change, and your environment will change. Therefore, a periodic review and response to the questions asked in this chapter will help you evaluate your original decision. This review may result in a modification of your educational plans but should not result in permanent deferral of a college education or advanced degree.

IGNATIUS COLLEGE OF FORDHAM UNIVERSITY is a private university based on the Jesuit tradition of education and is located in New York City. Ignatius College was established to meet the needs of nontraditional students. These include recent high school graduates working their way through college, graduates of community colleges, and working adults. The typical student takes about six years to complete a degree. Fordham has approximately 15,000 students, and enrollment in Ignatius College is about 500.

The college follows a somewhat traditional degree model that requires students to complete courses by attending classes. However, the classes normally meet once a week from 6:30 to 9:15 P.M. and on Saturdays from 9:00 to 11:45 A.M. In addition, administrative offices and services are open one to two nights each week to accommodate working students' schedules. Many of the academic policies have been developed with adult students in mind. For example, a student unable to take a final exam in a course—but otherwise in good standing—can be awarded an ABS grade and complete the exam as soon as possible. The college also has a special scholarship program for students who attend evening classes.

Ignatius puts an emphasis on preparing a "well-educated person" through a traditional liberal arts degree program. There is a core curriculum of 63 credits (in which students have some choice about courses), a major of 30 credits, and electives of 27 credits. Students can receive up to 18 hours of credit for prior learning experiences. Ten majors are available in several of the traditional liberal arts and sciences areas.

The college is a good example of how a traditional degree program can be structured and adapted to meet the needs of adult students. It is able to offer a high-quality education in the liberal arts tradition to adults.

Chapter 3

College Education—The New and the Old

Colleges have been responding to a variety of changes in our society. In order to avoid major cutbacks in programs, faculty, and staff, they have found it necessary to expand their constituency. The changing demographics of the population have a major influence on higher education. During the 1960s and '70s, colleges had a large population of traditional students—students under 20 who enrolled in college immediately after high school, lived on campus, and attended classes full-time—as a result of the baby boom generation graduating from high school. These traditional students provided an adequate base from which to recruit students. However, the number of high school graduates began to decline during the '80s, and colleges began to focus more attention on adult students and their particular needs.

Additional changes in higher education have been driven by several social forces. Political, business, and educational leaders have recognized the need for innovative approaches in higher education to better prepare the workforce for competition in a global economy. Many colleges have worked cooperatively with these leaders to create new degree programs that accommodate the needs of business, employees, and higher education. Further, many educators have recognized the potential offered by technology for innovative educational programs and have developed new degree programs. Another factor driving change is the rise of student consumerism.

Degree programs that respond to the needs of adults—and to the many societal changes mentioned—have proliferated in the past few years. Nontraditional degree programs exist in every part of the country, and there are many degrees you can obtain from colleges across the country from your own living room. There are more types of degrees, a greater variety of degree programs, and more innovative methods for obtaining a degree than ever before. This chapter describes the various degrees that are available, and explains the many options today's students have for degree programs. It also defines some academic terms and concepts for those readers who have not attended college before.

A College Is a College—Right?

The words *college* and *university* are often used in a very casual manner. Businesses and institutions that are peripherally involved in educational activities sometimes use these names—such as McDonald's Hamburger University. As you begin to consider higher education, it is important to understand the difference between the various types of institutions and what is meant by the terms college and university.

From an academic viewpoint, a *college* is an institution that grants degrees to students who demonstrate a mastery of knowledge appropriate for the degree awarded. In addition, a college or university is not regarded seriously unless it has been recognized by an independent organization called an *accrediting body*. (An explanation of *accreditation*— what it means and how it is done—is included in the next section of this chapter.) There are degree mills that—for a fee—will award anyone a degree, but they are not recognized as legitimate institutions of higher education, and the degrees they award are essentially worthless to a person's career. In this book, we have used the term college in a generic sense—applying the name to all institutions of higher education that award degrees.

Community Colleges and Junior Colleges

Community and junior colleges provide college-level studies that typically lead to a two-year associate degree. The term *junior college* has gradually given way to the more popular name—*community college*. However, junior colleges that are privately owned and financed still use the name. Community colleges are almost always funded by state governments. Some private junior colleges do not award degrees but, rather, prepare students to enter a four-year institution with junior status.

There are several advantages to attending a community college. One is convenience. They normally have been established in locations not served by four-year colleges and universities. Another advantage is lower cost. Community colleges usually are funded by the state government, don't equip themselves to conduct costly research, and hire few faculty with doctoral degrees. All of these factors keep expenses low. A further benefit of attending a community college is that the educational philosophy is more suited to adult needs. Community colleges focus on preparing students for careers, use faculty with work experience in course content areas, and schedule courses at times convenient for adult students. This may account for the fact that more than 50 percent of all students attending community colleges are over 25 years old.

Four-Year Liberal Arts Colleges

These are institutions that emphasize the bachelor's degree and award the majority of their degrees in liberal arts fields. The focus of the faculty is on teaching and the intellectual development of students. Liberal arts colleges emphasize a well-rounded education with less concentration on preparation for a specific career. Students typically major in fields such as English language and literature, foreign languages, life sciences, physical sciences, mathematics, the arts, social sciences, or religion. Most liberal arts colleges are private institutions, and a large number are associated with churches. Since private institutions don't receive direct government assistance, the cost to attend a four-year liberal arts college can be high.

It may seem that this sort of college isn't the best for a career-minded adult. However, there has been a raging debate among business leaders about the best educational preparation for the world of work, and a significant number prefer the liberal arts degree. The reason is that liberal arts students are typically well prepared in oral and verbal communication, have good analytical skills, are effective problem solvers, and are able to work with diverse groups of people.

In the past 15 years, many traditional liberal arts colleges have shown a great willingness to provide innovative and nontraditional education programs to meet the needs of working adults. The degree programs are often in career fields like business management or nursing. Many of these colleges have also begun offering the master's degree in a limited number of areas, such as education and business.

Four-Year Colleges

Four-year colleges graduate a majority of their students with a bachelor's degree in a professional area. These areas often include engineering, business, and nursing. As liberal arts colleges have begun to offer more professional degree programs for adults, there has been a blurring in the distinction between liberal arts colleges and other four-year colleges.

The four-year college usually is private and doesn't get state funds. Therefore, it costs more than most state institutions to attend. Many four-year colleges have faculty with well-developed connections to professionals in their field. This can result in a competitive advantage for graduates who are seeking employment. Another advantage is that many of these colleges have developed outstanding reputations for producing well-prepared professionals.

Universities

Many four-year colleges have changed their names from college to university in recent years—often in an attempt to distinguish themselves from junior and community colleges. However, a *university* has traditionally been an institution of higher education that awards graduate degrees. A comprehensive university offers bachelor's, master's, professional, and doctorate degrees in a wide variety of disciplines. Other universities concentrate on graduate work at only the master's level or offer a limited number of degree programs at the doctoral level.

Graduate education is usually expensive to provide, and for this reason the majority of universities are state-supported institutions. The focus of a university is usually on research. Teaching students is important, but not as high a priority as research. Also, many university faculty prefer to teach graduate students and so assign teaching assistants—who are graduate-level students—to teach undergraduate courses.

The benefits of attending a university can be found in several forms. One benefit is the library system, which has been developed to support research and provides access to a large number of resources useful to college students. Universities also offer a wide variety of degree programs. Because universities are typically state-supported, the cost of a college degree is lower, and they are the best source of a high-quality, low-cost graduate degree. In addition, most universities have high name recognition, which can be beneficial when you are looking for employment. At the graduate level, you will have an opportunity to study with some of the most highly qualified and well-recognized experts in your chosen field of study. Unfortunately, quite a few universities have been reluctant to institute innovative degree programs for adult students.

The Importance of Accreditation

Accreditation is conferred on an institution of higher education by an accrediting agency and is important for several reasons. First, a college must be accredited by a body recognized by the U.S. Department of Education for students to qualify for federal financial aid programs. Second, employers—particularly larger corporations—will not recognize a nonaccredited college as legitimate. They often don't consider a college degree from a nonaccredited school acceptable in meeting basic job requirements. In addition, most employers that provide tuition assistance won't reimburse workers unless the college is accredited. Third, credits earned at a nonaccredited college usually will not transfer to an accredited college. Likewise, entrance into a graduate program at an accredited college normally requires a bachelor's or master's degree from an accredited college. Finally, accreditation ensures that the quality of education a student receives meets the standards the college claims to have set for itself. Thus, accreditation is a good guide to quality education.

For accreditation to be legitimate, it must begin with recognition by the federal government. The Department of Education recognizes accrediting bodies that can confer accreditation on colleges. It is important to recognize that these accrediting bodies are governed by the colleges and institutions that they accredit. In essence, the higher education community works together in a form of self-policing to protect the public and ensure that colleges are conducting themselves in accordance with established standards.

Accrediting bodies do not stipulate a long list of rules, policies, and procedures that colleges must follow. Rather, they establish broad standards that each institution is expected to follow in setting their own goals, objectives, policies, and procedures.

The regional accrediting bodies are the most highly respected of all accrediting groups. Whenever possible, a college will seek accreditation from one of these bodies. The United States has been divided into six regions, and each body provides accreditation for colleges within its region. The six regions and their accrediting bodies are listed below:

Middle States Association of Colleges and Schools
Delaware, District of Columbia, Maryland, New Jersey, New York, Pennsylvania, Puerto Rico, the Virgin Islands

New England Association of Schools and Colleges
Connecticut, Maine, Massachusetts, New Hampshire, Rhode Island, Vermont

North Central Association of Colleges and Schools
Arizona, Arkansas, Colorado, Illinois, Indiana, Iowa, Kansas, Michigan, Minnesota, Missouri, Nebraska, New Mexico, North Dakota, Ohio, Oklahoma, South Dakota, West Virginia, Wisconsin, Wyoming

Northwest Association of Schools and Colleges
Alaska, Idaho, Montana, Nevada, Oregon, Utah, Washington

Southern Association of Colleges and Schools
Alabama, Florida, Georgia, Kentucky, Louisiana, Mississippi, North Carolina, South Carolina, Tennessee, Texas, Virginia

Western Association of Schools and Colleges
California, Hawaii, American Samoa, Guam, the Commonwealth of the Northern Marianas, and the Trust Territory of the Pacific Islands

A college must seek accreditation from the regional body responsible for its state of residence. It is possible for a college to seek accreditation from another body, if the college administrators don't think that the regional body will understand the college's mission, philosophy, and structure. One accrediting body that oversees many nontraditional colleges is the Distance Education and Training Council. This body is responsible for accrediting home study schools granting associate, bachelor's, and master's degrees. In the past, this was relevant only to colleges offering correspondence degree programs. However, with the advent of video, television, and computer technology, this body is now responsible for overseeing some of the most innovative programs in adult higher education.

An institution filing for accreditation and deemed suitable normally is given preaccreditation status—sometimes referred to as candidacy—until it graduates its first class of students. Once the first class graduates, it is reviewed again to determine its ability to comply with the accrediting body's standards. Only then is it eligible for full accreditation.

A college that has received accreditation is reviewed periodically—commonly every 10 years—to ensure continued compliance with standards. Whenever an accredited college offers a new degree at a higher level, that degree program must be reviewed for accreditation. The new degree status will be preaccredited but doesn't receive full accreditation until the first group of students graduates from the program. Thus, a college can be accredited but may only be a candidate for accreditation for a particular degree. It is possible to receive financial aid from the federal government for a college or degree that has been preaccredited by a regional accrediting body.

Colleges also must be recognized and approved for operation by state agencies of higher education. The names of these groups vary, but typically they use the words commission or regents in their title. A state agency is often concerned with protecting its citizens against fraudulent institutions. Some state agencies rely on the evaluations by regional accrediting bodies to determine the status of an institution. Other state agencies are more proactive and review each institution according to their own standards. Thus, it may be possible for an institution to operate in a state without accreditation from a regional body. Some colleges without regional accreditation will advertise that they are approved by the state commission or board of regents. This status is not sufficient for the institution to qualify for federal financial aid. However, state recognition may allow students to qualify for state financial aid programs.

Each individual must decide whether to attend a nonaccredited college. The benefits and advantages offered by the college may offset its lack of accreditation. Creative and innovative degree programs usually undergo more scrutiny and may take longer to get accreditation even though the offered degree is of high quality. Furthermore, some colleges and degree programs lack only a graduating class and otherwise meet all standards. Students pursuing degrees from an institution in this situation may feel confident that their degrees will one day be recognized as having come from an accredited college. These students are usually the pioneers who make up the first graduating class that leads to an institution's accreditation.

College Degrees

The ultimate goal of most college students is a degree of some type. The degree represents an accomplishment in the student's life. Employers typically require degrees for certain jobs and see two advantages in hiring people with degrees. One advantage is that a degree demonstrates a person's ability to establish and accomplish a major goal. Another is that a degree indicates that a person has developed a general knowledge base and has specialized knowledge about some subjects.

A college degree can and should be more than just preparation for a career. It helps the individual become a more knowledgeable citizen able to contribute to society. This includes government, charitable organizations, the arts, and community activities. A degree by itself doesn't make a person a more capable citizen but, rather, the learning that accompanies the degree. A degree is a tangible means of recognizing the learning that has taken place in the life of an individual. Colleges and universities offer different types of degrees. The length of time needed to complete the course work varies with each degree.

Undergraduate Degrees

There is a hierarchy of degrees that consists of two basic levels. Typically a student must first complete one degree level before advancing to another. The first is the *undergraduate* level. An *associate degree* may be earned with two years of full-time college credit. The *bachelor's degree* may be earned with four years of full-time college work. It is not necessary to complete an associate degree before advancing to a bachelor's degree. Both associate degrees and bachelor's degrees are referred to as undergraduate degrees, and credits earned toward them are called undergraduate work. Each type of degree is explained more thoroughly to help you determine the most appropriate goal for yourself.

The Associate Degree

The associate degree is a recent educational creation and was originally developed for junior college and community college graduates. However, many four-year colleges now offer associate degrees. An associate degree usually requires two years of full-time classes—about 60 semester hours or 90 quarter hours. Some associate degrees require three years to complete. Associate degrees are often directly connected to an occupation, such as early childhood education, respiratory technology, or electronic technology. Community colleges, junior colleges, technical schools, and many four-year colleges offer associate degrees.

For many adult students, an associate degree is attractive because it offers a degree in a shorter time. Many people obtain an associate degree at a community college and transfer those credits to a four-year school. An associate degree is generally like having completed the freshman and sophomore years of college; however, the student receives a diploma. Knowing that you have a diploma can be a real confidence booster as you continue your educational process. An associate degree is recognized by many employers as a significant accomplishment that can improve your career opportunities. Statistics from the Department of Labor indicate that workers with associate degrees have average annual earnings that are $5,000 higher than high school graduates.

The Bachelor's Degree

Typically, a bachelor's degree is what most people think of as a "college degree." Earning a bachelor's degree at a traditional college usually requires four, and frequently five, years of full-time work—about 120 semester hours or 180 quarter hours. The most common bachelor's degrees are the Bachelor of Arts (B.A. or A.B.) and the Bachelor of Science (B.S.). Traditionally the Bachelor of Arts degree emphasizes the humanities and arts and requires foreign language study, whereas a Bachelor of Science degree places more emphasis on science courses, with advanced mathematics being part of the program.

These traditional distinctions have become blurred on many college campuses, so you will need to question the academic advisors at a college to determine the distinction made by that college.

Some other bachelor's degrees include Bachelor of Fine Arts (B.F.A.), Bachelor of Business Administration (B.B.A.), Bachelor of Liberal Studies (B.L.S.), Bachelor of Professional Studies (B.P.S.), Bachelor of Science in Nursing (B.S.N.), and Bachelor of Social Work (B.S.W.).

Graduate Degrees

Graduate degrees are the second degree level, and include *master's degrees, professional degrees,* and *doctoral degrees.* To be accepted in most graduate programs a student must have earned a bachelor's degree. Some master's degrees are considered terminal, which means there is not a higher degree to be obtained in their area of specialty: an example is the Master of Library Science. Many master's degrees are designed to prepare students for doctoral-level work. Professional degrees frequently are required for entry into a specific profession like law, dentistry, or medicine. The doctor's degree is the ultimate educational degree. It is possible to obtain an academic doctorate—normally a Ph.D. or an Ed.D.—or a doctor's degree in a professional field.

The Master's Degree

Master's degrees usually are academic degrees focused on preparing students for research and teaching at the college and university level—often with the intention of the person pursuing a doctorate. However, some have been developed to prepare students for specific professions.

Most academic master's degrees take one year of course work--about 33 semesters hours or 45 quarter hours—and many also require a written thesis. Typical academic master's degrees include the Master of Arts (M.A.) and Master of Science (M.S.). Professional-level master's degrees typically require one and a half to two years of course work—45 to 60 semester hours or 75 to 90 quarter hours. Professional degrees at the master's level include Master of Business Administration (M.B.A.), Master of Library Science (M.L.S.), Master of Public Administration (M.P.A.), and Master of Public Health (M.P.H.).

There are many nontraditional master's degree programs for adults. In fact, educators seem to have a more liberal attitude about innovative approaches to the master's degree. This is because they know that a graduate of a master's program is required to have a bachelor's degree from a regionally accredited institution. Therefore, the student has already demonstrated a reasonable level of competence in satisfying academic requirements at the college level. There is also immense pressure from consumers to modify master's degree programs so that they accommodate adult learner needs—almost 80 percent of all graduate students are over 25.

The Professional Degree

Some professional degrees require three years of academic study, but these are usually doctoral degrees. This type of degree normally requires a bachelor's degree but doesn't require a master's degree. The emphasis of the degree program is preparation for a profession. Examples of this type of degree are Doctor of Medicine (M.D.), Doctor of Veterinary Medicine (D.V.M.), Doctor of Ministry (D.Min.), and Juris Doctor (J.D.)—to practice law.

Less innovation has been demonstrated among professional degree programs than at any other level of higher education. (Exceptions to this are degrees in religious ministries programs.) Most occupations requiring a professional degree are tightly controlled and licensed by both professional associations and state agencies. Qualifications for licensing are based on educational requirements that are based on traditional models. This severely limits the ability to originate degree programs designed to accommodate adult needs.

The Doctorate

A doctorate is the highest academic degree that can be earned. It is normally awarded as a Doctor of Philosophy (Ph.D.) or a Doctor of Education (Ed.D.) Traditionally, the Ph.D. has placed more emphasis on research, including mastery of a foreign language that could be used in research. However, the requirements distinguishing the Ph.D. and the Ed.D. have begun to break down at many universities.

An earned doctorate includes course work, a dissertation based on original research conducted by the student, and comprehensive written and oral exams evaluated by a committee of university faculty. A doctoral degree is usually earned after a master's degree and requires three years of study beyond this degree. However, some programs will accept a student with a bachelor's degree and award both a master's and a doctor's degree on completion of the program. Other doctoral degrees have been developed over the past century, including Doctor of Business Administration (D.B.A) and Doctor of Public Administration (D.P.A.).

Many institutions have created doctoral degrees that are nontraditional, and many of these degree programs are accredited. However, there has been some reluctance on the part of the larger academic community to recognize the quality of these degrees. Since one of the major career opportunities for people with doctorates is teaching at the college level, it is vital for future employment that the academic community recognize and approve of a degree program. This shouldn't be your only consideration when reviewing nontraditional doctoral programs, but it certainly is one primary factor that should be included in the decision-making process.

A Major

A student earning a bachelor's degree has a major area of study. The student concentrates on this area, and one-fourth to one-half of his or her course work is taken in this discipline. A minor area of concentration may also be required. A minor requires about one-half the number of credits needed for a major. Not all majors and minors require the same number of credits to complete.

Your major is important for two reasons. First, it affects your eligibility to enter some graduate programs. For example, graduate degree programs in areas such as biology, mathematics, and psychology usually require that you have a bachelor's degree with a major in that area. In addition, your major determines how employers evaluate your eligibility for jobs within their organization. For example, an accounting firm is not likely to hire someone for an accountant position unless that person has a bachelor's degree with a major in accounting.

It is best to select a major as soon as possible. A major is governed by a department in the college that teaches the courses needed for that major. For example, a chemistry major is governed by the chemistry department. So, in most institutions, faculty members in the chemistry department vote to determine the courses that a student majoring in chemistry must take to obtain a degree. This applies not only to courses in chemistry but also to related courses that the faculty feel are needed in areas like physics and mathematics. (Usually, the university establishes a core of general education courses that all students are expected to take, and this core is incorporated into the department's guidelines for its majors.)

Deciding on a degree early in your academic career means that you can follow the course guidelines established by the department. It also means that a faculty member from that department is assigned to be your academic advisor. The academic advisor provides guidance and counsel about the courses you should take to meet the degree requirements. This person usually has a much better understanding about departmental policies regarding a major than a general advisor assigned by the college.

JOHN is 30 years old. He has been married for two years and has no children. He has an undergraduate degree from a conservative, reputable university. John is the head of a consulting firm available to entrepreneurs interested in small businesses. He is active in church and community activities. His life is full.

As John has done his consulting work, he has realized that a graduate degree is becoming an industry standard. For that reason, he has enrolled in a graduate program at a major university. John has taken some adult education courses. He believes that graduate classes should be taught to adults as learners. He is disturbed by the fact that many of his classes are taught exactly like the undergraduate classes he took seven years ago.

Working on the degree has affected every part of John's life. His lifestyle has changed. He has made adjustments in his commitments at home, in the community, and on the job. His goal is "to graduate with honors without having a nervous breakdown."

As John nears graduation, he reflects on the question, "Is it worth it?" His answer is simply this: "I grow and learn every day; it's just that, to be acceptable and recognized by society, I must do it in a formal classroom setting. I'm willing to conform so that later I might be able to influence a change in society's view."

The Traditional College Degree Program

There are several traditional assumptions colleges have made in this century when planning degree programs, and they continue to shape the way most degree programs offered today are structured. The most fundamental assumption is that students reside on the college campus and attend classroom lectures given by instructors. From this perspective, a college is a community where members live and work together toward a common goal: the discovery and sharing of knowledge.

Another assumption is that courses must be delivered in a standard format. It is customary to divide an academic year into "terms." These terms are usually semesters—15 to 18 weeks in length—or quarters of 11 to 12 weeks. A course is assigned a specific number of "credits" based on the amount of classroom contact time. (Contact time implies that the student attends a class meeting held by a college instructor.) One credit equals a specific number of classroom hours. For example, one semester credit equals 15 hours of classroom contact. Therefore, a course that a student takes for 3 semester hours of credit meets for approximately 45 hours during the semester. The number of semester hours is usually divided into class meetings of 50 minutes for three days a week or 75 minutes for two days a week.

A further assumption on which traditional college programs are based is that students fit a traditional demographic profile. This profile characterizes students as recent high school graduates pursuing a degree full-time, living on campus, and proceeding through courses at a continuous pace until a degree is obtained. This assumption translates into several common practices on college campuses. Most courses are offered between 7:00 A.M. and 4:00 P.M. A course is scheduled for class meetings two, three, and sometimes even four times a week. Faculty members hold office hours when students can meet with them, usually between 8:00 A.M. and 5:00 P.M. Administrators keep the same hours for important functions such as registration, advising, career advising and placement, and the bookstore.

Educators and administrators also assume that learning for which students receive credit must occur in a college classroom. This means that strict policies are developed governing the way credits are earned. College faculty and administrators review and approve the curriculum to determine that all academic policies are met. Strict guidelines are developed for the transfer of credits accumulated by students at other colleges. Transfer policies usually specify that courses must have been taken within a recent time period, come from another accredited college, and be equivalent to a course taught at the college.

Colleges also have a tradition of helping students develop a "liberal" or "general" education. Specifics on how this is accomplished have changed throughout history. Originally, most elements of a student's education were devoted to the development of a liberal education. Over the years, the time spent acquiring a liberal education has become much smaller. In most colleges today, approximately 25 to 33 percent of a student's college education is devoted to a liberal education. Critics of higher education often focus on the lack of emphasis on a quality liberal education. General education requirements at a college consist of the courses the faculty and administration consider to be important in defining a liberal education for students.

KANSAS STATE UNIVERSITY is a major state university supported through state funds. It is located in Manhattan, Kansas, and has a student body of approximately 20,000. The Division of Continuing Education offers a Non-Traditional Study Program available to anyone in the United States. The goal of this program is to help students obtain a bachelor's degree. The program is particularly focused on students who don't have ready access to a college, who have experienced lapses in their college education, who need a more flexible schedule than traditional programs offer, and who have job and family responsibilities hindering a return to college.

Most of the students are older than the traditional student, who is 18 to 22. The ideal person for this degree program must be self-directed, flexible, and capable of integrating learning experiences.

Individualized programs are developed between the student and university advisors. Most students are able to work on a Bachelor of Science in interdisciplinary social sciences or a Bachelor of Science in agriculture, animal science, and industry. Students can earn credits toward the degree by courses taken at other colleges and transferred to KSU, and by military training, portfolios of prior learning experience, guided study, exams, and other nontraditional methods. At least 30 hours must be earned through courses from the university. Students set their own pace, although the university's promotional literature says that the average student completes a bachelor's degree in two to six years.

Colleges traditionally have hired faculty with strong academic credentials. The emphasis is placed on hiring faculty with doctoral degrees, with a preference for Doctor of Philosophy degrees. Faculty are expected to earn tenure—a lifelong guarantee of a job—by conducting research, teaching, and participating in service to the university and community. It is also possible for faculty to be promoted without moving into administrative positions. Faculty ranks—from low to high—are lecturer, instructor, assistant professor, associate professor, and professor. Members of the faculty play an important role in setting policies for the college.

Guide to a Traditional Degree Program

The first step you must take to obtain a traditional college degree is to gain admission to a college or university. There is a formal procedure that the admissions office administers. There are specific dates for submitting an application and for notification of acceptance. Your high school must submit a transcript of your courses and grades to the college—or evidence of a GED (the high school equivalency exam). Many colleges require that the applicant receive an acceptable score on either the SAT (Scholastic Aptitude Test) or the ACT (the American College Testing program). (Addresses to get information on these tests appear at the end of this chapter.) Sometimes a written essay is required. You must coordinate the completion of all entrance requirements so that the college receives them by the application deadline.

Admission to a college allows you to register for courses and pursue a degree. You must discuss your plans for registration with an advisor, who will give you a curriculum guide for your major. This guide shows all the courses required for graduation within your departmental major and states the number of courses required for graduation. It may also recommend a schedule for the entire degree program. This can be helpful, because many courses will have prerequisites. These are courses that must be completed before you can register for a course. Recommended schedules also help you determine the number of courses that are electives and when they can best fit into your schedule. The selection of a major early in your college career will help you more effectively and efficiently plan course schedules.

You will register for courses one term (semester or quarter) at a time. There are usually several time periods established when you can register for courses. These may be designated as early registration, advanced registration, preregistration, open registration, or late registration. A course schedule, or course listing, is usually published by the college a few weeks before the first registration opportunity.

You need to balance the courses you want with the days and times that classes are scheduled. Figure 1 illustrates a typical college registration schedule and shows all of the issues that must be weighed when you put together a class schedule for a semester or quarter. You must avoid conflicts between courses with classes scheduled on the same day and at the same hours. You also need to consider where the class is located, because there may be too much distance to walk from one class to another between the scheduled periods.

Often an advisor must approve your schedule. Then you take it to the registrar's office, where it is entered into a computer system to verify that all classes are open. (Some colleges now have campuswide computer systems that allow advisors or departmental secretaries to enter the information and confirm that all classes are open; others allow students to register by phone or computer). When a class is closed, you can register for the same course at another time and period. However, if there are no openings for a class, you usually must return and get the advisor's approval to take a different course. This can be a cumbersome and time-consuming process.

Figure 1
*Sample College
Registration Form*

University of Examples **Registration Form**							Form No. 1012
Course Number	Dept.	Course Title	Credit Hours	Days	Hours	Building	Room
		Total Hours					

Student's Signature   Date   Advisor's Signature   Date

There are some useful tips to consider when you register for classes. It is always best to register as early as possible to ensure that you get the courses you want, at the times you want, and with the instructors you want. Courses scheduled at the most convenient times and assigned the most popular instructors will fill up quickly. Some students avoid early registration opportunities because they often must also pay tuition earlier. You need to balance the availability of money to pay tuition with the need or desire to get a class at a particular time.

When a class is full, you can still sometimes get in with approval from the instructor. Many instructors will accommodate your request to get into a class, but some are adamant about not exceeding the class limit. If you request entry into a full class, have a good reason for needing the class and be able to explain the reason clearly. It also is helpful if you can demonstrate that the circumstances that prevented you from getting the class weren't entirely your fault. Don't register for classes late and expect to find many sympathetic instructors.

Registration for classes is followed by payment at the bursar's office. At many colleges, early registration is followed by an invoice mailed from the bursar's office, and you can pay by mail. However, open and late registration usually require immediate payment at the bursar's office. This often means standing in long lines and increases the time needed to complete the registration process. Failure to pay for registered classes ordinarily results in the cancellation of your registration, and your name will be removed from each class list.

After you have registered for classes, you can go to the bookstore and get the textbooks, supplemental reading books, curriculum packets, laboratory supplies, and other items required for a course. The bookstore has records from each instructor about the books and materials required for each course. Financial aid can be used to purchase books, and the bookstore may have a procedure you need to follow to use this aid.

There are three types of bookstores. One is the college-run bookstore, which is directly administered by the college. Another type is sponsored by the college and is on campus, but the college contracts with a private firm to operate the bookstore. The private firm pays a fee to the university for the privilege of operating the bookstore. Still another type of bookstore is a private one operated at a location somewhere near the campus. At colleges where multiple bookstores are available, it is sometimes beneficial to compare prices at both a campus and noncampus bookstore.

At the beginning of each academic year—normally the fall semester or quarter—there are some additional tasks that must be performed during registration periods. You need to have your identification photo taken and an identification (ID) card issued to you. ID cards are typically used for admission to sporting events, concerts, and plays, and for using the library. If you want to park a vehicle on campus, you must get a parking permit. Parking permits are usually issued by the campus security office and must be posted on your vehicle.

After a term begins, you usually have a specific time period in which a course or courses can be added or dropped. This is normally in the first one to two weeks of a term. Adding a course should be done as soon as possible, because you will miss class assignments. Dropping a course may be necessary if you discover there are course assignments that are not possible for you to complete because of conflicts with other classes, work, or family life. Normally, the longer you wait to drop a course, the greater the financial penalty will be. For example, you may be able to get a full tuition refund if the course is dropped during the first week of classes, but the refund may drop to 80 percent the second week and 70 percent by the third week. Usually a course can be dropped without approval from an advisor, but the advisor may need to approve a course that is added.

At some point in your college career—normally during or after your sophomore year—you will be required to declare a major. The major should be selected because it will help fulfill your career goals. You will find yourself attracted to certain majors because you enjoy the courses, respect the faculty, and find the department faculty and staff cooperative. A faculty advisor will periodically meet with you to review the progress you are making toward a major. Whenever you have any questions, doubts, or concerns about courses you should take, contact your faculty advisor.

Most colleges require that you apply for graduation at the beginning of your last term. You may receive a notification from the registrar's office about this, or there may be a general announcement in the class schedule book. Application for graduation allows the department and registrar to review your records and verify that all required courses have been completed and that a minimum grade point average has been achieved. You will then be notified about your graduation status. It is important to monitor your progress in completing degree requirements so that there isn't an unpleasant surprise at this point in your academic career.

Academic procedures and policies vary greatly from one college to another. Each college has a catalog that explains all policies and procedures and describes the requirements for completing degrees. This catalog is important because it is considered a contract between the college and you. Generally, a student is allowed to follow the policies and degree programs given in the catalog that is current at their initial enrollment in classes. You may be given an option to switch to a newer catalog during your academic career whenever it offers more flexibility. However, you are assured that more restrictive policies cannot be applied before you graduate.

It is important to read your college catalog and become familiar with its contents. Discuss items you don't understand with other students to get a practical perspective about the policies and procedures—just realize that the only authoritative information comes from college administrators and faculty. Based on the experience of some students, it may be wise to get critical points clarified in writing so that no misunderstandings occur and you have documented proof about what you are told.

*While in high school, **MITZI** took business and typing classes. After high school she worked as a secretary. She found that her high school classes had prepared her for her secretarial position.*

However, at age 32, Mitzi, a single mother of a 13-year-old son, wants more than just a job. She has enrolled in a computer-aided drafting program at a local technical college and has completed four semesters of the six-semester associate program. Her goal is to complete the CAD program and be accepted in the civil engineering program at a large university nearby.

Mitzi wants to design and build streets and roads. She believes that her career goals will earn her "status, title, and more money."

School is Mitzi's life. Each night she and her son study together—an experience Mitzi sees as role modeling for her son. She works part-time at the technical college through the work-study program, which is based on financial need. Mitzi appreciates the financial aid and the work-study program available through the college. Recently, she was elected vice president of the student senate. She is proud of this accomplishment. Mitzi's learning experiences have brought her a feeling of greater worth.

Nontraditional Degree Programs

Nontraditional degree programs take many forms. In fact, many colleges offer innovative ways to accomplish traditional programs. The degree programs described in this section have been designed specifically with adult students in mind. There are several nontraditional adult degree models explained, along with an example of each model. Before you consider these descriptions, compare the nontraditional programs with the basic assumptions made by traditional degree programs. This provides an insight into the rationale behind the development of most nontraditional models.

A primary distinction is the perspective that nontraditional programs have about the learning process in higher education. Nontraditional degree programs assume that learning equivalent to a college education can occur in a variety of situations and places. It is not necessary that classes take place on a college campus or that students be residents of the campus.

Traditional schedules for course delivery are not considered important. Courses may be offered in blocks of three to four hours one day a week or may take place for two to three days over a long weekend. Structure is not usually a primary concern for nontraditional programs. In fact, a predetermined course structure may not exist; the structure may be planned in a cooperative effort between the instructor and students. An instructor is not always needed, and learning may be self-directed.

The most important difference between the traditional and nontraditional viewpoints is the recognition that many college students are adults and, as such, have unique needs and bring mature attitudes and learning skills to the educational environment. Nontraditional programs recognize that most adults have full-time jobs and family and community responsibilities. In addition, adult students are seen as customers who can and do demand responsiveness to their needs.

In response to these needs, administrative offices are kept open during hours convenient to students. Courses are offered at times most appropriate for adults. Registration is typically done by phone, by a remote computer connection, by fax, or by mail. In fact, registration may be unnecessary, because course schedules are predetermined and classes conducted in a lock-step fashion. Books and supplies may be distributed in the classroom, and students are directly billed for the books.

Classes are often held at locations most accessible to adult students. A class may be located at an office or factory and held as soon as the workers conclude their work day. Colleges that are located at a distance difficult to commute to might establish classes in outlying communities. The inconvenience of parking on campus has led some universities to hold classes in shopping malls, churches, and other facilities closer to and more convenient for adult students. New technologies, including video, television, and computers, make access easier for adults. Students may access courses through these technologies at work or home.

Nontraditional degree programs often allow students the opportunity to accumulate credits for life experience that is equivalent to college learning. This may be done through exams that test the student for knowledge commensurate with a college course. In addition, many colleges have been more willing to accept the transfer of college credits regardless of when they were earned. An organization called the Council for the Advancement of Experiential Learning (CAEL) has promoted many concepts designed to acknowledge learning by adults through experiences outside the college classroom. One concept that CAEL has promoted is the learning portfolio. This is a written compilation of adult learning experiences that are comparable with college-level learning. (Procedures for earning college credit without attending classes are described in Chapter 4.)

Nontraditional programs often have fewer general education requirements or may define general education more broadly than traditional college programs. For example, rather than require all students to study sociology, the program may allow a student to take any social science course. There are usually no foreign language requirements and limited mathematics requirements—two areas that many adults dread. In fact, students may be allowed to define their own general education. Frequently, it is possible for adults to meet general education requirements through exams or prior learning portfolios.

Faculty who teach in nontraditional programs usually have a different background from traditional college faculty. Often they have advanced degrees but are practitioners. A practitioner is someone employed full-time in a nonacademic job. The job is frequently in the professional field related to the course that the instructor teaches. An example would be a police captain teaching criminal justice courses. Many times the faculty have master's degrees rather than doctorates, but they have valuable knowledge—accumulated through experience—that is more current and relevant than the information traditional faculty can bring to the classroom. The course content often stresses practical issues rather than theoretical and research issues.

Modification of the Traditional Degree Program

Many colleges use a traditional model but modify it so that it is more convenient for adult students. SAT and ACT scores may not be required for admission. This acknowledges that such exams often fail to assess accurately an adult's learning capacity or potential for success in a college degree program. Procedures for the transfer of credits are often less stringent than those of traditional colleges. Arrangements often are made for students to get credit for prior learning—usually through examinations. All general education courses are offered during hours more convenient for adults, often at night—after 5:00 P.M.—and on weekends. Selected majors offer all courses needed to complete a degree during time periods convenient for working adult students. Registration procedures are frequently designed so that adults do not have to make a special trip to campus to complete the process. Office hours are extended past 5:00 P.M. so that adults can conduct their business after work.

An example of this type of college is Indiana University-Purdue University at Fort Wayne (IPFW). Located in the northeast corner of the state and more than 100 miles from either of the main university campuses, the institution provides a convenient campus location for the second most populated area of the state. Enrollment at the university is near 12,000 students, with the majority attending part-time. There are no dormitories for residential students. The university offers degrees at the associate, bachelor's, and master's levels.

Like a traditional university, IPFW provides classes during the day. But most courses offered by the university also can be taken after 6:00 P.M. Classes usually meet for 90 minutes two nights per week or about three hours one night per week. In addition, a weekend college program makes some majors available by taking courses only on Saturdays and Sundays. Courses are available in some outlying communities—reducing the need to drive to campus for the entire degree program. Two 15- to 16-week semesters occur during the fall and spring. In addition, two shorter summer sessions of 5 to 6 weeks are provided. This approach demonstrates that, with some reasonable adjustments to a traditional model, a college can easily accommodate the needs of adult students.

Using a Learning Contract

The *learning contract* is the basis of many nontraditional adult degree programs. It may also be called a study contract, a study plan, or a degree plan. A learning contract is a legal agreement between the student and the school. It states the goals the student is expected to achieve, the way in which the student plans to reach these goals, and the action that the school will take when the student has reached these goals. In most cases, the school will either grant a stated amount of credit or award a degree when the student completes the requirements stipulated in the contract.

Since the learning contract is legally binding on both the student and the school, it provides an excellent way to avoid misunderstandings concerning the work that must be done. Within the contract there are usually clauses calling for binding arbitration by an impartial third party if a dispute should arise.

Learning contracts may be initiated by the faculty or by a student. Negotiating the learning contract is a normal expectation in this type of program. Since there are no rigid rules concerning the contract, one student might negotiate and receive more credit than another student doing the same amount of work—although administrators strive for consistency. Some learning contracts are written for an entire degree program. Others are used for portions of the program. For example, different contracts might be written for each subject area being studied in the process of obtaining a degree.

The statements in a learning contract are very specific. A simple learning contract consists of the following parts:

Educational goals the student expects to accomplish.

A description of the methods that will be used to achieve the goals.

A stated method for evaluating the learning outcomes.

An explanation of the way problems and disagreements will be resolved.

One advantage of a learning contract is that it allows the student to share in planning the content of the degree program, the study methods and materials to be used, and the evaluation process.

In this model, the student becomes a partner in the learning process. A learning contract allows the student flexibility. It may be started or terminated at any time. It doesn't have to be linked to semesters or quarters. When a student signs the learning contract, he or she agrees to meet some stated objectives. The student has a clear direction in which to work. A learning contract allows a student the convenience of studying at a comfortable pace. The method of learning may be traditional or nontraditional, depending on the agreement.

Skidmore College's University Without Walls is an example of this type of program. It is a private, nonprofit, nonsectarian college located in Sarasota Springs, New York. In 1971, the college established its University Without Walls (UWW) to meet the individual needs of adult students. The program awards either a Bachelor of Science or a Bachelor of Arts degree to its students.

The program accepts credits from previous college work and assesses prior learning experience for credit. Students admitted to the program meet with advisors—on campus—to determine an individual curriculum plan. It is possible to accumulate credit through courses at other colleges, distance education courses, internships, work-related assignments, independent study under the guidance of a qualified instructor, and self-directed study. As each "learning experience" is completed, the student and instructor evaluate the student's accomplishment. The student can choose whether the instructor's assessment should become a permanent part of the recorded evaluation. Independent projects are reviewed and evaluated by products submitted by the students as demonstrations of their accomplishments.

Three on-campus meetings are required, but otherwise there is no residency requirement. At the first meeting two advisors review the applicant for admission. A discussion about the program and its appropriateness for the applicant takes place, and within two weeks the applicant is informed of the admissions decision. The student then meets with two assigned advisors to evaluate his or her prior learning experiences, determine learning needs, establish goals, create strategies for reaching the goals, and develop a specific plan to complete the degree. When the degree plan has progressed to its later stage, the student meets with the UWW Committee—which consists of six faculty members and two administrators—for final approval of the learning plan. When final agreement is reached between the student and committee, an actual contract is completed. To graduate, the student must meet the goals established in the contract.

Accelerated Degree Programs

Throughout the United States, adult-oriented colleges and universities are offering accelerated degree programs to adults. This type of program has been implemented by a large number of small—600 to 3,000 students—liberal arts colleges. Typically these programs admit adult students who are over the ages of 23 to 30 and have significant work experience. Usually the programs require students to have a minimum of 60 hours of college-level credit. Often this can be earned through a combination of credits transferred from another college, exams, and prior learning assessment. The class schedule and methods of teaching are geared to adult learners. Much of the class work focuses on the real world in which adult students function. Normally, these schools offer a limited variety of professionally oriented majors, such as business, counseling, nursing, or education.

Admission is typically open-ended, so that students can begin courses at any time when the university starts a class. Normally, a class starts whenever 18 to 22 students at one location have been admitted to the degree program. This cohort of students takes all courses required for a degree together. Courses usually last for five to six weeks. Classes meet one night a week—or on the weekend—for four hours. This schedule continues for 16 to 22 months until all courses are completed. The sequence of courses is often focused on a major area like business. Students are expected to complete all the reading and homework assignments that would be required in a normal academic term. There are usually few breaks from the time a student begins the first courses until the last course is finished. This intense schedule can be grueling but allows students to earn a degree in a shorter time than is possible through traditional programs.

LeTourneau University in Longview, Texas, operates a degree program—LeTourneau Education for Adult Professionals (LEAP)—that is an example of an accelerated degree program. The university is a private, nonprofit, nondenominational, evangelical Christian college. It awards degrees at the associate, bachelor's, and master's levels. A Bachelor of Science in Business Management and a Master of Business Administration are available through the LEAP program. Admission requirements include 60 semester hours of credit earned from a regionally accredited college; CLEP exams, military training, and prior learning assessment can be applied toward this requirement. Applicants must have a minimum of four years of work experience in an occupation related to the degree.

Students are admitted to the program on an open-ended basis and begin taking courses when a group (class) of 16 to 22 students have been admitted at a class location. Students can attend classes on the main campus and at centers in the Dallas-Fort Worth area, Houston, and Tyler. In addition, courses are sometimes offered at business locations where an employer provides classroom space. Classes meet from 6:00 P.M. to 10:00 P.M. Mondays through Thursdays, and some classes meet on Saturdays.

Students in the bachelor's degree program complete a total of 43 credit hours of business courses in approximately 18 months. Students are assigned to study groups of three or four, work with the group to complete major assignments—in addition to individual assignments—and frequently make group presentations. The emphasis on group work and class presentations is excellent preparation for team work and communication of ideas in a business setting. The student's practical work experience provides a daily laboratory for the testing of new concepts learned in a course.

The Virtual Campus

An innovative program now operated by several state university systems, as well as some private colleges, might be called the virtual campus. These colleges do not have a campus—other than administrative offices—and offer no classes. They provide students with an alternative means for accumulating credits and earning a degree. Credits are typically earned through a combination of college credits, prior learning assessment, exams, military service school courses, and correspondence courses. Students can take courses at any accredited higher education institution and transfer the credits to the college. There usually is a variety of majors that students can pursue in completing a bachelor's degree.

Typically, there are established requirements for each degree program, but a student can devise specific strategies for meeting these requirements. For example, to complete a major in psychology, a student may take correspondence courses and attend courses at a nearby college. This type of degree program is particularly beneficial to adults who are frequently transferred in connection with their work. Repeated transfers can result in the accumulation of a large number of college credits but never enough from one college to meet the minimum credits earned in residence. It also is ideal for adults who benefit from pursuing a variety of learning strategies.

Charter Oak State College was created by the Connecticut legislature in 1973. The college's purpose is to provide adults with an alternative means of earning a college degree while maintaining the quality and rigor expected from an accredited institution. It offers Associate in Arts, Associate in Science, Bachelor of Arts, and Bachelor of Science degrees. There are 25 concentrations available for the Bachelor of Arts degree and 7 concentrations for the Bachelor of Science degree. Each student develops an individual plan of study with the guidance of an advisor. This program establishes the courses that a student will take to earn the required credits for a degree and specifies how the courses will completed.

Students complete course requirements at their own pace. Courses can be taken at accredited colleges and will be accepted if a passing grade is received. Correspondence courses from accredited colleges are accepted if the student receives a passing grade. Some noncollegiate courses offered by the military, business, professional groups, government, and nonprofit agencies may be eligible for credit. Certain programs have been evaluated by the college for credit and can be taken with the knowledge that the college will grant credit for them.

For example, up to 30 hours can be earned through the Chartered Life Underwriters examination program. Credit can be earned through examinations like CLEP, ACT, DANTES, GRE, and others. Prior learning portfolios can be submitted by a student for the assessment of credits. Charter Oak offers a limited number of courses that students can take through guided study—only 11 courses were offered during the 1994-95 academic year.

A well-known institution similar to Charter Oak State College is Regents College of the State University of New York. There are some colleges that offer degree programs that resemble the virtual campus programs. However, these programs are operated by traditional colleges. An example would be the Non-Traditional Study Program operated by Kansas State University.

Distance Education

Distance education is the application of technology to move learning beyond the walls of the college classroom and bring it to learners at a distant point. Print technology was first used to accomplish this in the mid-1800s with the introduction of correspondence courses. In the 1930s, the first application of electronic technology to distance education was instituted with radio broadcasts devoted to learning. These humble beginnings were only a precursor of how modern technologies can dramatically change the availability of college education and bring it to large numbers of people anywhere in the world. Today, audiotapes, videotapes, telephone lines, television, and computers are used in a wide variety of ways to deliver college education. Education can be delivered to either individuals or groups. Distance education has the potential to make college education universally available in the same way that telephone service has been made universally available to all residents of the United States.

Printed text, audiotape, and videotape programs are frequently used to provide courses to individuals. Often lectures are recorded and used to supplement textbooks and other reading materials. There are many colleges and universities that provide correspondence courses, but a more limited number offer degrees that can be completed with this method. Eastern Oregon State University is one college that offers a bachelor's degree in liberal studies through correspondence courses. Computer-assisted instruction (CAI) has also been used by some colleges to deliver courses. Many programs rely on the telephone for advisors and instructors to communicate with students as they complete their course work. A few colleges have degree programs that can be completed through videotaped lessons. One of the drawbacks of all these methods is the lack of interactivity between students and instructor.

Computer-based degree programs provide for more interactivity and are a hybrid. Students can participate in classes from home or work over a computer linked by telephone with a computer at the college. However, courses are often taken in conjunction with a class of students, so the methodology is also group-oriented. Messages can be sent from the instructor to students and from students to each other. Course assignments are distributed over the computer, and interactive computer conferencing is often a component of these degree programs. Students can log into the campus computer system and view messages from the instructor and other students any time of the day or night. Examples of colleges using this technology are Atlantic Union College, with an associate degree in general studies, and the University of Phoenix, with a Master of Business Administration. New developments and innovations now occurring on the Internet and other online services have the potential for making many other exciting degree programs available to adults with access to personal computers.

Some colleges provide degree programs through televised courses viewed by individuals at home or work. And many colleges have established interactive-video programs for the delivery of courses to groups of students. Classes are broadcast live, and there is either an audio link from the outlying classes with the instructor or, in some cases, a video link. The audio link allows interactive transmission of voice, but the interactive video allows the college to duplicate the actual classroom in several locations at one time. Classes for interactive video courses are frequently held in a business or local high school and sometimes even have a course facilitator present to help students with problems that can't be addressed by the interactive video link.

Mind Extension University (ME/U) is an interesting program that represents distance education programs and their potential to reach large numbers of people. This institution does not actually provide degrees but coordinates the activities of a group of colleges. ME/U broadcasts courses over a cable television network that reaches more than 26 million households in 8,500 communities. Courses are available from more than 30 regionally accredited colleges and universities, and it is possible to obtain associate, bachelor's, and master's degrees from some of the colleges—only degree-completion programs are available. Students can view lectures, demonstrations, interviews, and educational videos in the convenience of their own home. It's possible to videotape class sessions when you can't view them live or to make arrangements to have videos of classes mailed to you. It's also possible to communicate with instructors and other students through ME/U's electronic bulletin board and voice mail systems.

Adults interested in earning a degree must apply for admission to a specific college associated with ME/U and can receive assistance in this process through ME/U's Education Center. Tuition fees for courses vary, depending on the college delivering the course. Financial assistance is based on applications to the specific college in which you enroll. Books and course packets are mailed to students prior to the start of the course's broadcast schedule. Some colleges offering degrees through ME/U include Washington State University, Regis University, George Washington University, and Seattle Central Community College.

The Final Word

Back in olden days, a college degree meant day classes on a university campus for at least four years; but times have changed. You no longer have to think of a degree as a four-year process. Colleges and universities are looking for students. They need you. So look for a program that fits your needs and go for it!

Addresses for College Entrance Examination Programs

Scholastic Aptitude Test (SAT)
College Board
45 Columbus Ave.
New York, NY 10023-6992

American College Testing (ACT)
P.O. Box 168
2201 North Dodge Street
Iowa City, IA 52243

Graduate Record Exam (GRE)
Educational Testing Service
P.O. Box 955
Princeton, NJ 08541

Graduate Management Admissions Test (GMAT)
Educational Testing Service
P.O. Box 955
Princeton, NJ 08541

Law School Admission Test (LSAT)
Law School Admission Council
Law School Admission Services
Box 2000
Newtown, PA 18940

Chapter 4

Speeding Up the Process

As you think about becoming a college student, time becomes a very important factor. After all, you're no "spring chicken"; you've been hatched for a few years. At this point, investing four or even five years of your life into being a college student may seem overwhelming. If you are the typical adult, you can attend classes only part-time. Finishing a bachelor's degree or a doctoral degree may seem centuries away. The prospect of spending the rest of your life pursuing a college degree may make you feel like saying, "Forget it! It's too late for me."

Don't be discouraged! Many adult students have found ways to speed up the process of accumulating enough credits to meet graduation requirements. This chapter investigates several ways that adults can earn college credit for learning that they have accomplished through their personal life experiences as well as through past formal education. This is often called *documented learning*. Several methods for accelerating a college degree program—specifically developed for adult students—are introduced in this chapter. Today, many adult students are earning degrees in less time by speeding up the process, and you can too.

Selecting the Right Program

As the first step in speeding up the process of getting a degree, determine what you want from your college experience. Set specific goals, and it will be easier to accomplish them. Not every adult attending college wants a degree. This is why the need for career planning and decision making was discussed in Chapter 2. Perhaps you just want to explore some courses to find out if you like a particular school or subject area. In this case, you might want to audit a college course. You would pay a nominal auditing fee and attend classes but wouldn't take exams or be required to complete the written work. Of course, you would not receive any credit for the course. Noncredit courses are also available through continuing education and community education classes. This may be the best method for getting the skills needed to implement your career plans.

If you want to improve your work skills and obtain some type of verification of your credentials, a *certificate program* might meet your needs. Certificate programs deal directly with specific work skills. They may involve five to ten courses—usually 15 to 30 semester hours—and typically require a few months to a year to complete. Normally, students must pass a proficiency exam to receive a certificate. Certificate programs provide a quick way to gain needed skills, but it is important to be sure that the school you attend offers a quality education.

If you want a degree as soon as possible, an associate degree might be the choice for you. An associate degree can be earned in less time than a bachelor's degree. Some adults choose to get an associate's degree and then complete a bachelor's degree later. Gaining a degree at the halfway point in their college work acts as a motivator for many people.

If you are interested in a graduate degree, you will want to investigate some graduate school catalogs. By taking the necessary courses for an undergraduate degree, you can avoid taking the courses later in order to get accepted into a graduate program. Some majors lead to graduate degrees. For example, many psychology or social work undergraduates continue their studies in graduate schools because it is difficult to gain entry into the profession without a graduate degree.

Think of most academic programs as stepping stones. It often is possible to begin with a certificate program and then transfer the courses into a degree program. An associate degree provides an interim step to a bachelor's degree, and the bachelor's degree is a prerequisite for the master's degree or professional degree. Most doctoral degree programs require a master's degree. The step to each new stone will be easier to take with careful planning and thought. Seek out advice from faculty and others in your profession as you make these plans.

Past College Credits

Did you attend college back in prehistoric times? Did you earn some credit hours? Those credits may be transferred to the school you plan to attend. The college that you attended still has your transcript on file. Your college transcript is the official record of all the courses you took, your grades, the number of credits you received, and any degrees you were granted. The *registrar* is the person responsible for keeping these records.

To obtain a copy of your transcript, contact the office of the registrar at the school you attended. Usually you will be charged a few dollars for each transcript you request. A telephone call to the registrar's office will provide you with the information needed to obtain your transcript. The office will want to know when you attended the school, the name you used during that time, and your Social Security number. The registrar will need your signature on a form to release your transcript to another institution.

The school will send you an unofficial transcript. Having an *unofficial transcript* will help you discuss the transfer of credits with an advisor at the college you plan to attend. However, the school will probably ask for an *official transcript* as documentation of your earned credits to be sent directly to the admissions office. An official transcript has the college seal imprinted on it and is mailed only from one college to another.

What if the grades on your transcript show that you weren't seriously into academics 20 years ago? Since college admissions officers generally understand that people tend to be better students as adults than they were in their youthful days, lower grades aren't something to be concerned about. However, any courses that appear on your transcript as failed will not be transferred. Some colleges will not accept courses with a grade of "D." You may be given a "probationary" admittance in order to prove your academic ability.

The registrar will determine what credits may be transferred and applied to your degree program. Colleges and universities differ about the amount and kinds of credit accepted. Some schools set a limit on the number of transfer credit hours they will accept. They may accept credits for subjects only outside your major area, or require that the course be similar to one in their catalog to receive credit. Some schools will not accept credits that are considered too old. This is especially true in areas of study such as science or technology, where new knowledge may have been discovered over the years.

If some credits are not accepted, you might be able to make a logical appeal to the registrar, stating reasons for your previous college credits being both valid and current. The registrar often confers with faculty for advice about such appeals. With polite persuasion, you might be able to gain some college credit from the past. Don't be afraid to shop around for the college that accepts the largest number of transfer credits. This approach also puts you in a stronger position to negotiate credit from the college you really want to attend.

Credits from Other Classes

You might be able to get college credit for courses you have taken at your workplace, a community college, or a proprietary school. Schools sometimes have *articulation agreements* through which they will accept one another's credits without question. This may be the case between a community college and a university in the same region, a proprietary school offering a strong program that the university does not offer, or even between a college and a corporation's employee training program. Courses taken as part of military training may be another source of college credit.

If you have taken courses in any of these situations, you might be able to obtain college credit for your prior classes. Check with the school to learn what documentation is required. Usually a DD214 form contains the information that the college needs. Most colleges will use the American Council on Education's (ACE) *National Guide to the Evaluation of Educational Experiences in the Armed Forces* for guidance about the credits you should receive for military training.

There are some corporations, unions, and professional associations that offer sophisticated training programs. ACE has established the Program on Noncollegiate Sponsored Instruction (PONSI) for the evaluation of noncollegiate courses by faculty experts. Many of these programs have been assessed, and appropriate course and credit information determined. This information is available in the *ACE National Guide to Educational Credit for Training Programs*. Consult with the personnel director or training director at your place of employment to find out how you can obtain a transcript from the ACE Registry of Credit that records PONSI courses you have taken.

In cases where the college won't transfer credits from another college or other source, it still may be possible to obtain credit through a portfolio process. The concept of a portfolio and its use in speeding up the process of getting a degree are discussed in the next section.

Prior Learning Assessment

To speed up the process of earning a degree, many adult students enroll in colleges or universities that have programs of prior learning assessment. *Prior learning assessment* is a method that a college or university uses to evaluate learning that a student has gained through life experience and to determine whether that learning is equivalent to courses taught at the college level. College credit is awarded for such learning if it is evaluated as equivalent to the college course. For example, through workshops offered by his employer and hands-on experience, Rich learned how to use a word processing program and several other business-related computer programs that are taught in an Introduction to Personal Computers course. Through prior learning assessment, Rich received college credit for his knowledge.

The prior learning assessment program allows adult students to save both time and money. Gaining credit without attending and paying tuition for classes is a double benefit. Prior learning assessment also helps the adult student to recognize areas of study that may need remediation or review. Prior learning assessment is a fair, systematic way of recognizing learning outside the academic classroom. In addition, the student gains a feeling of self-worth by getting college credit for individual learning.

The prior learning assessment process has been greatly influenced by an organization called the Council for the Advancement of Experiential Learning (CAEL). Founded in 1974, CAEL aids colleges and universities in developing their evaluation programs. In addition, CAEL sets academic standards for assessment programs that are being used currently nationwide. There are also useful publications available from CAEL that describe the process for obtaining credit through prior learning experience.

What Is Your Assessable Learning?

Too many adults believe they have stopped learning. In their minds, they might see learning as taking place only in a formal classroom. Stop and consider yourself as a child. Think of all the learning that took place. How did you learn to walk? How did you learn to talk? How did you learn to ride a bicycle? Obviously, none of this learning took place in a formal classroom, but learning definitely took place.

Adults also have many different opportunities to learn through experience. For example, you just bought a new VCR. You need to know how to connect it to your cable TV. You want to be able to record a basketball game tomorrow night while you are away from the house. What do you do? You read the manual that came with the VCR. You experiment with the VCR and the TV. If you have real problems, you consult with a friend who has a VCR. Eventually you know how to program the VCR. Learning has taken place. There is a large amount of research that demonstrates adults regularly engage in what is termed "self-directed" learning. Almost 80 percent of adults in the United States spend an average of 150 hours each year engaged in self-directed learning projects.

As an adult, you are an active learner. In fact, you may well be a more skilled learner as an adult than you were as a student in elementary and high school. Why? You have matured. You have skills as an adult that you did not have as a teenager. You have past experiences and knowledge to use in problem solving. You know what you want to learn and have a reason for learning. You are ready to make a sacrifice of time, money, and lifestyle to go back to school.

Adults learn in a variety of environments, including home, work, and the community. Focus on one thing you have learned in the last year. Maybe you learned how to use a wok, install wireless fencing, put together the church newsletter, lead a team of workers, or use a new computer-assisted drafting software program. Think about that experience and answer the following questions.

1. What was your learning experience?

2. What was the goal or outcome that you set for yourself?

3. How did you learn? Through books, videos, a class, friends, etc.?

4. Where did this learning take place? At work, home, school, church, etc.?

5. What were the final results of the learning experience?

6. How has the learning experience affected your life?

Some learning experiences are not equivalent to what you would learn in a college course, but there are many learning activities that are. There are many colleges that recognize the significance of this learning and give adult students credit for it. There are several ways that your prior knowledge can be assessed and granted college credit by an institution.

Credit Through Examinations

Tests are not the joy of the college student's life; however, for the adult student, testing may be a good way to earn college credit. Many colleges and universities use equivalency tests to measure the knowledge adult students have in a particular area of study. An *equivalency test* is similar to taking the final exam in a college course. The CLEP and PEP examinations are the two most commonly used standardized tests.

Colleges and universities do not have a universal method for awarding credit through examinations. Each school sets its own standards for accepting examinations, defining a passing grade, and awarding hours of credit. Some schools have a limit on the number of credits they can award based on exams. In some cases, schools will not grant credit for the test, but will allow a student to bypass an introductory class and begin at a more advanced level.

Before you enroll at an institution, you should determine its policy on credit by examination. These policies can make a crucial difference in the time it takes to earn a degree. Since colleges and universities vary so much on the exams that are acceptable, be sure to check with an admissions officer or academic advisor before you spend time and money taking an exam. Specifically question the advisor about the name of the exam and the subject areas for which you can get credit. Sometimes a college accepts an exam covering one subject area but will not grant credit for the same exam covering a different subject. Often a college or university will not accept or transfer credits that were awarded at another college for the exam programs described in this section. Ask questions! Request a reply in writing.

College Level Examination Program

The College Level Examination Program (CLEP) is a widely used test designed to validate adult students' learning outside the formal classroom. CLEP is available at approximately 1,200 testing sites throughout the United States, such as community colleges and large public libraries. CLEP is also available in foreign countries if requested. The addresses for this and other programs described are listed at the end of this chapter.

CLEP offers two types of exams. The *general exams* deal with areas of study covered in the first two years of college. For example, one of the general exams covers mathematics. A passing grade for each general exam can be worth three to six semester hours of credit.

Subject exams cover information in specific subjects typically taught in undergraduate courses having similar names. For example, Introductory Microeconomics is one subject area exam. A passing score on a subject exam usually results in an award of the same amount of credit that a student would earn by passing a similar course at a college. However, remember that each school makes the decision concerning the amount of credit awarded; more credit may be granted by one school than another.

There are 35 examinations available through CLEP. Each takes 90 minutes to complete. The cost for each exam is approximately $40. Most of the exams are multiple-choice although a few also include some essay questions. The CLEP may be taken every 6 months. You can ask that the test score be sent only to you. The test score does not have to be reported to the college or university unless you decide to enroll.

Seven years ago, after completing two years of college, WAYNE became very confused. It was time to declare a major, and he had no idea what direction he wanted to follow in his career. His solution was to quit school.

Wayne found a job selling cars in his hometown. His parents had only one question when he told them about his new job: "When will you finish college?" Wayne promised to return to complete a degree when he knew what he wanted to do with his life.

Wayne has been quite successful as a salesman. He is now married and the father of two small children. From time to time, Wayne has thought about completing his degree. His parents have occasionally asked when he plans to complete his degree.

This fall he enrolled in an accelerated degree completion program. By transferring credits from his former college, CLEP tests, and a learning portfolio, he plans to complete his degree in approximately 18 months. The classes he takes will help him complete a major in business management. Transfer credits, credits from exams, and portfolio credits fulfill the general education requirements for the degree. Wayne's parents are looking forward to graduation day.

Proficiency Examinations Program

An alternative exam program accepted at some colleges is the Proficiency Examinations Program (PEP). This program contains examinations for about 40 subject areas. Adult students may use each test to show knowledge gained through their work, life experiences, and their own study. The exams cover such varied subjects as nursing, business, education, arts, and sciences.

PEP exams are usually four to five hours long. Most are multiple-choice. Some exams contain a few essay questions and short written answers. A few are entirely essay. Each exam is based on a course outline that is available in the PEP Study Guide for that subject.

The Graduate Record Exam

The Graduate Record Exam (GRE) is normally required for students entering graduate school. Occasionally, the GRE is used in assessing prior learning at the undergraduate level. One general aptitude test is available. The advanced exams have been developed to test knowledge at the bachelor's degree level in a given field of study. Subjects that may be tested include English literature, education, music, history, and psychology. The GRE is offered twice each year at various locations throughout the United States.

Advanced Placement Credit

The Advanced Placement Program was one of the first designed to give college credit on the basis of an exam. It tests 13 subjects and is usually used for high school seniors entering their freshmen year of college. However some schools use this program as part of the prior learning assessment. Colleges and universities may use their own examinations to determine advanced placement credit. Sometimes no credit is given. The student is simply allowed to take a more advanced class rather than spend time in a class that is not challenging.

Other Standardized Examination Programs

There are other programs for obtaining credit through examinations that are standardized (that is, uniform). For individuals who have mastered a foreign language through travel or work in another country, the New York University Proficiency Testing in Foreign Languages can be taken to obtain credit for this skill. Other programs are listed at the end of this chapter, along with addresses to contact for more information.

College and University Examinations

Colleges and universities occasionally use exams that have been developed by the institutions, departments, and faculty members. These tests are not standardized. They are based on the lecture content and textbooks used for particular courses. The philosophy of the school and of the faculty members designing the tests is reflected in the exam. Ask the department chairperson for information about policies and preparation for these exams.

Challenge Examinations

Suppose that, through your work experience, you have gained a knowledge of accounting. You believe that your knowledge is equal to the information learned by students taking the Introduction to Accounting course at the university. You may request an opportunity to take a challenge examination for the introductory class. To learn about the policy and procedure used by the school to make the request, you should talk to an advisor. Challenge examinations are used for the following purposes:

To grant credit for the course being tested.

To prove that the knowledge you gained from a similar course taken elsewhere is transferable.

To know what level of course you are ready to attempt.

To excuse you from taking an course, allowing you to take an advanced course

Because challenge examinations are based on the learning in a specific course, you would be wise to talk to the instructor before taking the test. Reviewing the material in the text used for the course will help in your preparation.

Oral Examinations

Sometimes rather than offering a written test, a college may ask you to interview with a faculty member or members. Some interviewers may simply discuss the topic with you to determine your mastery of the subject. In some cases, a list of questions may be asked. Through the interview the faculty member will review your prior learning and your understanding of the subject. The interview may be very informal or very structured, depending on the approach taken by the interviewer. Before taking an oral exam, you should discuss this option with an advisor.

Defense Activity for Non-Traditional Educational Support

The Defense Activity for Non-Traditional Educational Support (DANTES) is more than an examination program. DANTES provides a testing program, an evaluation system for military technical training, and a system for documenting learning experiences gained through military service. This program, set up by the Department of Defense, is especially useful for active and reserve military personnel. Information about its services may be secured from the educational officer on your military base.

The DANTES Subject Standardized Tests

The DANTES Subject Standardized Tests (DSSTs) were developed for use by active military personnel. The tests are now available to anyone who chooses to participate in the examination program. The testing program includes about 50 different exams. The material tested covers information typically learned in a one-semester freshman or sophomore college course. The topics cover such varied subjects as Introduction to Carpentry, Marketing, and Physical Geology.

The tests are not timed but usually take 90 minutes. The DSSTs are given at the convenience of the test administrator and the student.

In addition, DANTES provides about 100 proficiency exams free of charge to military personnel. These include many of the exams we have discussed, as well as others.

Other DANTES Services

Through the American Council of Education, DANTES maintains the quality of military training programs at a level that makes them acceptable for credit at many colleges and universities. Civilian educators evaluate the programs.

Another DANTES program helps military personnel gain college credit through the use of a portfolio of their learning experiences. The portfolio may include examinations, documentation of completed training courses, and work done in the military and based on training courses.

Professional Certification

Many organizations offer certification or licenses to their members as an indication of their continued learning within their occupational field. The certificate usually is awarded based on the individual's work experience, course work, and examinations. Examples of this type of certification are a chartered financial consultant, a certified life underwriter, and a certified professional secretary. Many professional certification programs have been evaluated by ACE PONSI.

Prior Learning Portfolios

Colleges and universities use different processes to evaluate prior learning. Some of these methods are already documented. However, part of your learning may not be neatly documented by a transcript, an examination, or an evaluated program. You may need to develop a *portfolio* showing your past learning. If this is your situation, you will want to find a school that has a portfolio assessment program.

Prior learning assessment requires that a learning experience be specific. It is not enough to state, "I am good with numbers." Instead, it is better to say, "I have kept the financial records for my company for five years." It is not enough to say, "I lived in France for three years." It is better to indicate that learning took place as well: "I learned to speak French while living in France for three years." Credit is given for only college-level learning. The learning must be well documented and organized.

A portfolio is a written record presented by the student requesting college credit for learning outside the classroom. A portfolio provides a list of personal accomplishments. It allows the student to think of skills in a broader sense and identify skills that can be translated into academic areas. The portfolio also provides an awareness of skills that might be developed through a degree program. A portfolio is useful in demonstrating to a college reasons for granting credit for specific life experiences. Later the portfolio can be used in obtaining a job or continuing one's education. It provides a record of one's accomplishments.

Most colleges require that you pay a fee for a portfolio assessment. Payment of the fee in no way guarantees that you will receive college credit for the portfolio. However, most adults over 25 have had significant life experiences for which they can earn college credit. After the college determines the number of credits you should receive for prior learning, you might be required to pay a modest fee for credits. CAEL discourages this practice because it might appear that the college is selling credits. The prior learning assessment fee is quite nominal in comparison with tuition payments that you would make to take the course at the college. Development of a well-prepared portfolio takes a significant investment of your time and frequently can be the most costly aspect of the process.

Writing Your Portfolio

Some schools that use a portfolio assessment program offer workshops to adult students that provide guidance in writing portfolios. Such a workshop can be an orientation for adult students. The portfolio can be helpful as a tool in designing a student's individual degree program. It is helpful as the student forms individual goals.

The actual format of a formal portfolio will differ from school to school. As you read about the portfolio, you should realize that the school you attend may require a different format; however, the basic information most schools require for a portfolio is contained in the following discussion.

A well-constructed portfolio must be organized in a logical way and should be consistent. For example, if topics in one part are listed alphabetically, an alphabetical listing should be made throughout the portfolio. It should be written so that the reader can understand the points being made. Each section of the portfolio should be connected with transitional statements. Neatness counts in the preparation of a portfolio. Using a word processor is the best approach, although a typewriter can be used. A portfolio should never be handwritten. It is important to use excellent grammar. The portfolio represents you to the institution, so it must make a good impression to receive the most positive evaluation.

A Working Portfolio

To begin your portfolio, you must first identify your prior learning. Preparing a *working portfolio* allows you to evaluate your skills. Using the working portfolio as the starting point, you will write a formal portfolio to submit to the college or university you are attending. Preparing the working portfolio will involve not only writing but gathering information and documentation of your learning. You might need to do some research work to verify your learning. If you already have a job resume, you will find it helpful in providing information for your portfolio. Also, some of the exercises you completed in Chapter 2 should help you identify skills and achievements that can be documented in the portfolio.

THOMAS EDISON STATE COLLEGE is a four-year school located in Trenton, New Jersey. The college was founded in 1972, and was charged with enlarging educational opportunities of adult students. There were 8,619 students enrolled in the fall of 1994, and their average age was 39. Students can live just about anywhere while earning credits in 118 subject areas leading to 11 bachelor's and associate degrees. The school grants credit for passing scores on national proficiency exams and uses a portfolio assessment program. Portfolios are evaluated by one of the 300 professors from accredited regional colleges and universities. Course credits transferred from other colleges are another means of accumulating credits for graduation.

There are several resources that Thomas Edison offers for earning credits. One is through courses offered by PBS's Going the Distance *program. Students who don't have access to the courses through a local PBS station can order the course on VCR tapes. The college's Directed Independent Adult Learning Program (DIAL) makes courses available through independent distance learning. Work is completed in a 16- or 24-week semester and is based on weekly readings, video and/or audio tapes, and written assignments. Midterm and final exams are required, along with periodic evaluations conducted by faculty advisors.*

Another innovative resource is the Online Computer Classroom. *This allows students to take guided courses by computer from home or work. Students can communicate with other distance learners and their faculty mentors through the computer. Students in essence attend weekly classes by computer and use computer conferencing for class discussions. Written work is submitted by e-mail. Course materials such as books and tapes are mailed to the student's home. A direct link with the college is possible, or the program can be accessed through the Internet.*

To receive credit for a course, a student must have documented proof that the learning is equal to what a student attending the class for a semester would have gained. The student's work is compared to that normally taking place during a semester in the classroom. If the learning is evaluated as being equal, the student is given a passing grade and credit for the course.

Your Formal Education

Remember that a portfolio must be specific and documented. As each part of the portfolio is discussed, fill in the information about yourself. Some educators suggest that you create a file for each category. In the file you place both your list of accomplishments and the needed documentation.

Start with your formal education. List each college or university you have attended. List each course you have taken. (It doesn't matter if the course was taken in pursuit of a degree.) Be sure to include any classes you might have taken without earning credit. Don't worry about how long it has been since you attended the class. Obtain a photocopy of the transcript from each school and place each photocopy in the file.

Some course titles do not adequately explain what was learned. This makes it difficult to evaluate and match with a course at the college. In this case, it is helpful to get a catalog description of the course or a syllabus that explains what material was covered in the course. The registrar's office can provide photocopies of the course descriptions from the catalog during that academic year.

Complete the following information about yourself for each course that you've taken.

School Attended	Date Attended	Course	Unites	Grade	Comments
_____	_____	_____	____	____	_____
_____	_____	_____	____	____	_____
_____	_____	_____	____	____	_____

Your Education Outside the College Classroom

Throughout your life you've had educational experiences outside the college classroom. This learning may have taken place through job-related training, military training, or organizations with which you have had contact. This kind of learning may be worth college credit. You will need official documentation from company records, military records, certificates, or some other type of credentials. This documentation should be placed in your file along with your written list. List training even if you don't have documentation. The school may be able to suggest methods you can use to obtain documentation.

Fill in the following information about any company training you've had.

Course/Subject	Description	Date Attended	Certificate/Proof	Comments
_____	_____	_____	_____	_____
_____	_____	_____	_____	_____
_____	_____	_____	_____	_____

Fill in the following information about any military training and experiences you've had.

Service Branch _____ Discharge Date _____

Assignment/ Military Training	Dates	Rank	Comments
_____	_____	_____	_____
_____	_____	_____	_____
_____	_____	_____	_____

Fill in the following information about any certificates, credentials, licenses, or awards you have received.

Type	Date Issued	Organization Issuing	Comments
_____	_____	_____	_____
_____	_____	_____	_____
_____	_____	_____	_____

Many colleges and universities will evaluate these institutions, using information from the *Guide for the Program on Noncollegiate Sponsored Instruction* from the American Council on Education. As mentioned earlier, this program provides evaluations for training programs conducted by hundreds of businesses, unions, and government agencies. It suggests the equivalent course and credits an applicant should receive for each specific training program.

Your Work Experiences

If you have a job resume, you might find it useful in compiling some of this information. Remember, however, that this does not include just your job experiences. This section should also include volunteer work, hobbies, and special accomplishments, such as building a home, organizing a community fundraiser, writing a newsletter, or playing a musical instrument.

If you do volunteer work at your child's school or your church, list that work and describe what you do. If you have organized and managed a softball league team or taught piano lessons to residents at a nursing home, list the activity and describe the skills involved. Does this job involve organization such as scheduling? Do you have to do any writing? Do you use any psychology as you interact with coaches, team players, or piano students? What responsibilities have you had? How have they influenced your learning? It is important to recognize that CAEL guidelines stipulate that the documented activity for which you are seeking credit should be equivalent to college-level learning.

List all of the jobs you've had since high school.

Job	Location	Date	Responsibilities	Major Accomplishments
_____	_____	____	_____	_____
_____	_____	____	_____	_____
_____	_____	____	_____	_____

List all the volunteer work you've done.

Volunteer Work	Agency	Date	Describe Work	Major Accomplishments
_____	_____	____	_____	_____
_____	_____	____	_____	_____
_____	_____	____	_____	_____

List your hobbies.

Hobby   **Describe What Your Hobby Has Helped You Learn**

_____   _____

                        _____

_____   _____

                        _____

_____   _____

                        _____

List your special accomplishments.

Accomplishment   **Describe What Each Accomplishment Has Helped You Learn**

_____   _____

                        _____

_____   _____

                        _____

_____   _____

                        _____

Some learning is self-taught. People learn by reading both fiction and nonfiction books, newspapers, and periodicals. Computer-assisted instruction and educational videos are some modern resources for learning skills and information. In addition, many people teach themselves certain skills. To document these skills, you might need photos or actual completed work. Because of the difficulty in documenting and verifying self-learning activities, many colleges have policies that are very difficult to satisfy.

List books, newspapers, periodicals, computer-assisted instruction, and educational videos that you have used recently or use regularly.

Title of Publication/Program/Video   **Author/Publisher**

_____   _____

_____   _____

_____   _____

List any skills you have taught yourself.

Skill	**How Do You Use This Skill?**	**How Did You Learn This Skill?**
_____	_____	_____
_____	_____	_____
_____	_____	_____

The information you have compiled gives you an idea of information that should be contained in your portfolio. After a few days or weeks, you should review it. You may want to add more information to the list. This information can act as the basis for your written portfolio.

The Essay

Most portfolios will include an essay or narrative section. In the narrative, you will need to tell about yourself. It is a way of introducing yourself to the individuals who determine the amount of credit you will receive for prior learning experience. The essay should state your goals and experiences and tell why you are asking for this credit.

It is important to edit your essay, since it will be your first communication with the faculty evaluating your request. Having someone else edit it for you is a good idea. Your essay needs to be organized and clear in its meaning. You should read the college's description of the essay to know exactly what should be written.

SHEILA is 32 years old. She left high school at 16 to marry her high school sweetheart. After the birth of her second child, Sheila earned a General Equivalency Diploma. Following a divorce, Sheila became tired of working in low-paying jobs with no future. She decided to enrolled at a local technical school.

Sheila was very apprehensive about attending classes. Her last formal learning experience had been high school. She was afraid she would not be able to function successfully in the classroom. She was afraid she would feel awkward.

Despite her fears, Sheila has actually enjoyed her classes. She feels better about herself now. She enjoys the learning atmosphere provided for adults in her school. The availability of computers for student use makes learning easier. Sheila believes this hands-on learning is much better than the traditional methods of lecturing, note-taking, and testing.

Sheila is proud of her grade point average. As a short-term goal, she wants to keep her grades as high as possible. Completing her degree is her long-range goal. She would find nontraditional programs useful in completing her degree more quickly.

Documentation

Documentation can be in two forms. *Direct documentation* is the strongest evidence of your skill or knowledge. Examples of direct documentation are reports, photos, paintings, videos, audio cassettes, or blueprints. *Indirect documentation* is information provided about your experience. Types of indirect documentation are letters of recommendation, official personnel evaluations, and program notes about your performance. Indirect documentation should be on company letterhead and is typically given more credence when it is from a supervisor rather than a peer.

If you need to write and request documentation from someone, be sure to allow the person sufficient time to return the documentation to you. While documentation is needed, don't overwhelm your evaluators with unnecessary and burdensome amounts of documents.

The Credit Request

Knowing how much credit to expect may be difficult. In most cases, the college will have a policy. The decision will be made without your input. Some colleges require that a student's knowledge be comparable to a specific course. The credit is determined by the credit awarded for that course. Since each institution is different, you will need to know how your school assesses learning. Talk to other students from the school who have completed the portfolio process. Ask about what to include, how to present the information, problems to avoid, and the credits the students were awarded based on their portfolio.

Some schools allow students to cluster their learning into learning components. A *learning component* refers to what a student knows and can do. It cannot be compared easily to a specific college course. Students can obtain credit in this way if they list the skills, competencies, and accomplishments that are equivalent to course work conducted at a college level.

The college catalog is a good source to use in comparing your learning experience with course requirements. If the courses were taken through workshops sponsored by organizations, colleges sometimes use the Carnegie Formula to award credit. This means that for every 15 or more hours in the classroom and 30 or more hours of work outside the classroom, one credit hour is awarded. So if you can prove that the 30-hour seminar you attended involved 60 hours of outside work such as report writing, research, and reading, you can ask for two credit hours. If the course is listed in the ACE Guide, the college may use its credit recommendation.

You should expect to get help from your college in evaluating your credit request. The help may be available through a portfolio workshop. If not, you should get help from an assessment counselor or faculty member.

A Formal Portfolio

Each institution has its own portfolio format. Within each portfolio, you should expect to find these parts:

The Cover Page

The cover page identifies the educational institution and the name of the program in which you are enrolled. Provide identifying information about yourself: your name, address, telephone number, and the date of the portfolio's submission. See Figure 1 for a sample cover page. Make sure that the cover has an attractive appearance.

Figure 1
Sample Cover Page

**Portfolio for Prior
Learning Assessment**

Submitted to

SEASIDE COLLEGE

ADULT DEGREE PROGRAM

by
Isabella DeRio

March 13, 1996   1412 Ranchero Avenue
Santa Maria, CA 33333
(444) 777-6666

The Table of Contents

The table of contents is simply a guide to the portfolio. It is an overview of the portfolio. No doubt, the table of contents will need some revision when the portfolio is completed. Be sure to use the correct page numbers. It is a guide for evaluators who want to locate information, so make it easy to understand and use.

The Essay or Narrative

As explained above, this part enables you to present your impression of yourself. The essay should be about the learning you have experienced and its value at the college level. It should also reflect any lack of knowledge that you perceive and suggest ways you intend to overcome this inadequacy through future studies. Your assessors need to understand how your prior learning experiences are related to your future studies.

Learning Experiences and Documentation

This is the main part of most portfolios. First, make a list stating each learning component, the documentation for that component, and the amount of credit being requested. Identify each component by a number or letter. This number or letter should be used to identify the documents that support it. For example, in the following example a CLEP transcript would be labeled with the letter A.

Learning Component	Documentation	Credit Requested
A—Beginning and intermediate Spanish	CLEP test transcript	6

Following the list, include a one-page competency statement for each component, including information about how the learning took place, as well as a description of what was learned or what skill was acquired. The request for credit is placed at the bottom of the page. The actual documentation follows.

Submitting Your Portfolio

Be neat. Check your work carefully. Ask a knowledgeable friend to check it one more time. Then review the information again. Keep a copy for yourself. You may want to use a three-ring binder that allows you to move pages and dividers easily. If you have included keepsakes such as photos or letters, you will want to protect them with plastic covers. The school may accept copies rather than the originals. You should never submit original copies of important documents like licenses because they might get lost. Deliver your portfolio to the proper college office. Relax and wait for the assessment to take place.

Assessing Your Portfolio

The assessment of your portfolio will be done by a committee of faculty and administrators. They will read your documents and decide if the learning is equal to that done at the college level. They will check the documentation to make sure it reflects that the appropriate learning has taken place. They will make sure you are not using the same learning component to request credit in more than one area or duplicate previously transcripted work. They will judge the learning from the standpoint of your degree program. Then they will consider the credit request to see if it is reasonable.

You may be interviewed by a faculty member or administrator to provide a face-to-face evaluation of the learning you have done. This may be very casual or more like an oral examination. It is a part of the evaluation process. Sometimes students are granted additional credit hours following the interview.

Mission Accomplished

After your portfolio has been assessed, a number of hours of credit will be recommended. The committee will notify you of the results. In addition, the registrar and possibly a dean will be given the results

The registrar will record the number of credits awarded on your college transcript. The transcript will show the number of credits awarded for the courses or learning components to which your learning has been applied. This transcript becomes a record of your college career.

You may want to check your transcript to make sure it is correct. To do this, ask for a copy of your transcript from the registrar's office.

A Source of Help in Documenting Your Learning

For many people, learning has been a scattered experience. Gathering the documentation for a portfolio may be very complicated. If this is your problem, the Regents Credit Bank may offer a solution.

The Regents Credit Bank was established by the University of New York. It acts as an evaluation and transcript service for people wanting to put all of their academic records on one transcript. The Credit Bank will evaluate and accept credits from the following seven areas:

1. College courses through a residency or correspondence from accredited U.S. schools and their equals in foreign countries

2. Scores from equivalency exams

3. Military schools and occupational specialties accredited by the American Council on Education

4. Courses offered by companies, seminars, and in-house training that are evaluated by the American Council on Education or the New York National Program on Noncollegiate Sponsored Instruction

5. Pilot training licenses and certificates issued by the Federal Aviation Administration

6. Approved nursing examinations

7. Prior learning assessment through interviews or a portfolio and independent study

The Regents Credit Bank charges a fee to register. If some type of work is not judged to be worthy of credit, it may be listed as noncredit work. If you have taken a traditional course and failed or received a low grade, you may request that it not be recorded on the transcript. It is actually possible to obtain a degree from Regents College by accumulating sufficient credits through the sources mentioned in the preceding list. Additional credits can be earned and added to your transcript as the learning experience is completed. For further information, write to Regents College at 7 Columbia Circle, Albany, NY 12203-5159; or call (518)464-8500.

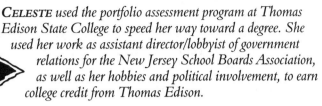

CELESTE *used the portfolio assessment program at Thomas Edison State College to speed her way toward a degree. She used her work as assistant director/lobbyist of government relations for the New Jersey School Boards Association, as well as her hobbies and political involvement, to earn college credit from Thomas Edison.*

One of Celeste's hobbies was antique jewelry. She became certified in the areas of gemology and diamondology. She used her certification to document her knowledge of mineralogy, earning college credit for this course. She was able to earn additional credits through her portfolio in data processing, political science, business and advanced business writing, and communications. These credits were awarded for such skills as her self-taught word processing abilities, her work as a state legislator's aide, her writing of business proposals, and making presentations to groups. Using her portfolio, Celeste was able to speed up the process of earning a bachelor's degree, and so can you.

Contact Information

Proficiency Examination Program (PEP)
American College Testing Program
2255 N. Dubuque Road
Iowa City, IA 52243
(319) 337-1000

Advanced College Placement Program (APP)
Educational Testing Service
Princeton, NJ 08541
(609) 771-7300

College Level Examination Program (CLEP)
CLEP
P.O. Box 661
Princeton, NJ 08541-6601
(215) 750-8420

Student Occupational Competency Achievement Tests (SOCAT)
National Occupational Competency Testing Institute
409 Bishop Hall
Ferris State University
Big Rapids, MI 49307
(616) 796-4695

Defense Activity for Non-Traditional Education Support (DANTES)
DANTES Program Office
Educational Testing Service
Princeton, NJ 08541-0001
(215) 750-8328

New York University Proficiency Testing in Foreign Languages
Foreign Language Program
NYU School of Continuing Education
2 University Place, Room 55
New York, NY 10003

Ohio University Examination Program
Lifelong Learning
309 Tupper Hall
Athens, OH 45701

Thomas A. Edison State College Examination Program (TECEP)
Office of the Registrar
101 West State Street CN545
Trenton, NJ 08625

Council for the Advancement of Experiential Learning
223 West Jackson Boulevard, Suite 510
Chicago, IL 60606

Chapter 5

Getting Over the Financial Hurdle

The cost of financing a college education is one of the biggest hurdles that all college students face. Adults are financially independent and typically don't have Mom or Dad to fall back on for tuition payments. With their other financial obligations, many adults dismiss the possibility of attending college because of the cost. However, a college education will provide a higher return on investment than almost any other financial venture you can make. This chapter explores ways of reducing costs for college and financing a college education. It addresses one of the two reasons most adults cite for not participating in educational programs: money and time.

The Price Tag

What will your education cost? Since people don't have the same income, assets, and expenses, you must answer this question by looking at your own financial situation. Every student must pay tuition. The amount depends on the academic institution you choose. Books and supplies are expenses that vary with the major you choose. Some schools encourage students to purchase personal computers. In some cases, the school includes the price of a computer in tuition fees. For most adult students, room and board are not expenses; however, in some situations these expenses may be a factor. In lieu of room and board, you might find a need to eat out more while attending classes, and housekeeping help might be needed. Childcare, elderly care, and reliable transportation to and from classes are additional expenses that adult students may have.

As an adult, you already have some financial responsibilities that won't disappear when you enter those hallowed halls of ivy. Your creditors aren't interested in your academic pursuits. The monthly bills will still be delivered to your mailbox. The mortgage payment or monthly rent, the car insurance, and the utility payments will still be due. If you have been the financial provider for your family, that responsibility doesn't go away.

Paying the monthly bills while meeting all of your education expenses may seem like an impossible feat. Each year college tuitions increase. You may be asking yourself, "Why even try to overcome this financial hurdle? Is a college degree really worth all these dollars and cents?" Remember, statistics show that a college degree is worth your financial investment for two reasons: earnings and employability.

Education and Earnings

The U.S. Bureau of the Census recorded the following average annual incomes by education level.

Level of Education	Average Income
High School	$21,241
College	$34,355
Master's	$40,666
Professional	$67,131

According to this chart, a college graduate earns over $13,000 more each year than a high school graduate. There are 40 to 50 working years in the typical career span. This means that a college graduate will earn between $520,000 and $650,000 more than a high school graduate by the end of his or her career. To calculate what a degree might be worth to you, determine the number of years you plan to work before retirement and multiply that number by $13,000. This is obviously a rough estimate, because you can't expect to achieve the average earnings immediately upon completing a degree. However, many adults with significant work experience are able to get better jobs more quickly than a traditional, 22- to 23-year-old graduate. Do you want to earn more money? A college education is a wise investment.

Education and Unemployment

A college education means that you have a stronger possibility of being employed. Suppose you were an employer. You interview Jeff and Kurt for the position you want to fill. Both men have experience. You are equally impressed with them. You would feel comfortable working with either person. There is one difference: Kurt has a college degree. Whom will you hire? When hiring individuals of equal abilities, a college degree often is the deciding factor.

A college education doesn't guarantee freedom from unemployment, but statistics do show that a college education means fewer periods of unemployment. Eighty-five percent of women college graduates are part of the labor market, whereas only 47 percent of the female high school dropouts are part of the labor market. Ninety-five percent of male college graduates are part of the labor market. Only 78 percent of male high school dropouts are part of the labor market. With fewer periods of unemployment, college graduates are assured of earning more during their working lives. A college education is a wise investment.

Reducing the Cost of Education

Before you decide to attend a school, investigate the costs of all educational opportunities available to you. You may be able to reduce the cost of your education by using some innovative strategies.

The primary item to target in reducing the cost of a college education is tuition. To accomplish this, you must understand how colleges charge tuition. Most colleges base tuition fees on a per-credit basis. In other words, one credit hour may cost $150. Another typical price structure is a sliding scale that charges less per hour as the number of hours increases. If you attend weekend, evening, or summer classes, you may be given a discount at some colleges and universities. The savings may be as much as $300 for a course. Several adult degree programs have created innovative price structures that can save you money over the more traditional methods for tuition charges.

Some schools offer an "older student discount." The definition of "older student" varies from one school to another. Normally age 50 or 60 is the magic number; however, some schools will give a tuition discount to students as young as age 24. Many public colleges and universities offer free tuition—depending on course availability—to senior citizens residing in the state.

Classes at community colleges are almost always less expensive than at four-year schools. By earning an associate degree at a community college, you may obtain a job promotion or the opportunity to qualify for a better-paying job. You could benefit in two ways. First, you have spent less for the first two years of your education. Second, you have more money to pay for the next two years. If you plan to continue your education and earn a bachelor's degree at a four-year school, check with that school to see what credits will be accepted. That way, you avoid some confusion and additional expenditures for credits that are not transferable when you enroll at the four-year school.

Another way to reduce the cost of an education is to examine carefully the number of hours that it takes to complete a degree. Most bachelor's degrees require 120 to 130 semester hours for graduation. However, some majors require significantly more hours. You should determine whether there is more than one major that can help you achieve your career goals, and select the one with a lower number of required hours. The number of hours required for degrees and majors varies among colleges. Comparing the total number of hours required by various colleges can help you identify cost savings.

Some additional investigation may help you reduce transportation costs. Check to see whether off-campus classes are offered. By attending classes in your community, you save both time and money. Many universities are offering classes at job sites, in local school buildings, and at other public facilities. Some schools lease office facilities. The staff at these off-campus sites can register students for classes and handle other advising. Students might graduate without ever attending an on-campus class. The classes are taught by professors who travel from the main campus or by community professionals hired by the university.

Some classes are taught through telecommunications. Interactive television allows a professor to teach the class from an on-campus classroom. The students at the satellite campus can see and speak to the professor as if they were in the same room. Classroom interaction is still taking place, despite the distance.

Learning at home is another innovative way to earn college credit. Correspondence classes are available through many schools. Public television stations and cable television systems have agreements with universities to offer courses to viewers. Two such programs are the Mind Extension University and the Public Broadcasting System's Adult Learning Service. It's important to be sure that the course you are taking is a credit course.

Your telephone line, a computer, and a modem can also bring a classroom to your home. Thomas Edison State College in Trenton, New Jersey, mails its students textbooks, videos, and software to make phone connections. Each student and a mentor correspond through e-mail. Class discussions, paper submissions, and assignments are also handled through e-mail.

Another way to reduce the cost of education is to speed up the process. In Chapter 3 we discussed some of the nontraditional adult accelerated programs. Gaining credit for life experiences is another way to complete the degree faster. In a traditional college setting, a student can accelerate the educational process by attending full-time through-out the year. Accumulating credits through exams and prior learning portfolio assessment costs much less than tuition for the same courses.

Having more than one family member attend the same school can decrease the cost of your education. Some schools offer family discounts: If more than one member of a family is attending the college, a rebate or lower tuition is charged. Some schools simply reduce the tuition by a set percentage for additional family members. At the University of Santa Clara, California, if three members of the same family are enrolled, one person pays no tuition. Pace University in New York City offers free classes (on an availability basis) to the parents of its undergraduate students. Getting a degree along with a spouse or child can be a real bargain.

Some schools offer free tuition in unusual situations. For example, if the major wage earner in a family becomes unemployed, an institution might offer free tuition to students in the family. Other schools offer one year of free tuition to farmers who have been forced out of farming because of financial problems.

As you contemplate your college education, there are some important strategies to consider to save yourself money. If your college offers a discount as the number of course hours increases, structure your plans to take as many hours per semester or quarter as possible. If you plan to transfer to another college to complete your degree, make sure that all credits will transfer and count toward the credits required for graduation. You don't want to pay for college credits that won't count toward your degree. Another strategy is to avoid dropping classes. This almost always results in a loss of tuition payments.

The Adult Student and Financial Aid

Adult students are often reluctant to apply for financial aid. As a responsible adult, you have been financially independent for several years. Asking for financial help might not be attractive to you. But think about this: Most of the financial aid available comes from taxes. As a taxpayer, you have been paying for other people's education for several years. Maybe it is your turn to receive the benefit of all those tax dollars you have paid.

Some people believe that financial aid is available only to younger students. This is not true. Aid is granted without regard to age. You are considered an independent student. Your financial aid will be based on your earnings, and your spouse's if you are married.

If you are unable to attend classes full-time, you might not receive as much aid. Each institution defines what is meant by a full-time student. The definitions can and do vary from one college to another. In some cases, simply adding one more class may allow you to qualify as a full-time student. Some schools offer students a unique way to qualify as full-time. Courses are offered one at a time in a way that allows students to complete three courses during a semester. The class meeting is usually one or two nights each week for three to four hours. Before you decide to attend a college, find out the institution's definition of a full-time student, because it can affect your financial aid.

Finding Out About Financial Aid

The local library has several books about financial aid. If you have not chosen a college, this is a good way to conduct an initial investigation of financial aid opportunities. Your state's department of higher education is another source of information on state aid that may be available.

If you are thinking of attending an institution, visit its financial aid office. The financial aid officer will provide information about any aid that might be available to you. In order to receive any type of financial help, the college will ask you to fill out a form called the Free Application for Federal Student Aid (FAFSA). Much of the information will come from your income tax return. It is important that the information on the form be accurate. The forms must be filed by the deadline. You can get help in filling out the form through the financial aid office or by calling (800) 4FED-AID. You also can also get general information about federal financial aid programs. About 750 schools require an additional form called the Profile. For further information about this form, contact The College Board at 45 Columbus Avenue, New York, NY 10023, or phone (212) 713-8000. The two forms are similar in the information requested.

Grants, Loans, and Scholarships

Financial aid is available through the federal government, state governments, colleges and universities, and private organizations and associations. Financial aid may be given in three different ways.

1. Grants are a form of financial aid that do not require any repayment. Grants are given according to the economic need of the student. They may also be dependent on the student being enrolled in an eligible school and maintaining a certain grade point average.

2. Scholarships are another kind of financial aid that are not repaid. The college may offer scholarships. Scholarships may also be available through associations and organizations interested in education. In some cases, scholarships have been set up specifically for adult students. Scholarships may cover all or part of tuition expenses. A stipend may be included to pay for books or housing expenses.

3. Student loans must be repaid. They are considered financial aid when the interest rate is below the market interest rate, and repayment is not required until the student leaves college. Subsidized loans do not start accruing interest until the student leaves school. Such loans are based on the student's need. Unsubsidized loans accrue interest while the student is attending college. Depending on the loan agreement, the interest may or may not be paid while the student is attending classes at the college.

How Is Financial Aid Given?

Grants, some scholarships, and student loans are based on need. To receive financial aid based on need, a student is required to prove that a need for aid exists. Colleges use information from the Free Application for Federal Student Aid or the Profile to determine how much you can financially contribute for your own education.

Some scholarships are granted on the basis of merit. Such scholarships might be given for maintaining a certain grade point average or for outstanding athletic or artistic abilities. In some cases, a student must meet requirements such as belonging to a certain organization, being from a certain ethnic group, or preparing for a certain occupation. Some scholarships may be renewed from year to year. Others are awarded just once. Scholarships are available from federal agencies, state governments, educational institutions, and organizations interested in education. Some aid is available that is not based on financial need—such as Stafford Loans—but applicants must first exhaust their eligibility based on need.

Am I Eligible for Federal Financial Aid?

Before you apply for financial aid of any kind, you need to determine whether you meet the following basic requirements.

1. You have a high school diploma or have passed the GED test.

2. You are a U.S. citizen, a U.S. national, or a permanent resident of the United States.

3. You have a Social Security number (unless you are a noncitizen).

4. You are enrolled or are enrolling in an accredited college or university. You must be a regular student—not admitted as a special student—and must be enrolled in a qualifying degree program.

5. If you are a male, you must be registered with the Selective Service.

6. You have never defaulted on any other federal financial aid.

SHERINE *is a 29-year-old Hispanic female. She is employed as a secretary/bookkeeper at a social service agency that is operated by a religious association. She has a 9-year-old son and has never been married.*

Sherine decided to go to college for both personal and economic reasons. She feels that higher education will help her become more disciplined and focused on her future. She wants to be a role model for her family and for other Hispanic people. She is working on a bachelor's degree in criminal justice and hopes to continue work toward a Master of Social Work degree. Sherine attends college part-time and works full-time.

Money has been a problem for Sherine, but she has been able to manage college expenses with the help of a Pell Grant. The Pell Grant has provided enough money to pay for half of her tuition. She pays for books and the remaining tuition from her earnings. She doesn't have a lot of money to spend on "fun" things, but she manages. Her goal is to graduate in the next two years, and she has made getting the degree her priority.

Federal Pell Grants

If you decide to apply for federal financial aid, the first step is to apply for a Pell Grant, The Federal Pell Grant is the largest need-based federal program available to students seeking their first undergraduate degree. All eligible students receive Pell Grants; however, the amount of the grant will vary depending on each student's need. For the 1995-'96 school year, a student could receive a maximum of $2,340. The amount of the grant is either credited to the student's account or given directly to the student by check.

To qualify for a Pell Grant, you must meet each of the following criteria:

1. Your Expected/Estimated Family Contribution (EFC) must meet the required level set by the federal government.

2. You must be attending an eligible school in an eligible program.

3. You must not have previously earned a bachelor's degree.

4. You must meet all application deadlines.

5. You must be a U.S. citizen or a permanent resident.

To apply for a Pell Grant, you must submit the Free Application for Federal Student Aid. This form is available from the college's financial aid office or from your state student assistance office. The form should be sent to the address listed as soon after January 1 as possible. It is extremely important to meet the deadlines for these applications. Missing a deadline means that you receive no aid. If the form is not filled out correctly, you will have to resubmit the information. This will delay the processing. If the information is correct, you will receive your Student Aid Report (SAR) in about six weeks. This report will tell you if you are eligible to receive a Pell Grant. The SAR must be submitted to your college's financial aid office before any money will be awarded. Again, your school will have a deadline for this submission. Since this varies from school to school, check with the financial aid office for the deadline. If you miss it, you will get nothing.

Federal Supplemental Education Opportunity Grants

The Federal Supplemental Education Opportunity Grant (FSEOG) is an additional need-based federal grant. While the funds for the grant come from the government, the school administers the money. Usually students who qualify for Pell Grants are given priority in receiving the FSEOG. To be eligible for the FSEOG, you must meet the following requirements:

1. You must attend a school that grants FSEOGs.

2. You must, in the view of the school, have a great financial need.

3. You may be either a part-time or full-time student, but institutions typically give higher priority to full-time students for receiving an FSEOG.

4. You must not have previously earned a bachelor's degree.

If you are interested in obtaining a FSEOG, you should talk to your financial aid advisor as soon as you are enrolled in college. Find out how to apply, what forms you need to complete, and when the financial aid office will begin accepting applications. When you return the completed forms to the financial aid office, ask how long it will be before you are notified about your award. It is important to apply early. Schools tend to run out of this type of money.

In 1995-'96, students receiving an FSEOG could receive up to $4,000, depending on their need. Normally, a student's account is credited or the student receives a check (or a combination of both) at least once each quarter or semester.

Federal Perkins Loans

The Federal Perkins Loan must be repaid. It is a low-interest loan—5 percent fixed rate—that may be subsidized. The college is the lender and makes the decisions concerning the loan. The money comes from the federal government, but application for the loan is made to the school. This loan is based on need. A student who has received a Pell Grant has a good chance of obtaining a Perkins Loan as well.

To be eligible for a Perkins Loan, you must meet the following requirements:

1. You must be an undergraduate or graduate student.

2. You must be attending an institution that receives funds from the Perkins Loan program.

3. You must be at least a half-time student.

4. You must be working toward an undergraduate or graduate degree.

The amount of the loan will depend on the student's need and the amount of aid the student already receives from other sources. Since the school receives a set amount of financial aid money from the federal government, it is important to apply early. Once the school runs out of money, no more will be loaned. To apply for the loan, talk to a financial aid advisor at the school.

An undergraduate student can borrow up to $3,000 for each year of study. A maximum of $15,000 can be borrowed by an undergraduate. For a graduate or professional degree, up to $5,000 can be borrowed for each year. A maximum of $30,000 can be borrowed; however, this total includes any money borrowed for an undergraduate degree.

To receive the loan, a student must sign a promissory note. This is an agreement in which the student agrees to repay the loan. The loan must be repaid even if the student doesn't graduate or isn't able to find work after graduation. Since the loan is subsidized, the loan repayment does not begin until nine months after graduation or after a student drops out of school or becomes a less than half-time student. Interest does not accrue until the repayment period begins. The loan can be paid back at one time, or over a period of ten years. In some cases, all or part of the loan may be canceled.

Federal Stafford Loans

The Federal Stafford Loan program is the largest financial aid program funded by the federal government. Loans made through this program must be repaid. The loan is borrowed through a lending institution such as a commercial bank, a credit union, or a savings and loan association. Some colleges are also approved lenders. Your state guaranty agency has information about the Stafford Loan program in your state. Call the Federal Student Aid Information Center's toll-free number (800-433-3243) for information about loans and your state's guaranty agency.

A Stafford Loan that is need-based is subsidized by the federal government. The government pays the interest on the loan while the student is enrolled in school and up to six months after he or she leaves school. The student is required to begin making payments six months after departure from school. The payments include both principal and interest and must be repaid within ten years.

Unsubsidized Stafford Loans, which are not based on need, are also available. In this case, the interest is paid by the student while he or she is in school. Sometimes the financial institution will delay the payments and add the interest to the loan. The loan is repaid in monthly payments, which may be made over a ten-year period.

During the 1995-'96 school year, an independent undergraduate student could borrow $6,625 as a first-year student enrolled for at least one academic year. A second-year independent student enrolled for a full academic year could borrow $7,500. In both of these cases, $4,000 of the amount must be in unsubsidized loans. After completing two years of study, an independent student may borrow $10,500 for each full academic year. At least $5,000 of this amount must be unsubsidized loans.

Federal Work-Study Program

The Federal Work-Study Program is another type of financial assistance. This campus-based program allows students to earn money to help with educational expenses. The federal government pays 75 percent of the student's wages. The employer pays the remainder. Either on- or off-campus work is available, and jobs must be with a nonprofit private or public organization. Usually, the employer is the college or a community nonprofit organization. Sometimes a private for-profit employer is used if the job is related to the student's course of study.

The salary must be at the current federal minimum wage. Undergraduates are paid by the hour. Graduate students are paid hourly or by salary. Payment must be made to the student at least once each month. Each student is awarded a maximum of work-study money that may be earned during an academic year. A student cannot receive more than this amount of money.

An adult student who is not working full-time might be interested in the Work-Study Program. The program has several advantages: First, it offers the adult student an opportunity to become a part of the campus atmosphere. Second, the hours are usually set with the student's class schedule taken into consideration. Third, it offers students the opportunity to learn more about their field of study. Fourth, earnings are excluded when filing for federal aid in the following year.

The benefits that can result from an adult student using financial aid are illustrated in an article that appeared in the August 12, 1994, issue of The Wall Street Journal. *It reported on a 40-year-old man named* RANDY KOHRS. *In June, 1991, Mr. Kohrs found himself jobless again. With only a high school diploma, minimum-wage jobs with no health insurance benefits were the only available jobs for this husband and father. Unable to keep up with their mortgage payments, the Kohrs family lost their home. They moved to Cedar Rapids, Iowa, where Mr. Kohrs managed a video store for $13,000 a year. His wife worked as a cashier at an auto dealership. Three years later, when the video store closed, Mr. Kohrs was once again unemployed.*

In desperation Mr. Kohrs went to the counseling center of the Kirkwood Community College. He was given an aptitude test which showed that the health care field would be a good career choice. He wanted to enter Kirkwood's two-year respiratory therapy program, but money was a stumbling block. Tuition was about $900 per semester, plus $250 for books. Mr. Kohrs found help at Kirkwood's dislocated workers office. Through a combination of federal grants, loans of about $10,000, and *unemployment benefits, Mr. Kohrs was able to pay for his education and help support his family. His wife continued to work at the auto dealership and took a second job at a local Wal-Mart. The family took heart in knowing that their situation would not last forever.*

Randy Kohrs graduated from Kirkwood Community College with an associate degree in respiratory therapy. He now works in Iowa City as a respiratory therapist and earns $26,000 a year. He enjoys the challenge of his new job. And he has health insurance.

State Financial Aid

All 50 states offer some type of need-based financial aid. Many offer merit-based awards, as well. In addition, some states offer special loans similar to the Stafford Loans. To find out about your state's financial aid program, contact the state department of higher education. Ask for a handbook with descriptions of the various programs available and the application forms for these programs. Having the forms will save time when you are trying to meet deadlines. Because different figures are sometimes used, you might qualify for state aid even if you didn't meet the requirements for federal aid.

Some states use the Free Application for Student Federal Aid to determine eligibility for state grants and loans. Others require a different form that is processed by the state department of higher education. Generally, state aid is given to students who are enrolled in public universities or private colleges within the state. In some cases, a state has a reciprocal agreement with other states, so that a student may attend a school in another state and still receive aid from the state of residency. Depending on the state, the financial aid may be available only to legal residents, or it may be offered to out-of-state students attending colleges within the state.

OHIO UNIVERSITY *is a state school located southeast of Columbus in Athens, Ohio. It has a student body of approximately 18,500. It is a traditional college—established in 1804—with a nontraditional outlook. The university offers several programs that serve adult students in Ohio, nationally, and internationally. Almost 6,000 adult students are served through the university's Lifelong Learning Programs.*

An External Student Program is designed for students who cannot attend a college on a residential basis. Students can earn associate and bachelor's degrees through this program without attending courses on campus. Degree programs are individualized and can be completed by earning credits through exams, prior learning assessment, independent study, correspondence courses, and courses from other accredited colleges. Ohio University offers one of the most extensive programs available for earning credits through examinations.

Many classes are offered in the evening and in summer workshops. For students who live too far to make regular trips to campus, there are special residential learning opportunities. A summer institute provides courses for one- or two-week periods, and students can stay in a dormitory on campus. The winter institute occurs the first week after Thanksgiving and includes week-long courses, but participants must stay in private lodgings or hotels. Courses in these institutes require that students prepare assignments before attending and complete additional course assignments after returning home.

Other Sources of Financial Aid

There are two programs funded by the federal government but administered at the local level that can be used by special populations. Neither of these programs is designed specifically to provide financial aid for college, but they can do so when it is an appropriate strategy for helping a person gain employment. One is the Job Training Partnership Act, which is designed to help people who are economically disadvantaged and those who have suffered dislocation in their employment for a variety of reasons. To find out more about this program and determine your eligibility, contact a local Private Industry Council (PIC).

Another specialized program is the Vocational Rehabilitation Program, which can provide financial assistance to students who have mental or physical disabilities. You can get more information on this program through your state or regional vocational rehabilitation office.

If you have been in the military, check with your state's office of veteran affairs to learn what kinds of financial aid are available. Check with the branch of the service in which you served for additional aid that might be available.

Some organizations and businesses that give scholarships will accept applications from adult students. A few scholarships are offered specifically to adults. For example, some community women's organizations give scholarships to women who are returning to school to complete their education. If you have chosen a field of study such as health care or teaching, funds may be available. Scholarship information can be obtained from the local library or the financial aid office of your school. Informative books as well as computer software programs list various scholarships, qualifications, and the application processes.

Orville Redenbacher's Second Start Scholarship Program is an example of a scholarship designated for adults. The Orville Redenbacher Company produces popcorn—all kinds of popcorn. The company is also interested in people, and has established a special scholarship program for students over the age of 30 who are working toward their first degree. The scholarship is offered to those who are returning to complete their college degree or those who are just beginning. The $1,000 scholarships are given in all fields of study. Applications are accepted between March 1 and May 1 of each year.

To find out more about this adult scholarship opportunity, write to Orville Redenbacher's Second Start Scholarship Program, P.O. Box 4137, Blair, NE 68009.

Employer-Assisted Education

Your employer might be a source of financial help in your quest for an education. According to *The Wall Street Journal*, only 7 percent of employees participate in company plans that pay for job-related courses. However, some research has shown that as many as 40 percent of all adult students are receiving some kind of employer assistance. Younger employees are more likely to use the benefit to complete a bachelor's or master's degree. This under-used source of financial assistance may be available to you. You need to understand your company's program. The following descriptions are typical of policies that companies often use when paying for employees' education.

An employer may set some requirements that limit a student's choice of colleges and majors. Sometimes, tuition will be paid only for courses that are related to the employee's work. Under this restriction, an office worker couldn't pursue a degree in nursing and be reimbursed by his or her employer. Often, students are reimbursed for tuition only at state-supported institutions; or the maximum tuition reimbursement offered is equivalent to the tuition fees at a state-supported college. Most employers require that the college be accredited. Most also limit annual payments to $5,250; this is the limit the federal government allows a business to take as a tax deduction for an individual employee. Tuition assistance that is less than this amount will not be considered taxable income for the employee. You should remain alert to changes in this tax regulation, as it is frequently reviewed by Congress.

Companies differ in their eligibility requirements for these programs. Some don't offer this benefit to newly hired employees. An employee may be offered the benefit after working for 90 days, six months, or some other set amount of time. Some companies offer assistance only to those employees at certain salary levels.

The dollar amount of tuition assistance also varies. Some companies allow an employee a set amount of money for a year, based on funds that are budgeted for tuition reimbursement. For example, a maximum amount of $1,000 may be offered to an employee for classes taken during one year. Another method uses the amount to pay a percentage of the tuition each year. A full-time employee might receive a larger percentage than a part-time employee. Other companies will pay tuition, registration fees, and books without setting a limit.

It is possible that your employer will require you to work with the company for an established length of time after you complete your degree; otherwise, you must repay the tuition.

An employer may pay the college directly for the student's bill. Others will reimburse the student only after the course is completed. For their records, employers will request verification from the school of the cost, the student's enrollment, and the final grade for the completed course.

Often, an employee is expected to receive a certain grade to qualify for tuition reimbursement. For example, it may be necessary to get at least a "C" to be reimbursed for a course. Another method used frequently is based on a sliding scale. Using this method, an employee might be reimbursed 100 percent for an "A", 75 percent for a "B", 50 percent for a "C", and nothing for lower grades.

Both small and large companies offer this benefit to their employees. Some employers encourage their employees to take advantage of it. In fact, some employers use it to attract new employees. Others don't advertise it, but it may still be available. It is certainly worth investigating. In fact, it may be worthwhile to try to get a job with a company that offers tuition reimbursement before starting your college career.

To find out about your employer's education assistance program, contact your company's human resource office. It's important to understand your company's program, because they can be complicated. To avoid confusion, get the information in writing before you start your educational program. You need to ask some questions and get answers based on the items listed below.

1. Find out exactly how much the company will pay and how the company will pay. Will you pay the bill and be reimbursed, or will your company pay the school directly?

2. Find out whether the company pays for any extras. For example, will it pay for books or supplies? What about lab fees? Will it pay for your bus ticket to campus or the gas for your car?

3. Find out whether the company must approve your class as a job-related course before reimbursing you. Will the company pay for Advanced Square Dancing? If the answer is no, you may want to register for Beginning Computer for the Office instead.

4. Find out who approves your study program and how often it must be approved. Must the program be approved every semester or quarter, or can it be done for the entire school year?

5. Find out whether your grades will affect your reimbursement. What if you get a grade lower than a "C"?

6. Find out whether the company must approve the school you plan to attend. Are courses at a nonaccredited school accepted in the program? Can you attend only certain schools? Will the company pay for seminars or a weekend class?

7. Find out how soon the company must be notified of your course of study. If you apply too late, you may have to wait to receive the help.

8. Find out whether the financial help has any strings attached. Not unfairly, your employer may expect a return for the investment made in you. Will you be expected to remain in the company for a set number of years? What happens if you must leave this job before that time has passed?

Be sure you fully understand your responsibilities and your company's policies before you enter your educational program. Get the details in writing to avoid confusion. Don't get stuck with the bills.

How important is this benefit to you? Is it logical to change jobs to gain financial assistance from an employer? Think about the following hypothetical situation.

MARILEE works at T-Shirt Creations, designing logos for the company. After two years, she has been given a nice raise. Her benefits include some health insurance and a week's vacation. She hopes to start attending the local community college next September. Her long-term goal is a bachelor's degree in graphic design.

A nationally known sportswear company is just opening in town. Their want ad says the company offers employees $2,500 of tuition assistance each year. When Marilee went for a job interview last week, she found that her salary would be $1,000 less than she is getting at T-Shirt Creations.

What's the logical answer to Marilee's situation? Simple arithmetic says $2,500 in school funds minus $1,000 in salary equals $1,500 of additional funds for her education. And remember, the entire $2,500 is not taxed. The question Marilee must answer is, "Can I make a lifestyle adjustment to eliminate $1,000 of living expenses?" If so, a job change seems reasonable.

Your Money

Spending someone else's money is not difficult. It's easy to spend Uncle Sam's money. Getting a scholarship is a real ego booster. It's not even hard to pay for your education with the boss's money. But it is possible that none of these methods of financing your education will be available to you.

The next step is to look at your money. What personal financial resources do you have to pay for your education?

Your Savings

If you have a savings account, start with it as the basis for paying educational expenses. You must decide how much of your savings you are comfortable investing in your education. No doubt you may not be comfortable completely emptying your savings account. Remember that your education should increase your earning potential, but it comes with no guarantee for doing so. Promising to replenish the savings account and keeping that promise is one way of approaching this problem. Naturally, if you are a family person, this matter must be discussed with other family members as well.

As a teenager, LEIGH became pregnant and quit high school. After the baby was born, she returned to school and graduated. Leigh chose to return to high school rather than get a GED. Her father encouraged her to enroll in college, but the birth of her second child made this impossible in Leigh's eyes.

When her marriage ended in divorce, Leigh's father again encouraged her to attend college. This year she completed her first associate degree in administrative office technology. She plans to start work on a second degree in computer information science this fall.

Leigh receives assistance from the welfare department, as well as child support. Her tuition is paid through benefits she receives as a child of a disabled veteran. A Pell Grant pays for her books and supplies. Her income is also subsidized through the college Work-Study Program.

Leigh finds living on a reduced income very stressful. She admits that she often is dependent on her parents for "extras." She is motivated to get her degree to provide a better life for her children. Because she is not planning to remarry, Leigh is even more motivated to succeed.

Your Friends and Family

Parents, grandparents, aunts, uncles, or friends may be willing and financially able to contribute to your educational expenses. As an adult, you might hesitate to accept this kind of financial help, especially from your parents. Many adult students interviewed for the background for this book said that one of the greatest influences causing them to return to complete their degree was a parent's desire to see it happen. So doesn't it seem reasonable to let your parents have the joy of attending your college graduation a little poorer? Or would you rather attend their funerals, knowing that your inheritance is a few thousand dollars greater? You may want to swallow your pride for their happiness.

Rather than a gift, you might ask for a loan from a relative, a friend, or even an employer. To avoid misunderstandings, work out a loan agreement with the person and put the agreement in writing. Include in the agreement the amount of the repayment, a date to begin paying off the loan, and any interest that is charged. Out of respect for this individual, honor it as if it were a bank loan.

Other Personal Resources

Some adults have accumulated other assets, such as stocks and bonds. You need to balance out the value of an education against the earnings that you expect from continued holdings of these assets. Maybe you have hobbies—such as stamp and coin collecting—that have resulted in the accumulation of valuable assets. Now may be the time to sell these items and invest in an education. The important task at this point is to measure the worth of whatever assets you have against the benefits that can be gained through an education.

Loans

Some people are very reluctant to use loans to finance their education. However, these same people might be making payments on an auto loan. The car is losing value each day. By the time the loan is paid off, the car will probably need some repairs. A college degree will not rust or break down. Its value will not depreciate. Using a loan to finance your education is an investment in you.

We have already discussed low-interest loans available through the state and federal governments. If you qualify, these loans are usually the best choice. However, it is sometimes possible to borrow against a 401(k) retirement program, and such a loan may offer rates competitive with the Federal Stafford Loan. Lending institutions are another source of personal loans. Interest rates vary among banks, so you will want to shop around. If you own a home, a home equity loan might be another source of an educational loan. A home equity loan will usually have a lower interest rate than a personal loan, and interest paid on it is tax deductible.

Credit cards are another form of loans. Most colleges accept major credit cards for tuition and fee payments. Likewise, college bookstores accept credit cards. It is possible to pay for an education using your credit card. This is more feasible when you have a credit card with a low interest rate. It might be possible to repay tuition and fees before a term is complete, thus freeing your credit limit for use in charging the next term's tuition, fees, and books.

Other Financial Options

To free up some money for your education, check your budget. How are you spending your money? Do you have discretionary money that could be used for your educational needs? Can you take a camping vacation this summer instead of a cruise? Can you drop your membership at the health club and use the facilities at the school you are attending? Can you hang onto your old car for a little longer to eliminate monthly car payments? Without making life miserable, what can you adjust to have more money for your education?

In your basement, garage, and attic live the "I know I'll need it some day" phantoms. Well, maybe the day you need them has arrived. Why not get rid of some of the things you don't need or never use? How many VCRs do you need? Are you really going to refinish that chest you bought five years ago at the garage sale down the street? Do you think your six-foot son would mind parting with his first tricycle? You might be pleasantly surprised at the amount of money your phantoms can bring at a garage sale or through newspaper advertising. At the very least, you might earn some book and supplies money.

Financing Is Possible

Financing your education is a challenge; but it is not an impossibility. You need to understand the cost and then plan the strategies you will use to finance your education. If you have a family, include their opinions in your plans. Try not to change your lifestyle abruptly. If you can't afford going to the movie every week, try some less expensive form of entertainment, such as going to a museum, renting a video, creating your own theater, or checking into activities on campus.

Don't let finances add more stress to your life. Plan ahead. Don't discount any aid that might be available. Talk to the financial aid people at the school you have chosen. Ask questions. Check into all of your financial opportunities. Most of all, remember you are making an investment in your future. Don't let finances stop you.

Chapter 6

Selecting the Right College

Once you've made the decision to get a college degree, it's time to choose a college. This choice is nearly as important as the decision to get a degree.

Selecting a college will affect your motivation, the cost of getting the degree, the effort and time required to complete the program, the quality of education and learning, and your career. This chapter explores issues you should consider in choosing a college and provides specific guidelines for making this important decision.

In addition, the second section of this book contains a guide to 240 colleges and universities. This section is a valuable resource in helping you select the right degree program and institution. You can use this information to identify a wide variety of colleges that can meet your needs. Frequently, adults limit their options by considering only colleges in their immediate vicinity. The college guide broadens your perspective on degree programs, delivery methods, and institutions of higher learning.

Adult Students' Needs

The adult student has many needs that should be considered when making a decision about college. As you read about these generic concerns, you may recognize some that apply to you. A better understanding of your personal needs helps identify the most appropriate match between you and the degree program offered by a college.

Limiting Disruption to Your Career and Job

A major concern for most adults is how to obtain a degree without seriously disrupting their career. Working adults must be realistic and face the possibility of a temporary disturbance in their career while attending college. Advancement in a job requires a focus of attention and time that attending college typically doesn't allow. You should be prepared for this possibility and not become frustrated when it happens. Finding a college that helps minimize career disruption is important. Search for a college that accommodates your current work requirements. Consider the following options and requirements:

1. It is important to find a college that allows you to take courses without relocating your residence. There might be a college in your own community that can accommodate your work requirements. A college located in another area might deliver courses in your community. Another possibility is to pursue a degree through some form of distance education.

2. It is also important that a college offers courses at a time when you can attend. Offering a limited number of courses that match your schedule isn't sufficient. Be certain that you can take all the courses you need to complete your degree at times convenient for your work schedule. Also, ask an advisor and other students how difficult it is to actually get courses that are offered. A course may be regularly offered at a convenient time but difficult to get into. Delays in pursuing a degree caused by heavy competition to get into a course can be costly. Some jobs require extensive travel and make regular attendance at scheduled classes difficult. If this is your situation, a degree through distance education might be the best option.

3. A required campus residency—even for a short time—must be fit into your work schedule. It might be necessary to use

vacation time and other authorized time off to spend time on campus. This will limit your vacation opportunities during the time it takes to complete the degree.

4. All working adults have experienced periods when their jobs required more time and attention than normal. Inevitably these periods cause conflicts with school work and attendance. Determine how understanding faculty at a college are about this problem. Are deadlines for submitting course assignments flexible when work schedules and workloads change? Is attendance mandatory, and does an absence from class significantly affect your grade? The more traditional a college and its faculty are, the more likely it is that these conflicts will result in a lower grade for a course.

Distance education courses offer the greatest versatility for working adults. You can read books, watch videos, log onto computer conferences, and complete assignments any day of the week, any time of the day. Often, the student establishes the rate of progress in completing a course. This means you can set aside school work if your workload becomes too demanding. The delay, of course, can be a disadvantage and prolong the process of completing a degree. Nevertheless, distance education is a practical solution for many working adults.

The faster you complete a degree, the sooner you can get on with your career. Opportunities for advancements and promotions that a degree brings will come about sooner. This makes any option to complete a degree quickly an important factor in selecting a college. Credit through exams, credit for prior learning experience, liberal acceptance of transfer credits, and accelerated courses are several strategies for accomplishing this objective. (These strategies are explained in Chapter 4.) Look for a college that offers the greatest number of options to complete a degree quickly. Individuals who have completed a year or two of college may find that degree completion programs are the best choice to earn a degree quickly.

Acknowledging Lifestyle and Family Concerns

The lifestyles of adults are full of commitments. Family responsibilities can make it difficult to attend college. Children and elderly relatives may require a great deal of care and attention. Spending time with your spouse is important. Your children's school activities require time. Housekeeping, shopping, cooking, home repair, car maintenance, and social activities all take up significant amounts of your time. Finding a college that recognizes these many roles and responsibilities and supports the needs of adult students greatly affects your ability to complete a degree.

Some colleges provide assistance with childcare but, beyond this service, not many resources are available to help adults cope with their responsibilities. What you can and should expect are procedures (such as class registration) that place minimal demands on your time. Offices and services should be available at times convenient for an adult's schedule. In addition, you should expect administrators and faculty who understand the problems adults typically encounter. Identify colleges that offer services designed to meet adult needs, because you are more likely to discover there institutions that understand the family needs of adult students.

Understanding Adult Characteristics and Learning Styles

As you consider a college, examine how well it accommodates adult learning needs. The field of adult education has developed several theories and concepts about the characteristics of adult learners. These ideas can be used to evaluate how well a college addresses the learning needs of adults.

An obvious fact—but one often ignored by college administrators and faculty—is that adults are more mature. Rules and procedures should reflect this level of maturity. Faculty should treat adult students with respect and acknowledge their abilities and needs. This includes recognizing the experience and knowledge that adults frequently possess about the subjects studied in a course.

Adults bring a wealth of work experience into the classroom. In some cases, adult students have more practical experience related to a subject than the instructor. Find out what a college does to promote faculty utilization of student experience. Can topics and projects from your job be integrated into class discussions and assignments? Does the college recruit adjunct faculty from practitioners in particular disciplines? Your learning experience will be stronger and more positive when these practices are used.

Adults are more problem-oriented than younger students. This means that adult students want to relate what they learn to practical issues and problems they face. Higher education is, by necessity, based on theory and research and not just application techniques. However, class subjects and assignments should reflect this need for problem solving. Look for a college that encourages faculty to help students understand how theory and research can be applied to solve problems common to adults. Community involvement, family and home activities, and work-related projects can play key roles in accomplishing this goal.

Most adults like to have some control over their learning environment. They are not as passive as younger students. This means that adult students are typically more vocal in expressing their opinions about an instructor's teaching and practices. Faculty who recognize this and treat students as peers in the learning process create a more powerful learning experience for students. Techniques that promote student choice and control are learning contracts, choice of class assignments, selection of course topics, flexibility in meeting course requirements, and self-paced activities. In addition, there should be opportunities in class for students to contribute to the discussion and relate their personal experiences to the subject.

Adults typically have better study habits than younger students. Several factors contribute to this situation. Adults are more motivated because they often expect immediate benefits to result from completing a college degree. They frequently are more disciplined than younger students. Adults who incorporate writing, reading, computers, and math in their jobs find it easy to transfer these skills to the college classroom. You should expect to find faculty who understand these study habits and use them to measure a student's understanding of subject matter.

Adults want to understand clearly what is expected by an instructor and what is required to get a good grade in a course. Look for colleges with faculty who recognize this need. One way college faculty can accomplish this is to provide a detailed syllabus. A *syllabus* is a paper that describes the course, learning objectives, class outlines, required texts and supplemental reading materials, other course materials, assignments, guidelines for grading, office hours and contact information for the instructor, and related course information. Ask the college for a sample course syllabus to see how complete it is. In addition, you should look for a faculty member who discusses course requirements in class and answers individual questions that arise as the course proceeds.

Financial Needs of Adults

It's important to find a college that gives adult students the same consideration for financial assistance as traditional students. Most institutions place a priority on providing scholarships to traditional students. However, some colleges award scholarships to adult students, and you should be diligent in seeking these out. In addition, it is important that they acknowledge the unique financial issues that adults have. One common issue relates to adult students who get tuition reimbursement from an employer. Most employers reimburse tuition once a course is completed. If this is your situation, you might want to look for a college that defers tuition payment until your employer reimburses you—some do this.

Many colleges recognize the unique needs of adult students and offer degree programs and services designed for adults. Examine a college based on how well it addresses the issues presented here. But additional factors— more specific and individual in nature—need to be considered.

College Status and Reputation

When you select a college, consider its status and reputation. How important this becomes for an adult is questionable, because employers evaluating applicants for a job or candidates for promotion consider work accomplishments more important than the degree. The degree is not ignored, but a person with an impressive work record and a degree from a lesser known college is likely to win out over a person with a degree from a better known college but with a less impressive work record. As a person gains more experience and shows steady advancement in a career, a college degree plays a less important role. Therefore, a college's reputation also becomes less important. However, when an employer finds your work experience equal to that of other candidates, the reputation of your alma mater may be a deciding factor.

A first step in identifying respected colleges is to determine the accreditation status of the college. Accreditation is an acknowledgment that peers from other colleges and universities have reviewed the institution and determined that it meets an acceptable level of academic quality. (Accreditation is discussed more fully in Chapter 3.) The most important level of accreditation comes from the six regional accrediting bodies. In addition, there are many accrediting agencies with a professional focus. For example, the Accreditation Board for Engineering and Technology (ABET) provides accreditation for engineering programs. It is possible for a college offering engineering degrees to have regional accreditation but not professional accreditation from ABET. Many employers consider a degree more valuable if it comes from a college with accreditation from both the regional and professional groups.

REGGIE is a 45-year-old white male nearing completion of a bachelor's degree in nursing. He is divorced and has two daughters living in another state. When he began the program three years ago, he had an associate degree in electrical engineering and another in nursing. Reggie has worked as a nurse in the emergency department at a hospital while working on his bachelor's degree. He believes the degree is important for advancement opportunities and higher earning potential. In addition, he anticipates that eventually all registered nurses will be required to have a bachelor's degree. He is contemplating continuing his education at the graduate degree level.

Reggie restructured his lifestyle to complete his degree. He has not done any serious dating. Peers and friends have been supportive, as have his daughters. He works the night shift at the hospital to achieve the greatest flexibility in selecting courses. Vacation time from work is often used to complete class assignments—particularly major projects.

Attending college has been a financial strain because Reggie selected a private college. He has paid tuition from his own earnings. He works overtime during school breaks to reduce this strain. In addition, he has taken out loans that he hopes to repay with increased earnings after completing his degree. However, as Reggie prepares to graduate, he feels that the degree has been well worth the time and sacrifices required, and he would make the same choice again if he had to do it over.

Colleges and universities that receive state funding are often better known by employers and the general public. In addition, they are more closely regulated because state commissions of higher education review their programs. The governing boards of state colleges and universities usually are composed of business, civic, and political leaders who are concerned about maintaining the reputation of the institution. In addition, access to state funds makes it possible for these institutions to ensure greater stability in their financial operations and the degree programs they offer. This is not to say that all state institutions provide high-quality education. Nor is it to imply that private colleges furnish lower-quality education. The point is that many employers within a state have a certain level of confidence in graduates from state-supported institutions.

You should balance out the strength of public colleges and universities against the fact that almost 70 percent of all students enrolled in graduate degree programs are graduates from private colleges. This demonstrates the strength of degree programs at private colleges. However, because the quality of education at private colleges varies greatly, it is important to scrutinize the reputation of a private college.

Several books and magazines are available to help you review the reputation of a college. Some books specifically rank colleges by reputation among employers, other colleges, and alumni. These are useful, but you need to consider the factors used by authors in ranking a college. In addition, magazines sometimes review colleges. One of the best known is *U.S. News and World Report.* Each September this magazine publishes an issue that reviews the status of colleges and universities, comparing institutions within specific categories, such as major universities, research universities, national liberal arts colleges, and regional liberal arts colleges. In addition, there is an annual issue that reviews graduate schools. These two issues have become important to employers and potential students as a source for determining the quality of a college. As you read this magazine, keep in mind that the writers are looking at the overall quality of an institution and are not considering its ability to meet the academic and service needs of adults.

Another way to evaluate the reputation of a college is by networking with coworkers, peers, and friends. Ask them what they know about a college and graduates with whom they've worked. Locate graduates from the college and question them about their college experience. Ask them to compare what they were taught with the skills and knowledge they actually need in the workplace. Contact the human resource department at your place of employment and question the staff about a college's reputation.

Getting the Degree You Want

The degree programs offered by a college are an important factor in the selection process—for our purposes, a degree program refers to a specific major that leads to a degree. The most important consideration is that the college offers a degree program that is accessible to adults. The availability of a degree doesn't mean that required courses can be taken at a time convenient for working adults. Specifically inquire about the practicality of an adult completing the program.

Selecting a college with a specific degree program is a balancing act. You need to find a college that offers a degree that will help you succeed in your chosen career. However, more than one degree program can provide successful entry into a career. There are some careers that require a specific degree. An example is elementary education: a person must have a major in that area to obtain a teaching license. However, other careers may be less restrictive in degree requirements. An example is business management, for which a variety of college majors may lead to a successful career. Typically, careers that require a license or certification also require degrees in a specific major and sometimes stipulate the courses included in a major.

You might want to look for degree programs that are likely to lead to a successful degree in a specific career. Some majors are more successful in helping graduates find jobs in a related field than others. The U.S. Department of Labor conducts studies every two years to examine the relationship between majors and related employment opportunities. The results of these studies are reported in the *Occupational Outlook Handbook.* Table 6-1 looks at the employment status of 1990 graduates, by major, one year after graduation. This table can be used to identify majors that have the greatest impact on employment. The rank—shown in column 5—is a quick indication of the major with the highest rate of employment.

Be careful how you compare majors, because some majors with low employment may be affected by a high number of students entering graduate school. For example, Biological Sciences ranks last in rate of employment. However, only 68 percent of its graduates are in the workforce; the majority of the remaining 32 percent are attending graduate school in a field such as medicine, dentistry, or pharmacy. Because of this, the impact of a major on employment can't be fully measured for another four to seven years.

Table 6-1 *Employment Status of 1990 College Graduates, One Year After Graduation*

Major	Employed Full-Time	Employed Part-Time	Unemployed	Rank
All Majors	74%	11%	4%	
Biological Sciences	51%	13%	4%	11
Business & Management	83%	6%	5%	2
Education	77%	15%	2%	4
Engineering	86%	3%	3%	1
Health Professions	81%	11%	1%	3
History	58%	15%	8%	10
Humanities	59%	19%	6%	9
Mathematics, Computer Science, and Physical Science	71%	9%	5%	6
Psychology	60%	14%	7%	8
Public Affairs	77%	11%	5%	5
Social Sciences	68%	12%	5%	7

Table 6-2 shows the results of a survey of 1990 graduates, one year after completing college, that asked the following three questions:

1. Does your job require a four-year degree?
2. Is your job related to your college major?
3. Does your job have career potential?

You might be discouraged by the statistics compiled from these questions: Only 56 percent of all respondents were working in jobs they thought required a college degree. However, it is important to consider that the majority of college graduates are traditional students who have no work experience in their profession. An adult student's work experience is likely to have a positive affect on his or her ability to get a professional job related to his or her major.

Table 6-2   *Relation of Current Job to Major Field and Career Potential, Class of 1990*

Major	4-Yr. Degree Required	Related to Degree	Career Potential
All Majors	56%	76%	79%
Biological Sciences	58%	73%	72%
Business & Management	53%	81%	83%
Education	76%	87%	84%
Engineering	81%	89%	90%
Health Professions	51%	95%	92%
History	37%	30%	60%
Humanities	43%	57%	66%
Mathematics, Computer Science, and Physical Science	67%	86%	85%
Psychology	47%	65%	69%
Public Affairs	46%	71%	71%
Social Sciences	48%	53%	72%

Many colleges with degree programs for adults offer majors in the business area. One reason is that there are more jobs in this field than any other area, increasing the potential number of students who can be recruited. Another reason is that adults working in business are more likely to have financial support from employers than those in other segments of the economy, thus overcoming financial obstacles to attending college. Finally, it is often easier to recruit instructors for business courses because they are more plentiful than in other areas such as mathematics or the physical sciences. Therefore, if you want a major in business, you will probably have several colleges to choose from. The number of colleges to draw from for other degrees is more limited.

It's also possible to find many colleges offering degrees in general studies. Technically, general studies is not a major but, rather, a degree program description. Usually general studies programs require that a student take three or four courses from several major fields. This program is offered by many colleges with distance education options. It has the advantage of giving a student a broad perspective and liberal education. Its major disadvantage is that it doesn't have a specific major an employer can match with job requirements. For jobs without specific academic requirements, this doesn't present a problem. However, it is unlikely to help a person seeking employment opportunities in professional fields with specific academic qualifications. This is one reason for taking the time to complete the career planning activities discussed in Chapter 2. Selecting a specific career goal can focus you on the most appropriate major for advancing your career goals.

REGIS UNIVERSITY is a private school operated by the Jesuit order of the Catholic Church and located in Denver, Colorado. Through the School for Professional Studies, the university provides an extensive range of options for earning a degree. Courses can be completed through an accelerated classroom format, guided study, or television (through Mind Extension University, discussed in Chapter 3). Moreover, 38 majors are available.

In the accelerated classroom format, students attend classes one or two nights a week for a five- to eight-week period. Classes are held at several sites throughout Colorado and Wyoming. There are also intensive weekend courses available: Students attend for eight hours a day, usually on two weekends separated by one or more weeks.

It is possible for students to take any course through guided independent learning. The course is designed by the student, a faculty advisor, and an outside expert who serves as course consultant. A learning contract is drawn up based on the design, and the work must be completed within a 16-week period. Students can obtain a Colorado or Wyoming teaching license by taking most courses in this format. Guided study can also include courses taken from other colleges.

Courses can be taken through Mind Extension University, a cable television network that is available to 26 million homes throughout the country. In fact, several undergraduate and graduate degrees are available through this format. A course is composed of five weeks of televised instruction and three weeks of guided independent study. Communication with faculty and other students by voice mail, telephone, and fax is encouraged.

Students can use any combination of these three course formats to complete a degree at the university. Regis also offers credit by exam and portfolio assessment of prior learning experience.

Cost of a Degree Program

Like any wise consumer, you want to obtain a high-quality product at the lowest price. It is important to find a good college that is within your personal budget constraints. A careful examination of benefits and costs is an important task in selecting a college.

A frequent mistake people make when comparing costs for colleges is to distinguish only between tuition rates—that is, the cost per credit hour. Another simple method is to determine the cost of a degree by multiplying the number of hours required for the degree by the tuition per credit hour. Add in additional estimates for books, class materials, and fees, and you have the total cost. It also is important to note that most colleges raise tuition and other fees annually, so factor in an increase of 3 to 7 percent for each year that you plan to attend before completing a degree.

This calculation provides only the gross cost, not the net cost of a college education. Comparing the cost of colleges using this simple method can be misleading. It leads to the conclusion that publicly funded colleges are always the least expensive option. A more accurate comparison is more complex than this. This section examines how to determine a more precise cost for a degree.

The first point to consider is the actual number of courses you will need to take in order to complete a degree program. The number of courses you need to take sometimes can be reduced, and this reduces the number of hours for which you must pay tuition.

Reducing the number of hours needed to complete a degree makes a significant difference in the cost. There are four common ways in which hours can be reduced.

1. The cost of earning credit through exams is normally much less than tuition. A college that allows for an unlimited number of credits in exams offers the best opportunity for lowering the cost of a degree.

2. Most colleges charge a minimal fee for assessing prior learning experience and granting portfolio credits. As with earning credits through examination, the more credits that can be earned, the lower the cost of a degree.

3. A college that accepts the greatest number of transfer hours—if you have accumulated any—reduces the total cost of a program.

4. Other methods for accumulating also reduce the total cost for completing a degree.

Another way to reduce the cost of a degree is to obtain financial assistance from the college. First consider the amount the college awards in scholarship money. These are funds that are not available unless you attend the institution. Therefore, they are important in comparing the cost of one college to another. Say you are interested in two colleges: The tuition for college A is $80 more per credit hour than for college B. However, if scholarship money from college B reduces this to a difference of only $20 per hour, it becomes more feasible to attend college B.

A second consideration is the amount of federal and/or state financial aid the college will award you. Normally the federal and state governments determine the maximum amount of aid for which you are qualified, but a college determines the specific amount of the award used at that institution. Determine the amount of assistance a college will give you. Grants should not be compared to loans because loans must be repaid. Only include money that doesn't need to be repaid. Sometimes a college is willing to negotiate an aid package when you inform them about awards offered by another college.

Another major cost you should consider might be called *opportunity cost*. This is the opportunities for promotions, raises, or general increases in earnings that are delayed by your work on a college degree. The longer it takes to complete the degree, the higher the opportunity cost. For this reason, you want to find a degree program that can be completed as quickly as possible. Chapter 4 details many strategies you can use to accomplish this. However, the strategies can be implemented only with the help of the college. Therefore, you might find it beneficial to seek a college that allows you to complete a degree as quickly as possible.

Assessing the cost of a college takes some time and effort to collect and analyze data. Use the following worksheet to calculate how much an actual degree program costs.

Cost for a Specific College Worksheet

Name of college

Line 1 — Total number of hours to complete degree   _____

Line 2 — Number of hours that can be earned through exams (estimate)   _____

Line 3 — Number of hours that can be earned through portfolio (estimate) _____

Line 4 — Number of hours accepted in transfer (ask college for estimate)   _____

Line 5 — Number of hours from other sources   _____

Line 6 — (Add Lines 2-5 together)   _____

Line 7 — Net number of hours to complete degree
       (subtract Line 6 from Line 1)   _____

Line 8 — Tuition Expense (multiply Line 7 by tuition per credit hour)   _____

Line 9 — Divide Line 7 by Line 3 (average number of hours per course)   _____

Line 10 — Multiply Line 9 by the average cost of books and materials
       per course (get estimate from college)   _____

Line 11 — Multiply Line 9 by the average cost of fees per course   _____

Line 12 — Cost for portfolio assessment and exams   _____

Line 13 — Degree expenses (add Lines 8, 10, 11, and 12)

Line 14 — Financial assistance—from college only

Line 15 — Net cost for specific college (subtract Line 14 from Line 13)

Line 16 — Financial assistance from other sources
       (federal govt., employer, outside scholarships, etc.)   _____

Line 17 — Incidental expenses, childcare, transportation, etc.   _____

Line 18 — Net cost of degree—out-of-pocket expenses
       (subtract Line 16 from Line 15 and add Line 17)   _____

Line 19 — Estimated number of years to complete degree   _____

Line 20 — Lowest number of years to complete degree (comparing
       all colleges)   _____

Line 21 — Differential in number of years to complete degree
       (subtract Line 20 from Line 19)   _____

Line 22 — Loss of earnings from not having a degree per year   _____

Line 23 — Opportunity cost (multiply Line 21 by Line 22)   _____

Total Cost of Degree Program (add lines 18 and 23)   _____

Personal Learning Style

A critical point to consider when choosing a college is your personal style of learning. Although a variety of structures for degree programs are available, not all structures work for everyone. An assessment of your personal learning style serves as a guide to the degree structure that best suits you. This section is designed to help you think more about your style of learning and use that knowledge in selecting a college that offers the best match with your style. There are many learning style models, and this section borrows several concepts from them. However, the focus is on learning styles that are important as you select a college that best matches your personal needs.

One factor to contemplate is your ability to learn independently. Independent study provides a great deal of flexibility and control over learning. With this control comes the need for discipline and concentration. There are often lengthy deadlines for completing course studies. This means that it is easy to put off assignments. Some independent study programs—those that allow guided study with a learning contract—also require more effort and time to design a course of study. Correspondence courses—whether in the form of written, audio tape, or video tape formats—typically require the greatest amount of independence and self-discipline. Distance education programs using television and computers for course delivery frequently are more structured and require less self-control and discipline. Answer the following questions to assess your ability to study independently. The more of these questions you can answer yes to, the more likely you are to succeed with an independent learning program.

1. Do you prefer to have flexibility in your learning schedule?

2. Do you like having primary responsibility for your learning?

3. Are you task-oriented?

4. Do you practice effective time management?

5. Do you feel comfortable conducting your studies with limited interaction with instructors?

6. Are you disciplined in the use of time?

7. Are you willing to expend the effort needed to plan your learning activities?

Another factor is the amount of social interaction desired. Many social dynamics occur during the *interactive learning* process. Group interaction often takes place in a classroom. Small group interactions can occur while you work on class assignments. Individual interactions both during and between classes can occur among students. Interaction between the instructor and students during class often creates a strong learning dynamic. The opportunity to interact with an instructor outside class is also important. Some students need these types of social interaction to learn. Social interaction and peer support are also important motivational tools for some people. Classroom-based educational programs are usually the most effective in providing social interaction. Interactive distance learning—through television, radio, or telephone—provides some of the interaction but in a less personal manner.

Answer the following questions to determine how important social interaction is to your learning experience. The more questions you answer yes to, the more important social interaction is to your learning.

1. Do you learn from class discussions?

2. Do you prefer group homework assignments to personal assignments?

3. Are you more motivated by social interaction?

4. Do you enjoy small group discussions and tasks?

5. Do you frequently talk with instructors about topics presented in class?

6. Do you frequently ask the instructor's guidance about assignments?

7. Do you find yourself energized by social interaction with other students in and out of class?

Another style is *visual learning*, which puts an emphasis on such tasks as writing and reading. Most visual learners are able to effectively use books to gain information. Writing down ideas helps the visual learner accumulate knowledge. Taking notes reinforces what has been said in lectures or discussions. Demonstrations and videos help visual learners understand concepts better. Everyone learns through visual input, but many people prefer this mode of learning over others. In fact, 70 to 80 percent of the population are visual learners. All college programs rely to some degree on visual stimuli to deliver course materials. If you are a visual learner, you will probably do better in a program that puts the greatest emphasis on visual learning. Classroom-based programs that emphasize reading and writing are effective learning environments for visual learners. Correspondence courses are also effective ways for the visual learner to learn. To determine if you are a visual learner, answer the following questions. The more positive answers, the more likely it is that you are a visual learner.

1. Do you learn better by reading than by having someone explain a concept to you?

2. Do you learn better from seeing a demonstration than from hearing someone describe a process to you?

3. Does watching someone role model a task help you learn better?

4. Do you better remember concepts you read in a book than those you hear in a lecture?

5. Do you prefer to review lecture material from notes than from a tape?

6. Do you find information from a video easier to learn than what you hear in a lecture?

Most people who are not visual learners are auditory learners. These people learn better by listening to someone, whether in a lecture or on a tape. While *auditory learning* is helped by a demonstration, it is the verbal explanation accompanying the demonstration that brings about learning. The use of classroom lectures is particularly effective for auditory learners. Discussion groups are quite useful as participants express ideas and explain concepts. The ability to engage an instructor or another student in conversation can be a powerful learning experience. Auditory learners find classroom programs that feature lectures and discussions to be effective learning environments. Distance education programs that are interactive also work well for auditory learners. The more affirmative answers you have to the following questions, the more likely it is that you are an auditory learner.

1. Do you learn better from a lecture than from reading course materials?

2. Are you able to learn more from listening to tapes than from using other methods of learning?

3. Do you learn better through small group discussions?

4. Do conversations with instructors and other students help you learn more than reading books and other materials?

5. Would you rather prepare for exams by reviewing tapes of lectures instead of studying notes and other written materials?

Another learning style that is effective for many people is called *experiential learning*. This is learning through actual experience. Practicums, internships, and cooperative learning opportunities are effective for experiential learners. Classroom activities that provide opportunities for role play and structured experiences help as well. Opportunities to give speeches, demonstrations, and presentations are beneficial learning experiences. Laboratory activities are also significant to experiential learners. Colleges that acknowledge experiential learning as a substantial educational tool will provide credit for students who design learning around work and community activities. Guided study courses often allow students to create learning projects based on experiential activities. Experiential learners should seek out colleges that allow the largest number of credits to be accumulated through these types of learning activities. Some classroom-based degrees emphasize experiential learning activities. Affirmative answers to the following questions help you assess the degree to which you are an experiential learner.

1. Do you learn more by doing a task than by reading or listening?

2. Are learning activities implemented through work assignments highly effectual?

3. Is a role playing exercise an effective way for you to learn new material?

4. Do you learn more from simulations and games than from other teaching methods?

5. Does preparing and giving class presentations and demonstrations help you learn better than other methods?

6. Are laboratory activities more helpful for learning than classroom lectures?

The final learning style to be considered is a relatively new one: *technological learning*. This is the ability to learn through a variety of modern technologies. These technologies include television, videos, and computers. Some people feel much more comfortable using technology-based learning than others. The person who can't program a VCR would be the opposite of the technological learner. Colleges that use computer-based education programs, multimedia software, computer bulletin boards, and computer conferencing would be good choices for technological learners. Also, colleges that use television or videos may have some appeal. However, use of a computer is the preferred learning method for most technological learners because of the computer's interactive nature. Answer the following questions to determine if you are a technological learner.

1. Do you enjoy working with computers?

2. Do you find that computer-based education programs are positive learning tools?

3. Do you feel comfortable using bulletin board systems or the Internet?

4. Do you learn better through multimedia software than by reading or listening to others?

5. Do you enjoy engaging in computer conferencing?

6. Are video and television presentations a good way for you to learn?

Most people use more than one learning style. As you read about these learning styles, you may have identified two or more that seem to fit you. It is common to have a dominant or preferred learning style that is supported by one or more other styles. Use the knowledge about your dominant style and supportive styles to select a degree program that provides the best opportunity to use these styles.

JENNIFER is a 50-year-old early retiree who worked for a major telecommunications business. When given the chance to retire, she took the opportunity to pursue a dream. She is now working toward a bachelor's degree in elementary education in order to start her second career. Her goal is to complete the degree, pass her National Teacher Exams, get a teaching license, and teach in one of the primary grades of an elementary school.

Jennifer, who is divorced and has two children, moved to a larger city in order to obtain the education she wanted. Because *of her retirement payments, she can take classes full-time, although she does need to work a part-time job to help with the additional expenses from school. Her former employer also provided a $3,000 grant toward her education that had to be spent within the first year of her retirement.*

During the time she worked in the telecommunications industry, Jennifer took college courses intermittently. Because of this prior college work, she can now complete an elementary education degree in approximately two years. The college she attends is attentive to the needs of adult students. She finds the professors to be quite approachable and easy to get help from. The teaching methods used are a good match with her learning style. Jennifer is excited about her decision to complete a college degree.

Admissions Requirements

Admissions requirements are important in determining if a college is the best choice for you. There are generally four or five admissions requirements that must be met for acceptance into adult degree programs. One is completion of high school. Most colleges that offer degree programs for adults will also accept a GED.

Another typical requirement is that the applicant be an adult. This is normally defined in one of two ways. Sometimes there is an age requirement, usually from 23 to 25 years of age. Another way to define an adult is through work experience. It is common to find this defined as three to six years of full-time work experience. A college may even require that the experience be in a professional or managerial position. Some colleges have both age and work experience requirements. A resume might be required to document an applicant's work experience.

There may be testing requirements. Most programs for traditional students set a minimum score requirement for either the SAT or ACT exams. A college that understands adult students usually doesn't have this requirement, as such exams are less valid in predicting the success of adults in college. It is more common to have an exam that measures the writing ability of the applicant. This exam is often used for prescriptive purposes, rather than to exclude applicants. In other words, applicants who do poorly might be required to take a specific sequence of English courses.

Some colleges require a written essay to assess a student's writing ability. The essay may also be used to evaluate an applicant's motivation for obtaining a degree. Colleges sometimes require students to obtain letters of reference from current and past employers to predict their level of motivation.

Frequently adults have some prior college credits. Many colleges require that applicants have a minimum GPA of 2.0. However, most colleges recognize that the grades adults received when they were traditional students are not an accurate reflection of their ability to do course work as adults. Therefore, it is not unusual for a college to have provisions for admitting a student on probation. If this is the case for you, be sure to understand fully the conditions placed on your probation.

Services and Accessibility

There are several services adult students need and should evaluate when comparing colleges and degree programs. The convenience of these services can be significant.

An important issue is how students register for courses. Registration is the process of enrolling in courses. You must select the days and times that the courses will be taken. Look for colleges that make this convenient by allowing telephone, computer, fax, or mail registration. Some programs have an established sequence of courses, and students are not required to register.

An important service related to registration is academic advising. Some colleges require students to talk with an advisor before registering for classes. This is often an inconvenience and treats adult students as it they were too immature to manage their educational program. You should expect access to an advisor when you need it, but should not be required to see one unless you feel it is necessary. Academic advising should be available at times convenient for working adults. It is usually necessary to obtain advice at the start of a degree program and as you get close to graduation.

The ease of access to courses is also important. For programs based on classroom learning, the primary issue related to access is parking. Many colleges require that cars be registered if parked on campus. This process can take time and usually costs money. Find out how far parking lots or garages are from classroom buildings. Satellite campus locations often make it more convenient to park and don't require car registration. Distance education programs should be evaluated on how easy it is to obtain course materials, access computer bulletin boards, and view television courses.

Look for the sensitivity of the college to adults and their concerns. Policies and procedures should reflect an understanding of adult students. Forms should be structured in such a way that they acknowledge adult students. College staff should treat you as a customer and provide high-quality service. Office hours should be set for times that suit working adult schedules.

Campus facilities are important in cases where you plan to attend classes. There should be areas set aside where off-campus students can study. These study areas should be located throughout the campus to provide easy access. Another accommodation is student lounges with tables and vending machines. Classroom buildings should have vending machines, and students should be allowed to take drinks and food into classrooms. This is particularly important when classes are offered during mealtimes. Also look for college cafeterias that provide hours and services to nontraditional adults. In addition, look for good security on campus, including a well-lit campus during night hours.

Books and course materials are needed for most courses. For this reason, having access to the bookstore with hours convenient for working adults is important. Some provide books directly to the classroom. This is normally the case when classes are held in remote locations.

Library services are another important consideration. Most college libraries maintain hours that are convenient for adults. However, for classes held at remote locations, it is difficult for students to get to the library. Does the library offer services to help these students? For example, some colleges make it possible to access the card catalog and journal databases through a remote computer link. Some have interlibrary agreements that make it possible for you to access libraries closer than the main campus library. Look for colleges where the library staff will copy and mail journal and magazine articles to students at remote locations. If you are planning to pursue a degree through a distance education program, identify library resources that will allow you access to materials needed to complete course assignments. It might be possible to obtain the resources you need through local colleges. Some states have policies that make library services from state-supported colleges and universities available to any state resident.

The final service you should consider is the career center. Many working adults don't think about this service because they already have a job. However, with downsizing and re-engineering, it's wise to keep in mind how the career center can help you. The focus for many career centers is traditional students, because they often act as a link between new graduates and corporations seeking entry-level workers. It is doubtful that such an approach will be useful to working adults. Determine what services the career center provides working adults. An emerging practice is to locate a career placement officer within particular schools. For example, a school of business might offer career assistance. An advantage to this approach is that the career staff have a better understanding of the skills a graduate has to offer. Determine whether assistance is available to students at remote class sites and to students participating in distance education programs.

As you investigate colleges and make comparisons, keep in mind that it is difficult to find one college that satisfies all your needs. The following worksheet will help you compare the colleges you are considering.

College Selection Worksheet

Write the names of the colleges at the top of the worksheet. The criteria used for selecting a college are listed on the left side of the page. Rate each criterion for a college on the basis of 5 (excellent) to 1 (poor). The final score for each college can be used as a rough guide in determining the one that is most appropriate for you.

	College 1	College 2	College 3
Potential disruption of career			
Acknowledges lifestyle and family concerns			
Positive atmosphere for adult learning			
Good reputation of college			
Good reputation of degree program			
Has a degree program that meets my goals			
Has a degree program with good potential			
College expenses are affordable			
Meets my personal learning style			
Reasonable admissions requirements			
Registration procedures are simple			
Advising is readily available			
Ease of access to classrooms is convenient			
There is sufficient space for parking			
Ease of access to services is convenient			
College is sensitive to adult concerns & needs			
Campus facilities are designed for adults			
Campus offices have hours for adults			
Staff treat adults as customers			
Books and materials are easily obtained			
Library services accommodate adult needs			
Career center meets needs of working adults			
Total Score:			

Chapter 7

Making It Work for You

No doubt you are already a busy person. Family, work, friends, and responsibilities compete for your time. Now you are adding the demands of attending college classes and meeting assignment deadlines. Going back to school creates many new challenges. This chapter gives some suggestions and hints about how to meet the many challenges faced by the typical adult student. It examines how to manage responsibilities and tasks at home, work, and school.

Returning to school will bring unavoidable changes in your life. Many of these will be welcomed. They may be the reason you have chosen to return to school. Others will bring new challenges. Changes may shake your self-confidence, disrupt your family life, or affect your work relationships. This chapter discusses some changes you can expect and the effects these changes may have on your family, friends, and coworkers. Positive ways to approach these changes are suggested to help you to reach your goal of getting a college degree with less stress and greater ease. The chapter also presents ways to help those around you deal with these challenges.

Balancing College and Family

A major concern for many people starting college is how to balance college and family life. Difficulties in working through family issues are frequently cited by adult students as reasons for not completing college. This section is designed to help you think about potential family problems and develop contingency plans to resolve them.

You and Your Spouse

If you are married, your spouse is an important source of support as you return to school. Your relationship should be a top priority on your list of important things to maintain as your life becomes busier. Neglecting your spouse is a big mistake. You will need each other during this time.

Before you enroll in school, the two of you should share in the planning. Discuss the classes you want to take, your class schedule, the financing needed, and any extra work you might expect to be doing. Listen to each other. Discuss the challenges you will both have to face. Communicate the feelings and worries you have about returning to school.

Realize that feelings of resentment are natural. View the situation through your spouse's eyes. He or she may be accepting more financial responsibility, more household work, and more childcare duties. You are meeting new people your spouse doesn't know. You are developing new interests your spouse may not share. All these factors need to be discussed honestly to overcome resentment. Be practical. Be aware that at certain times, such as during finals week or when a project is due, you need more time for school. Discuss how these times can be handled successfully.

Before you start attending classes, discuss how household duties will be handled. Who will pay bills? Do the laundry? Prepare meals? Pick up the kids from ball practice? Change the oil in the car? Being clear about who is responsible for what will help you avoid stressful situations in the future. Accept the fact that your spouse might do things differently than you would. Remember, towels can be folded in more than one way. The oil doesn't have to be changed precisely at 3,000 miles. Nutritious food can be served on paper plates. If your spouse accepts a responsibility, graciously allow it to be done.

Can you completely avoid stress and conflict? Probably not. Times of frustration will arise intermittently. But communicating feelings throughout the educational experience will help you avoid major misunderstandings. Daily communication is one secret of successfully reaching your goal with your marriage intact.

Including your spouse in your learning experience is another way to keep mutual support during this time. Share fun times together. Make it a part of your schedules. Take a 15-minute walk. Attend a school function together. Express your appreciation for your spouse's help. If your spouse has a dream, make an agreement to be the supporter when you have completed your goal.

You and Your Children

Your children need to be prepared for the changes that will occur in their lives. Sit down and make a list of changes that might occur. Let your children be an active part of this list making. In this way, you will find out both their conceptions and their misconceptions of what is about to happen. You can clear up any unfounded fears and deal with real fears.

Help your children understand what you are doing, why you are doing it, and how long you expect it to continue. Discuss what is practical to expect from you during this time. Help them understand that you might not be able to be their soccer coach or club sponsor right now, but you will still be at some of the games or attend a special Saturday outing.

Talk about ways that they can help you reach your goal. List some household work they can do. Instead of dictating jobs, sit down with your family and make a weekly chore list. Find out who will do each job and when it will be done. Even preschoolers can set the table or fold towels and washcloths.

Discuss your need for quiet study time. Older children can relate to this part of your educational experience. Some adult students have found that their children have become more interested in their own education after watching their parents study. Establish an area of the house where you can complete school work, and make sure other family members don't disturb papers or books in the study area. Inform the family that when you are studying, they are not to disturb you unless it is an important matter or problem.

Preschoolers live in a concrete world. Visiting your school is one way to help them understand what school is. It will help them have a concrete place to visualize when you talk about school. Older children might enjoy a visit to the library, the snack bar, or a walk across campus. Including them in your campus life is important.

Childcare

Childcare is a major concern for many adults returning to school. Knowing that your child is safe and happy in a childcare situation is important. Not worrying about your child will free you to concentrate on your studies. Childcare decisions need to be made before you start class. You will have to make the decision that is best for you and your child. In making the decision, your child needs to feel secure, be safe, and have nutritious food provided.

Working adults, who typically takes classes at night and on weekends, are often not able to find childcare centers open at the same time. You may be able to find friends or relatives who will care for your child while you are attending classes. It is also possible to locate individuals who will care for children at night. High school students can sometimes care for your child in your home. This can be a good solution when classes end at a reasonable evening hour.

Childcare is available in a variety of forms. Some schools offer daycare on campus. The university contracts with a fully licensed, state-approved childcare center. The university may use these facilities to help in training education students. Other campus-subsidized daycare centers may be run by not-for-profit agencies. In such cases, the college provides a guarantee of a minimum number of children and contributes financially to the center. Students attending day classes can often find preschool or nursery school programs that are available for a half day or a full day. For those adults who can locate childcare programs during class times, a visit to the childcare facility is an absolute must. No questions are improper to ask.

Student parents sometimes form daycare cooperatives—some are even located in student housing. A professional staff is typically hired, while student parents share the responsibilities of running the center. Drop-off centers for short-term childcare are sometimes available on campus. Reservations may be needed. Some childcare centers offer evening care for parents.

If your children are school aged, before- and after-school programs might be available at their school or at a local facility.

Transportation between the school and the facility is provided. Laboratory schools on college campuses sometimes offer reduced tuition rates to students' children. These schools are run as part of the university's teacher education program.

You will need a back-up childcare plan for emergencies. Plan ahead for situations such as school cancellations and delays, school vacations, sick children, or sick childcare providers. Let your child know what plans are made. Let your child know also how you can be contacted in an emergency. Have people lined up who will be responsible if you cannot be reached in an emergency. All these plans will relieve stress on you and your child when the unexpected happens.

Dealing with teenage children is a different area of concern. Teens engaged in extracurricular activities have less spare time to get into troublesome social situations. Encourage your children to participate in after-school activities. Set some rules for times when they are home alone. Call to check on them. Ask a neighbor to observe activities at your house when you are absent. Teens need the security of knowing that you love them enough to be concerned about their welfare.

Let teen children know your schedule. Some adults post a weekly schedule on the family bulletin board. Knowing where and how to reach you or other emergency back-up people is important for your teens' security. Providing this information will make your teens feel you respect them.

Children and teenagers often use times of change to test their parents' love. When you return to school, your child may resist the idea. For a preschooler or school-age child, the resistance may be refusing to go to daycare or complaining about the after-school care you have chosen. For your children's security, investigate their complaints. Talk about the problem with both the child and the care provider.

Teenagers may also resist the idea. They may rebel by simply being verbal, not coming home at curfew, or creating more serious problems. If real trouble is taking place, counseling may be available through student services.

Remember that your family is adjusting to a new lifestyle. Time and communication are needed. Some adult students schedule one hour each week to spend with individual family members to avoid neglecting anyone.

JULIA, a 33-year-old adult student, has worked as a nurse's aide in the detoxification unit of a social service organization for eight years. She has a real fear of drug addiction and alcoholism. Her father, who died when she was 2 years old, was rumored to be a bootlegger. Her mother and two brothers died early in their lives from drug-related diseases.

As a teenager, Julia dropped out of high school. Last year she earned her GED and enrolled at the university. She plans to become a nurse. Her dream is to participate in some type of cancer research.

At first, Julia's educational experience caused a strain in her marriage. The expense of college has made money tight for Julia and her husband. Her husband was upset because the housework was not always done. Cooking was no longer Julia's main concern. But he is now proud of Julia's accomplishments. He has become her greatest supporter.

Julia is determined to complete her degree, no matter how long it takes. She is working full-time and attending classes part-time. College has increased her self-confidence. Her heroes are the many African-Americans she knows who have paved the way for her and her family to have a better life. She gets real motivation from them.

Julia believes that she can use her brain as well as the next person. Her desire to help others and to have a better life makes her an excellent candidate for graduation. When she gets her diploma, Julia will be the first member of her family to graduate from college.

Older Parents

For some adult students, caring for parents is also a concern. If you are the care provider of an elderly parent, investigate the availability of adult daycare in your community. It may be provided through a community facility, a nursing home, or a church. Hiring a care provider to come to your home is another option. A family member might be willing to free you for a period of time on a regular basis.

A Place to Study

Having a permanent study area is important for two reasons. The primary reason is psychological: When you are in your study area, your mind is prepared for studying. Your family will also begin to realize that, when you are in this area, you should not be disturbed. Your family needs to understand that this is your area. You and the items in your study area should not be disturbed.

Another reason is that the study area is a place to keep the supplies you need when you are preparing for class. Textbooks, library books, video tapes, audio tapes, sources collected for research, papers, and notes can all be stored here. Family members should be instructed not to disturb anything in your study area in order to reduce confusion and improve time management. Supplies such as pencils, pens, stapler, notebooks, and paper should be kept in your study area. When you are ready to work, you won't have to waste time looking for these materials. A large calendar with your schedule recorded will help you remain on task and on time with projects and papers. Experienced computer users find that a personal information management system is an effective way to keep organized. A bookshelf with a dictionary, thesaurus, and other standard references is useful, as well.

An important study-area tool that makes college work easier is a personal computer. It is an absolute must for students taking courses through distance learning programs that have online access. You don't have to go out and buy the latest and fastest computer; look, instead, for one that can perform the specific tasks important for college. The most important function for which a computer is needed is word processing. This is useful to complete all the writing tasks that are an inevitable part of college. In addition, a presentation graphics program is useful for preparing graphics for class presentations. A good-quality printer is essential to produce the best possible copy for papers and graphics. The costs of ink jet and laser printers are now quite affordable, and both types of printers provide attractive copy.

Your study area doesn't have to be fancy. Some people use a flat door and file cabinets to create a desk. Bricks and boards can be used as bookshelves. A corner of a bedroom, a closet, or a storage area can become a study area. It's important that your study area be well-lit and undisturbed. Some people prefer music to block out other distractions. Others want silence. Make it both comfortable and functional, because you will spend a great deal of time in it before your degree program is complete.

SOUTHERN WESLEYAN UNIVERSITY is a private college operated by the Wesleyan Church and located in central South Carolina. The college was founded in 1909, and currently has a student body of 1,100. Its Leadership Education for Adult Professionals (LEAP) Program is representative of degree completion programs offered by scores of small liberal arts colleges throughout the country.

The university offers a Bachelor of Business Administration and a Bachelor of Science in the Management of Human Resources. It recruits students who are not traditional-aged and who have completed 60 or more hours of college credit. It provides an accelerated program over an 18-month period that allows students to complete all courses related to their business major. Students can get credit through exam programs such as CLEP and can receive portfolio assessment of prior learning experience.

A group of 18 to 22 students are enrolled and go through the program together. Each group or "class" of students is divided into study groups, with three to four students per group. Students are expected to meet weekly with their study group to complete major homework assignments. Students attend classes one night a week, four hours a night, for a five-week period. As soon as one course is completed, another begins, so there is no interruption in the process of completing a degree.

The university also offers these degrees: Associate of Science in General Business, Bachelor of Science in Elementary Education, Bachelor of Science in Special Education, Master of Arts in Management of Organizations, and Master of Arts in Christian Ministry.

Balancing College and Your Social Life

Probably the area of your life that will be most affected by your return to college is your social life. The basic reason for this is the setting of priorities. There are three areas in life where you can find the time to redirect to attending college. These are family, work, and social activities. Most adults place time with family above social activities. Work is a necessity for most adults because of income needs. Therefore, time is taken from social activities to complete college obligations.

Your Friends

Some of your friends might be very supportive of your choice to return to school. Offers of help from your friends should be graciously accepted. Friends might be willing to provide childcare in emergencies or offer to take on other responsibilities to help you gain that degree. Remember that you might be able to return the favor in the future.

Returning to school will affect your friendships. Time demands will limit the hours you have to socialize. With new demands on your time, you may no longer be able to go bowling every Tuesday night or join your friend for lunch on the spur of the moment. Your social life is likely to be less spontaneous and will need some preplanning. Some of your friends may find these changes hard to understand. Others will accept them.

In addition, your interests might change. It is likely that topics you are studying in class will become part of your everyday conversations. Talking about these interests might be threatening to some of your friends. Others will find your new experiences exciting. You will have to judge their reactions.

Another factor that affects your relationships with current friends is the addition of new friends. As you attend classes and join in school activities, you will form new friendships. Time spent with other students on group projects is a source of new friendships. Students who pursue the same major and enroll in the same courses are another source. Professors and other students will become friends. Forming friendships with other adult students gives you a support group. You can share your worries and dreams on an equal basis.

These new friends have a strong common bond: a college experience. Your current friends might feel somewhat strange and left out of discussions when they are around your new friends. To reduce potential awkwardness, try to bring up common interests and encourage a focus on these areas. You might find it necessary to get together with school friends at times different from those you spend with other friends.

Your old friends might find your new friends threatening or strange. They also may need time to adjust to "the new you." You might find yourself drifting apart from old friends. Recognize this as a natural part of life. All relationships change and some fade away. College will change you and your way of life. Friends will be part of this change.

Outside Interests

For many adults, volunteer work is a part of life. Being involved in scouting programs, children's school activities, sports programs, and church activities are important to them. In fact, interests developed through volunteering sometimes lead a person to seek education related to those interests.

If you are a volunteer, you need to evaluate the time you spend at your volunteer position. You may decide to play a less vital role in the organization but remain active. You may need to learn to say "No." You should not feel guilty in doing this. Remember, the learning you are doing will make you a better volunteer in the future.

You should also look for ways that college assignments can be connected with your social interests. A course on recreational management could yield assignments that can be worked into volunteer activities with a youth sports league. A political science course often provides opportunities to correlate class projects with civic projects. These examples should help you think of other ways that social interests can be continued by combining them with course assignments. However, it is unrealistic to expect to spend the same amount of time in volunteer activities as you did before starting college.

Balancing College and Work

Most adult students continue to work while attending classes. Employers are usually very interested in having their employees become better educated. Your employer might be very supportive. However, it is your supervisor who will deal most directly with you during this time. Your supervisor is daily affected by your work schedule and needs to know how your class schedule will affect your work schedule.

Before you sign up for classes, talk to your supervisor about your plans. Identify potential conflicts in the form of meetings, out-of-town travel, special projects, and coworkers' schedules. Getting support before you begin your academic pursuits is important. Discuss ways that you can complete your work with the least interference from your school schedule.

By preplanning, you might be able to avoid some conflicts. If your job requires more hours at certain times of the year, try to schedule a lighter school load during those times. Plan term papers and projects in advance to avoid having to leave work to complete them.

Whenever possible, relate class projects to your work. If a school assignment can be used to complete a task that helps your supervisor, you can demonstrate the immediate value of your education. If you must leave work to attend class, let your supervisor know. Don't just sneak away.

If your job involves traveling, you need to discuss this issue with your professor. Some professors are understanding about student absences; however, you might be required to do additional outside work when you miss classes. In some cases, credit for a course is not given if a student is not present in class a set number of times.

Try to schedule classes so that they will not interfere with your work schedule. Attending all morning or evening classes might help the schedule. Another possibility is scheduling all your classes on Monday, Wednesday, and Friday and using the other days for working. You might arrange to work a four-day week and attend a three-day or weekend seminar. Remember, classes don't all have to be taken from the same school. Taking courses at different schools might help you work out a better schedule.

Your Coworkers

Your choice to return to school may affect your coworkers. They might be asked to work a different schedule than normal. They might be asked to do work that you have done in the past. Some of your coworkers will view your experience positively and be willing to help you. Others may resent the "special treatment" they think you are getting. Some workers have a negative attitude toward higher education and will put down someone working toward a degree.

As you become more involved in college activities, you might find that you don't have as much in common with some of your coworkers. Some may feel threatened by your learning experiences. Others may be inspired to return to school through your example. You will need to deal with these relationships in your workplace.

You can make the situation more pleasant by consciously continuing to do your load of work. Attending classes should not be an excuse for not doing your job. If you leave early for class, try to make up the hours. Thank those who help you when you experience time management problems.

> **MARSHALL** *is a 43-year-old, full-time minister of a small, rural church. He graduated from a small Bible college several years ago. He is well read and has published several articles in various church-related magazines.*
>
> *Marshall wants to teach in a Bible college. That is why he enrolled in the graduate program of a large seminary in a city several miles from his home and church. He is near completion of his first goal: obtaining the first graduate degree. His next goal is to complete the doctorate program in five years.*
>
> *Marshall considers himself the old man in the program. Many of his fellow students are recent college graduates. In spite of his practical experience and knowledge, Marshall is looked upon as just another student. He sometimes wonders why his professors don't use his practical experience.*
>
> *Because the seminary's program is not geared for adult learners, Marshall has had times when he's had to make compromises to continue in the program. Some members of his church have voiced the opinion that the time required for his schooling has hurt the church. Still, Marshall believes that he will reach his goal.*

Coordinating Work and School Assignments

Look for ways to coordinate work activities and school assignments. There may be times when a class assignment directly relates to tasks you perform at work. Class assignments also can offer an opportunity to learn new tasks at work. For example, an assignment from a personnel management class might be to complete a new orientation handbook for the company's personnel department. This type of project improves your position with the company because you are doing something over and above your normal job duties. In addition, you develop skills that make you more valuable to the company. Furthermore, company managers see immediate benefits from your college work and are likely to be even more supportive as you pursue a college degree.

Attendance at professional conferences or company-sponsored training is another work function that can be coordinated with college courses. Discuss the conference or training with your professor. It might be possible to use the experience as credit for a major course assignment. For example, if you are taking a course on strategic management and the conference has several sessions related to this topic, it might be possible to write a paper about the sessions in fulfillment of a course requirement.

Many colleges have practicums and internships that can help you earn credits toward a degree. Discuss the requirements for these special courses with the professor. You might be able to use special projects you are conducting for work to fulfill practicum requirements. You might also be able to get a temporary assignment to another department in your company that will allow you to satisfy internship requirements.

Be on the lookout for creative ways to combine work and school assignments. It is not difficult to identify many ways in which they can be coordinated. Some professors are more open to these nontraditional arrangements than others. Talk with both students and faculty to identify professors who are likely to be cooperative.

Managing Your Time

One of the absolutes in life is that there are only 24 hours in a day. Managing those 24 hours will be very important to you as an adult student. Squeezing classes, study time, family, friends, and work into those hours can create stress. You can lessen this stress by being organized and practicing time management skills.

The starting point is to look at your life. To do this, keep a record of your activities for one week. Use the Time Management Inventory chart to record what you do each hour of the day for one week. Include everything: sleeping, meals, work, and leisure. Briefly note how you spend your time throughout each day. Be sure to include the time you spend in class, studying, and commuting to and from classes.

Time Management Inventory

	Sun.	Mon.	Tues.	Wed.	Thurs.	Fri.	Sat.
6:00 A.M.							
7:00 A.M.							
8:00 A.M.							
9:00 A.M.							
10:00 A.M.							
11:00 A.M.							
12:00 P.M.							
1:00 P.M.							
2:00 P.M.							
3:00 P.M.							
4:00 P.M.							
5:00 P.M.							
6:00 P.M.							
7:00 P.M.							
8:00 P.M.							
9:00 P.M.							
10:00 P.M.							
11:00 P.M.							
12:00 A.M.							

If you are not currently in school, block out the times you think you will be attending classes. Remember that for every hour you spend in the classroom, you should anticipate spending two to three hours studying. Some classes will require more time; others may require less.

Look at the schedule when you have completed it. Go through and review the activities. Are all of them necessary? That is, are they all truly important to you? Place a check by the activities that are *not* important to you. Can you eliminate some of these that are not so important, or delegate them to another person? How much time are you spending on the activities that *are* important to you? Are you allowing enough time for them? Are you spending too much time on them?

Now use the same chart to make up a schedule that you find usable. Using a pencil, start by filling in the activities you can't change. These might include work hours, class times, and commuting times. Next, add those activities you find important and don't want to eliminate from your life. Now, eliminate those activities that are not important to you.

Taking Advantage of Your Peak Time

When will you study? Most people have a peak study time. This is the time they are most alert. Some people study best in the early morning. Others find evening or even late-night studying better. As you plan your schedule, use your peak time for studying. Plan to use your down time for everyday, routine tasks. When you plan study time, recognize that you will reach a saturation point, and give yourself a break. Some people follow a 50-10 rule. They study for 50 minutes and break for 10 minutes. This 10-minute reward relaxes their minds for further studying.

Following the Instructor's Plan

Most college instructors will hand out a class syllabus at the first class meeting. This is your guide for the course. It will list the passages to be read and other work to be completed for each class meeting, the dates of tests and quizzes, and the due dates of term papers and projects. This guide will help you plan your study time. Plan to stagger extras like test preparation, projects, and term papers with normal class work. This way, you can avoid last-minute cramming and panic. It is helpful to plan a schedule for the entire term—semester or quarter—that designates the due dates for all course assignments and tests.

Using a large calendar for your family has already been discussed. Many students also find a pocket calendar helpful. If you choose this method of scheduling, begin by filling in the essentials for the week, month, and year. Go through the calendar and fill in obligations such as your class times, medical appointments, your children's school schedules, special family events, and any work obligations.

When you get the syllabi for your courses, record test dates and project due dates. Next, schedule the time that you will devote to the study and work needed to complete each assignment. The schedule should include all work assignments so that you avoid as many conflicts as possible. Don't forget yourself. Record your personal goals as well.

Keep the calendar with you so that you know what is happening in your life. Using the calendar will help you avoid overscheduling yourself and creating embarrassing situations. From your calendar, make a daily to-do list. Writing out the list before you go to bed at night is a good idea. Check off the items as you finish each one.

Some Helpful Tricks

Break large tasks into smaller parts. For example, if you have to read a 20-chapter novel by the end of a 10-week course, schedule two chapters each week into your study time. If you are writing a term paper, schedule library research time each week for note taking. When you have gathered enough information, begin an outline. Then you will have time to return to the library for additional information if it is needed.

Getting into a rut can be useful. Doing the same things at the same time each day can mentally get you into a routine, which can help you use time more efficiently. At the same time, you must prepare yourself for the complications and problems that are a natural part of life. Leave time in your daily schedule for the unexpected.

Going back to school is a challenging task that is never easy. The management of your family and work obligations becomes more complex when responsibilities for college are added. However, millions of people have been successful in doing all three at once, and so can you. Approach the situation with a positive attitude and personal discipline, and success will follow.

Chapter 8

Succeeding in College

Being in a classroom today is not like it was 20 years ago. New technologies, new teaching philosophies, and differing viewpoints may all be a part of your classroom experience, so be prepared to face some cultural shock. Have no fear, however, because new situations are opportunities to learn. Remember, learning comes from the sharing of ideas from a variety of sources. Use these new ideas to increase your knowledge.

In previous chapters, you learned about the many nontraditional college degree programs now available for adult students. In this chapter, you learn some study tips to help you deal with both old and new learning methods.

Essential Skills for the Modern College Program

This chapter concentrates on techniques you can use to improve your success in a classroom-oriented program. Statistics show that most adult students participate in this type of program. The classes may be accelerated, they may be at your place of employment, or they may be taken through an interactive video conferencing format. While nontraditional in nature, classroom-based courses continue to dominate. Therefore, it makes sense to concentrate on the strategies most adult students need to succeed at college.

You probably will find many things about college similar to what you encountered when you last attended school. However, many things have changed. College programs for adults often use four learning strategies to help students master course content. These are collaborative (cooperative) learning, class presentations, course papers, and research projects. Although they are still used in many colleges, there often is less emphasis on exams, quizzes to check that reading assignments have been completed, and regurgitation of an instructor's lecture. These latter methods are not effective with adults—some educators would contend they're not effective with any students—and often keep adults from enrolling in further courses. This section presents information to help you complete college course work successfully.

Cooperative Learning and Studying

Many adult education programs are developed around the concept of cooperative learning. This method of teaching allows students to play an active role in their learning. Research has shown that adults learn best when they can experiment and share in discussions and problem solving with others. Working together is a logical learning method for adults. In addition, the team approach is very much a part of the real working world in which adults function. Working on class assignments with a study group develops many skills that can be used in team activities related to your job.

The study group is one way that adults can work and learn together and can take one of several forms. In some cases, students are required to join a study group as part of their degree program. Attendance and participation in the group are as much parts of the academic experience as attending and participating in classes. In other situations, instructors form study groups to work together during a particular course. The group might be given a special assignment that members are expected to complete together. Or the instructor might require the group to work together on all course assignments. And sometimes, students form their own informal study groups as a means of support and help.

Study groups usually have three to six members. If the group is too small, there may not be enough diversity. If the group is too large, less communication is possible. Ideally, four or five students make up the group. Each member is expected to contribute his or her own knowledge, skills, and resources for the good of the group. It is best if no one person acts as the group leader. If the group is reaching the goals it has set, a leader is not necessary. On the other hand, if problems are occurring, a leader may emerge. Occasionally, if someone in the group has a great deal of skill in a particular course of study, a leader may appear for a period of time.

Formal study groups—those required by the college for participation in a degree program—are usually formed after students have had time to become acquainted. Normally, the instructor allows a few class sessions to pass before students are asked to form study groups. To foster greater creativity, students are encouraged to form groups with a diversity of backgrounds and personality differences. To make meeting together as simple as possible, work schedules and geographical locations may also be considered. After the groups are formed, the instructor becomes a facilitator. The groups function without interference. The professor may be a sounding board for group problems; however, the group is responsible for the solutions. Some additions or dropouts of group members may take place as students leave or join a program. The group is responsible for making these changes work effectively.

The group may be required to meet a certain number of hours each week and is responsible for deciding where and when to meet. Handling problems such as noncontributing members, conflicts within the group, and members with unequal abilities is the group's responsibility. The instructor may offer some guidelines to follow in problem situations, but the group chooses how to handle the situation.

The use of study groups for a particular course usually has standards set by the instructor. The professor's expectations for the group will set the atmosphere for group functions. The instructor explains what being a part of a study group means. Understanding the importance of each member's participation is important. The members' responsibility to each other is made clear. If someone is not able to contribute because of academic problems, it is the group's duty to help that individual to succeed. If someone is not contributing because of unwillingness to work, the group needs to know how to handle that situation. It is the group's responsibility to approach the individual about this problem. In some cases, the group can request that a person become a part of another study group. The difficulty in getting uniform cooperation and contribution is one reason many adult students dislike study groups. However, proper team management can resolve most difficulties and helps all group members become more proficient in the practice of team-building skills.

At the end of the course, students might fill out a confidential study group evaluation form. The instructor may use this information in evaluating the group and handling any problems that might be occurring. This method helps a group hold each member accountable for individual contributions. The professor may guide the group's progress by checking to see if the group is following a realistic schedule to complete a project, helping with any conflicts that are occurring, and checking that each member is contributing positively. Some groups want to divide a project among individuals. Working this way hinders the interaction of the group. The instructor can encourage group work by providing time for group meetings at the end of class, insisting that the project flow together rather than being short pieces of information, and giving a group grade.

A study group functions most effectively as members focus on the project as a group and not as individuals. A feeling of friendship and helpfulness encourages the group to work at a higher level. As members of the group debate, ask questions, and are actively involved in the learning process, the group becomes more productive. The group that works cooperatively rather than competitively is most successful. The study group provides supportive listening for its members and offers feedback when needed. Disagreement and difference are viewed positively; however, group decisions are accepted even when individuals disagree. The activities of the group are geared to accomplish specific tasks. At the end of a study group session, the members may review the meeting and discuss what has been learned through the process.

Being part of a study group will increase your learning. A study group can accomplish more in a shorter period of time than an individual can. For example, writing practice questions over a unit can be done much more quickly when members of a study group divide the unit and write questions. A study group offers both academic and emotional support. Members of your study group understand your frustrations when your child is ill and you miss class. Any class notes you miss will be available through your study group.

A study group offers you an opportunity to learn from other students. You will gain self-confidence as a contributing member of the group. Learning to work with deadlines will help you in the real work environment. Educators have observed yet another important function of study groups: They reduce the number of college dropouts. Students are motivated to continue their education when they have friends and acquaintances at school.

Making an Oral Presentation

One of the best ways to learn something is to teach it. Presentation skills are also fundamental for success in many jobs. For these reasons, instructors often use oral presentations on topics related to a course as a primary teaching method for adult students. Sometimes the instructor will assign topics to study groups. The presentation becomes a group activity. At other times, you might be required to make an oral presentation as an individual. You might be allowed to choose the topic of your presentation, or it may be preassigned.

Preparing an oral report is much like writing a paper. Two things are important when choosing a topic: First, the topic should be something you are comfortable speaking about. Second, it should be interesting to your audience. Whenever possible, select a topic related to your job and place of work. This helps to ease the tension that often occurs when a person isn't familiar with the topic being presented.

When the topic choice has been made, begin your research. You might want to make a list of questions or write a brief outline. Learn as much as you can about your topic. A speaker who knows a subject will get a more positive reaction from the audience. Think about the needs of students in your class and use these to guide your research on the topic. For example, you may identify a high degree of interest in total quality management among students in class. As you research a topic, determine how it relates to the implementation or improvement of total quality management.

The speech should contain an introduction, the main body, and an ending. Some experts suggest that you follow the adage, "Tell them what you're going to tell them, tell them, and then tell them what you told them." The introduction should get the audience's attention.

Involving the audience is one way of doing this. Ask a question. Give the class a sufficient amount of time to respond—and realize that what seems like several seconds waiting for an answer is often only fractions of a second. Listen to their answers and acknowledge them. Using a funny or moving anecdote is another way to introduce your speech. Quoting statistics that have a personal meaning to the audience is another introductory method.

As you write the body of your presentation, remember that the audience will recall only two or three main points. Repeating these main points throughout the presentation will help make this transfer of learning. Use detailed information as support for the main ideas.

Use visual aids—pictures, charts, and props—to help the audience remember better. Computer programs make developing visual aids much easier. You can easily produce overhead transparencies or display an image directly from the computer. Many students are now developing multimedia presentations with computers that combine sound, music, video, and written information. Use classroom presentations to learn more about the creation and use of visual aids.

Demonstrations, role playing, and drama are also useful in making your points. Products, procedures, and services can often be demonstrated. Enlist the aid of fellow students to role play or enact dramas. More creative methods like these should be discussed with your instructor to ensure that you are meeting her or his expectations.

The conclusion of your speech should remind the audience of the main points of your presentation. It should summarize the speech and leave the audience feeling uplifted or thoughtful. You may want to use a simple paper quiz or oral questions directed at the class as a way of summarizing the presentation.

Facing an audience is very few individuals' favorite activity. Clammy hands, sweating brows, a dry throat, shaking knees, and even nausea are common symptoms of stage fright. Actually the energy produced by the anticipation of being center stage can be helpful in making a presentation, if it does not get out of control.

SUZANNE works in the fast-changing field of computers. She is an instructor at a two-year technical college. At 57, she has returned to the university to obtain a master's degree in Computer Science. Her job requires the advanced degree, but Suzanne also has a personal desire to upgrade her knowledge.

Suzanne is a part-time commuting student. Because of the location of the university, she must commute to her classes. By the time she travels to the university and attends a class session, she has spent five and a half hours of her day. Suzanne commutes to her classes three days each week. Her weekends and three nights each week are spent studying. By her own estimate, Suzanne spends 40 hours a week pursuing her degree. In addition, she continues to work full-time.

Suzanne has completed about one-fourth of her degree. Although she wants this degree as much as she wanted her undergraduate degree, the time factor has placed limitations on her. As an undergraduate living in the dorm with her parents paying all of her expenses, studying was her main focus. Now, as a married adult working 40 hours a week, Suzanne finds working on this degree much more difficult.

Preparing well will help your confidence in making your presentation. Write out the entire speech. Read it aloud several times. You will begin to remember key phrases. Put these key phrases on 3" by 5" cards. Visual aids become a cue that serve the same purpose as cards. Use these cards to practice your speech. If possible, give the speech to family members or friends, ask for any suggestions they have. If you have been given a time limit, check to be sure you are within that limit. A brief speech will keep the audience's attention.

Go over your note cards right before you deliver the speech. Whatever you do, don't hold the cards in your hands during the presentation, because they interfere with the use of natural gestures. Relax. Breathe slowly. As you make your speech, use gestures, look at your audience, and move around the front of the classroom—without being frantic. Be in control but, at the same time, be enthusiastic.

Each time you make an oral presentation, your skills will improve. As your skills increase, you will gain more confidence. Even experienced presenters become tense when they get in front of an audience. View this tension as healthy, because it keeps you alert and prepared to do your very best. Presentation skills are needed in the work world as well as the academic world, so view this requirement as a positive learning activity.

Writing Skills

Writing is a skill you will use frequently in college. Like presentation skills, writing is an extremely valuable skill in the workplace. Employer surveys consistently list oral and written communication skills among the top ten skills for success on the job.

Adult professionals and managers typically write reports and other documents. However, for many adults, writing a class paper is a difficult assignment. If you are uncomfortable with your writing skills, check with your school. Many schools offer remedial writing courses or provide tutors for students. You will not be the only person needing this help. Don't hesitate to ask for assistance in this area.

To produce a satisfactory paper, you need to plan ahead. When you know that a paper is due, begin by scheduling time for research and writing. Make your own deadline a few days before the deadline set by the professor. This will allow you some extra time in case of emergencies. Waiting too long to start a paper can put unnecessary stress on you. You may not be able to get the resources you need if other students are writing on similar topics. You won't have time to revise and rewrite to produce the best possible paper. In the process, you may neglect other classes while you are trying to get the paper finished.

Before you begin researching, make sure you understand what is expected. Reread any notes or handouts you have about the paper. What is the instructor asking? How long should the paper be? Does the paper require any special topic or information? Is the paper to be written in any particular form?

If you can divide the paper into small segments of work, the task will not be so overwhelming. Make a list of the work you will need to do to complete the paper. This list could include these tasks:

Selecting a topic

Listing research questions

Researching the questions

Outlining the paper

Writing a first draft

Revising the first draft

Writing final copy

Set deadlines for completing each task. Mark these dates on your calendar.

Sometimes an instructor assigns a topic to each person or group in the class, but frequently you will be expected to select a topic. When you choose a topic, think about your interests. If you are interested in the topic, doing the work will be easier. Choosing a topic that your professor finds interesting is wise, because this one person is your audience. Talk to your professor about the topic. Make sure it applies to your class work. Ask for any suggestions or information your instructor has about your topic. Make sure that the topic is broad enough so that you will not have problems locating information, but narrow enough so that you can write a focused paper in the time and writing limits placed on you. Keep in mind the length of the paper. The subject of a 4-page paper should not be as broad as that of a 20-page paper. The topic needs to have enough resources so that you don't need to spend hours searching for information, but you should not be overwhelmed by the materials available.

After selecting the topic, determine what specific questions should be answered by the paper. Simply write a list of questions that, if answered, would cover the topic of the paper. Ask yourself the questions who, what, where, how, and why about the topic. Form more specific questions using these broad questions as a guide.

If you aren't sure what questions to ask, go to the library. Reading some general information about the topic usually will provide you with some ideas. An encyclopedia will give you a broad view of the topic. Skim some recent books or journals about the topic. Check with the reference librarian for any additional information sources.

Looking for information that answers your questions will be the basis for your research. As you read, you may find that additional questions need to be answered, or that some questions will be eliminated. This is no problem, since the questions are simply a rough idea of the information you plan to cover.

Knowing how to use your school's library is important to successfully writing papers. At many universities the library is now called the media center, the information center, or the learning resource center. These names are better descriptions of these facilities, which offer a much wider array of resources than simply books, journals, and magazines. Audio and video tapes, computers, tutorial programs, and many other resources are often available through the library.

College libraries usually have photocopy machines available for student use. Copyright law provides for "fair use," so that you can photocopy portions of books, magazines, and journals for scholarly purposes. The law, however, provides no clear definition of the term "fair use." What might constitute the "fair use" of published works? Photocopying a magazine or journal article; a small portion of a larger work (for example, a chapter from a book); or even an entire work if you cannot acquire a printed copy at a fair price. In no case, however, should you make copies for personal profit. You must use them for scholarly purposes only—such as for writing a college paper.

A student ID card is usually needed to use the library. A tour of the library will help you feel more at ease. You will want to know the library's hours, what materials can be checked out, what materials can be used only in the center, and the length of time an item may be borrowed. Remember, librarians are there to help. Don't hesitate to ask them when you need help.

Most library resource centers are computerized. The old card catalog has been replaced with a computerized system that allows you to use a terminal to search library sources. Like the card catalog, a terminal lets you make a search by subject, author, title, keyword, or call number. When you have found a source, you can immediately determine its availability. The computer will tell you whether the source is checked out and when it is due, or if it is on the library shelf. It will give a brief description of the source. The call number will help you locate it in the stacks. If you can't find the source on the shelf, check the area around it, in case the source has been reshelved in the wrong place. If you still can't find it, ask a librarian for help.

If you need a book that is checked out, you can fill out a request form. When the book is due, you will be notified. Some colleges allow professors and graduate students to check out books for longer periods of time than normal; but if someone requests the book, it must be returned. If the word "reserve" appears in the file, the source will be in a special section of the library called the reserve section. Professors sometimes place books in the reserve section to allow all the students in the class equal access. Check with the librarian if your source is marked reserved. You are typically limited to using the resource in the library— in some cases there may be a 24-hour time limit on using and returning the resource.

Online or CD-ROM databases allow you to look for journal or magazine articles about particular topics. Because periodicals require so much storage space, media centers use microfilm and microfiche cards to store them. Microfilm reading machines are very easy to use. However, with the rapid adoption of CD-ROM technology, many libraries have complete sets of journals stored on CD-ROM disks. A printout made from the CD-ROM disks is usually available for a small fee per page.

If you can't find the source you need in your library, the interlibrary loan system can be used. Check with the librarian to see if the source is available through another library. If the resource is available, it will be sent to your library, where you can pick it up. You return the item to your library by the due date. A small fee may be charged for this service.

If you have a personal computer with a modem, you might be able to check your library's resources without leaving home. Some libraries offer this timesaving service to their students. Be sure to check out your library's resources and use every service that will help you in your learning.

Keeping a record of your sources will save time and frustration when you begin writing the paper. One way to do this is by writing the bibliography information for each source on a 3" by 5" card. A card file system organizes the information so that it is available when you need it. You can use a number or a letter to identify each source. As you take notes from a source, place this ID code in your notes. When you need to identify a source in your writing, the information for citing credit is readily available. To indicate a direct quotation, place quotation marks around the words you found in the source. Write any other information in your own words. Write the source letter or number to identify the resource used on each card. Write one thought or idea on each card. Write as a heading at the top of the card the question being answered.

Whenever you quote an author, be certain that you do use quotation marks around the author's exact phrases and give the author credit. Failure to do this is called *plagiarism*. Plagiarism is the use of someone else's ideas as your own ideas. Pretending that someone else's ideas are your own is not only dishonest but also academic theft. If you plagiarize, you offend not just the reader but the person who originated the ideas you use without due recognition.

Be further warned that extensive paraphrasing of an author's work without giving the person credit is also considered plagiarism. There is common agreement that extensive quotations—more than a few contiguous paragraphs—should not be done without written permission of the author or publisher. Such permission is a must if *your* work should become published. Nor should you use so many quotations that they diminish your own contribution to a paper. Copying charts, tables, and graphs should be limited to those instances where they are only a small portion of the original work.

When you have finished researching the topic, sort the note cards by putting them into stacks—one for each question. Use the notes from these cards to write a detailed outline of the paper. Outlining allows you to organize your thoughts in a logical order where each thought builds on another. Using an outline, you can work more effectively. However, since this is a working outline, you may need to revise it.

Computer-literate students might find it easier to keep this information organized in the computer. In fact, the Cardfile tool found in Microsoft Windows works just like a 3" by 5" card system. The use of simple database software programs can also help you organize information.

Facing a blank page is often difficult for a writer. Before you actually start writing, try to get into a writing mood. Start by looking over your notes and outline. Gather all the materials you will need. Go to your study area and begin working. Put together an outline. List the major points that you want to make. Under each point list secondary items that need to be included. Many word processing programs contain an outline feature that can be useful in completing this task.

Try to write as if you were talking to someone. It is not necessary to use words or phrases that would not normally be part of your speech. Remember that this is the first draft of the paper. Right now you need to get your thoughts on paper. You will be revising the paper later to make corrections.

The logical starting point is the introduction. However, remember that, although the introduction may be read first, it does not have to be written first. If the introduction is not coming easily, start with an area that is more interesting and easier to write. You can write the introduction later.

As you write, show that your paper is backed up by research. Use short quotations, data, and specific examples to support your findings. Try to include only information that is relevant to the topic. Move through the paper, answering each of your listed questions as precisely as you can. Connect different answers with brief transition sentences. At the end of the paper, write a brief summary of the information presented.

Now you are ready to begin revising your paper. Start by checking the content. Read the paper aloud. Have you answered each question being asked? Do you need to rearrange any paragraphs to present your thoughts in a more logical order? Typically, you should introduce the ideas or concepts, beginning with the most important and proceeding to the least important. Look for overused words or terms. Make sure that the construction of each sentence is proper—students who haven't written much recently may forget that each sentence must have a subject and a verb that agrees with the subject. Make sure also that each paragraph makes a point. Review the introduction and summary to be certain that they achieve the desired results. The paper should have a smooth sound as you read it.

Read the paper aloud one more time. This time, check punctuation, grammar, and spelling. If your computer has spell-checking and grammar-checking programs, you should use them. Pay attention to and learn from the suggestions and corrections that these computer tools highlight. Be sure to check the paper visually, because a spell checker or grammar checker won't see every mistake. Once again, listen for any awkwardness in your writing. Make any adjustments that are needed.

If at all possible, have someone else read and correct your paper. Using a study group member is one possibility. (Some schools restrict collaboration between students, so be sure not to violate any honor system or ethical code guidelines). Your professor might be willing to look at your work before you hand in the final copy. The more feedback you receive, the better your writing will be. Revisions usually improve a paper. Therefore, the more editing you do, the better. However, time constraints place a limit on the reasonable number of revisions you can make.

If you have access to a word processor and are familiar with it, use it for the final copy of your paper. Follow all directions for structure and composition that the instructor gives. Often, detailed instructions are given concerning footnotes, references, and other documentation. If you don't have access to a word processor, most instructors require that a paper be at least "typewritten." If you don't know how to type, you should find other resources. Normally, bulletin boards around campus—as well as the campus newspaper—have advertisements for typists who will do the job for you for a fee. Another strategy is to put the word out around the office that you'll pay someone for typing your school papers. It usually isn't long before an interested person "volunteers" for the job.

JOHN F. KENNEDY UNIVERSITY, *located in Orinda, California, was founded in 1964 as an institution dedicated solely to adult education. It has a current enrollment of 1,850 students—the average age of whom is 37—and over 5,000 graduates. The university is organized into the School of Law, School of Management, Graduate School of Professional Psychology, Graduate School for Holistic Studies, and School of Liberal Arts.*

The university provides a wide array of bachelor's and master's degrees in both traditional and nontraditional subject areas. Examples of nontraditional degree programs are the Master of Arts in Career Development from the School of Business, and the Master of Arts in Transpersonal Psychology from the School of Holistic Studies. The university provides for several graduate articulated programs in which students can apply 18 to 24 undergraduate hours—completed at the university—to a graduate degree in the same field of study.

Students enrolling in undergraduate degree programs can obtain credit through CLEP, Advanced Placement exams, DANTES and military service, ACE (PONSI) approved corporate-training programs, and assessment of prior learning portfolios. It is also possible to earn up to 36 quarter hours through extension/correspondence courses from other colleges. An independent study program allows both graduate and undergraduate students an opportunity to study subjects not available through courses offered by the university.

Class schedules are established to be convenient for working adults. There are evening courses and weekend courses, and the Master of Arts in Career Development can be taken through a combination of correspondence courses, internships in the student's location, and an intensive two-week summer residency. Some courses are taught by full-time faculty, but over 650 adjunct faculty bring a balance of real-world experience into the classroom.

Basic Study Techniques

Every student discovers strategies and techniques for studying. This section provides some ideas you may find useful. Like any suggestions, some techniques will work for you and others will not.

Experiment with these techniques until you find ones that work for you.

Note Taking

Taking notes during class is one way to be an active listener. It allows you to use both hearing and sight in the learning process. You will develop your own method of taking notes. Some people abbreviate words and develop their own shorthand. They show importance by underlining or writing in larger letters. Some use an outline form for note taking. Writing clearly is important. The date and source of the notes should be written on the paper for later reference. Here are some suggestions for taking notes.

1. Don't write every spoken word. Write in your own words what you hear.

2. Listen for key words, such as "most important" or "remember this."

3. Listen for lists. For example, "Point number one is. . . ."

4. Write down anything the professor writes on the board or displays on an overhead projector or other projection device.

5. If the professor is excited about a topic, be sure to note it.

6. Be especially alert to anything said in the first or last five minutes of class time. The ideas presented in the first five minutes are often the basis of the class meeting. Ideas presented in the last five minutes may be the summary of the class meeting or something the professor considers so important that it must be squeezed into the class session.

7. Listen for words, phrases, or concepts in class that were also included in reading assignments. It is likely that the instructor is emphasizing them because of their importance in the study of the subject.

8. Avoid asking whether an item is important and will be included on a test. Most instructors find this annoying. It implies that items included in the lecture are unimportant and can be ignored when they are not going to be included on a test.

After class, you may want to spent 10 or 15 minutes reviewing your notes. This will allow you to make any corrections or additions while the class discussion or lecture is still fresh in your mind. If you have questions about your notes, ask the professor or other students to help you understand clearly what has been said. Reviewing your notes before the next class session will help you keep the information fresh in your mind.

Some students find it helpful to record an instructor's lecture. Always ask the instructor's permission before taping a class. If you use a recorder, still take notes during class. Use the recorded class material to review your notes and make sure that important points weren't missed. Some students record their notes and review them while commuting or doing other chores. Using recorded classes and notes is particularly helpful for the auditory learner.

Reading More Effectively

Reading is one tool you will use extensively while you are a student. Some experts estimate that as much as 85 percent of college work is reading. Graduate programs typically require much more reading than undergraduate programs. If you are uncomfortable with your reading skills, you should find some kind of help. Some people find it helpful to learn speed reading. You might be able to teach yourself or attend a class to learn this skill. Many colleges and universities offer students with poor reading skills help through remedial programs. Check with your college to find out what is offered.

Reading can be done in different ways, depending on the reason for reading. If you are reading to simply get the basic idea of the selection, you might find skimming the best approach. In skimming, read the introduction and summary sections of a chapter, read highlighted text, and review the first few sentences of each major section. If you are reading to gather information and details, read slowly and carefully. Reading to memorize requires more concentration. The use of highlighting pens can help when reading for details and memorization. Highlighting text helps fix the highlighted point in your mind and makes it easier later to review the material for a test or paper. Some students also find it helpful to write comments in the margin that record personal insights or reinforce a point made by the instructor.

The marking of textbooks raises an important issue. This action decreases the value of the books for resale. You may find that you don't want to sell your textbooks. Students often ask if they should sell or keep books. Usually this is based on your personal situation and preference. However, there are some useful points to consider when making this decision. Is it likely you will have a reason to use the book again? The probability of referring to a book in the future greatly increases when it is one used in your major field of study. For example, a business major is likely to refer to a book about marketing in a current or future job. Do you find the book interesting? You might want to keep some books just because they are enjoyable and can be reread or loaned to friends. Is the book a useful reference? Some books are good reference tools for work, home, or volunteer activities. For example, an English grammar book can be useful when you have future writing tasks for work, volunteer, or personal pleasure.

*After high school graduation, **NICK** enlisted in the U.S. Air Force, where he learned to be an electrician. After six years, Nick left the Air Force to open his own electrical business. His business has been established for 11 years.*

Nick has confidence in his skills as an electrician; however, as his company grew, Nick found that he needed more business skills. He wanted to know more about accounting as well as other business knowledge.

Six years ago Nick decided to start an associate degree in business. He chose a local technical college to meet his goal. By taking one class during the fall and spring terms, Nick has continued to pursue his goal. Because his business is busy during the summer months, Nick is unable to take classes then.

With a family and 12-hour work days, 37-year-old Nick admits that he sometimes experiences the same feelings about homework that he had as a high school senior. Time to concentrate on homework just doesn't exist. Life is too full. The temptation to "just get by" in class rather than be an active learner is always there. But knowing that his learning will improve his own business motivates Nick to reach his goal.

Using a Study Plan

Using a plan to study is helpful to many students. The SQ3R plan— **Skim, Question, and 3 R's: Read, Recite, and Review**—was developed by a professor at Ohio State University in 1941. Many experts consider this five-step plan a good way to learn the most in the least amount of time. Both practice and discipline are required to use this method.

Skimming and Questioning

The first two steps are skimming and questioning. Before reading a chapter in a book or a journal or magazine article, make a list of questions you want answered from your reading. Write the questions down. Check the beginning of the chapter or article for a list of questions written by the authors. These questions reflect the objectives of the author. Read the summary at the end. This gives you an idea of the purpose of the reading. Skim the reading by looking at the titles, pictures and captions, charts, and any highlighted words, phrases, and questions. When you have written your questions, you are ready for the next step, reading.

Reading

As you begin reading, set a goal. You may want to read a certain number of pages or chapters, or you may decide to read until you can answer a particular question or understand a concept. Check your concentration time. If your mind begins to wander after 10 or 15 minutes, give yourself a brief break. Stand up, walk around, or step outside briefly. Then return to your studying. Don't just quit.

To read with a purpose, use the questions you have written. Read quickly. Use headings, the sentences at the beginning of paragraphs, and the chapter summary to guide you quickly through the chapter. Remain active as you read. Read with a pencil in hand. Write out the answers to the questions you have formulated. If you find a word you don't know, use the sentences around it to discover its meaning. Write the word down. Check the dictionary for its definition.

Some students write their chapter questions on one side of 3" by 5" cards. On the other side they write the answers. Words and definitions are done in the same way. This is convenient for two reasons. First, these notes are ready when exam time comes. Second, the note cards can be carried around for those times when a few moments can be snatched for studying.

Reciting

After you have read a section, stop and state in your own words what you have read. Write down this information. Putting the information you have read into your own words makes it more personal. The information becomes a part of your long-range memory. Recitation involves two senses: sight and hearing. The more senses you use, the more potential you have for learning. If you have a study partner, recitation can be used successfully. Together you can share what you remember and discuss it. Asking each other review questions is also helpful.

Reviewing

Reviewing is the final step. When you have completed the reading, immediately look at what you have studied. Take five or ten minutes to go over the notes you have made. Since people tend to forget what they have read most recently, this brief review is important. It will reinforce what you have just read. When you are ready to study the next chapter in your book or another article, review your notes from the previous readings. By taking five or ten minutes to review the previous readings, you will be able to connect the information in the chapters.

Test Time

While some adult education programs use various forms to evaluate student learning, you will probably be faced with taking a written test at some point in your education experience. Many adult students fear taking tests. The thought of taking tests makes some people panic. If you dread taking a test, two factors might help you when test time arrives. First, you can avoid much test stress by continual studying rather than last minute cramming. Second, learning some test-taking tricks will give you more confidence.

Being Prepared

As you study, do it with a test in mind. Talk to your professor about when tests will be given. Find out what kind of tests your professor gives. The use of "objective questions" in the form of true/false, multiple choice, and matching and listing questions requires a focus on memorization. The use of short answer or essay questions requires more focus on concepts and developing ideas and conclusions from these concepts.

You can use different sources to make up practice questions. Professors sometimes give students old exams to use for review. Some textbooks have student manuals to use as study guides. Check with your professor or the bookstore about them. Talking to students who have taken the course will help you know what kind of questions to expect on a test.

Using this information, make up practice questions from your reading and class notes. Some students use 3" by 5" cards for these questions. Questions are written on one side and answers on the other. They make a file of questions and use them for weekly practice tests. Study groups can make up questions to ask each other.

By continually reviewing course material, you will be better prepared at test time. Cramming will not be necessary. You can approach the test with more confidence, less stress, and more sleep.

Taking Tests

Knowing how to take a test successfully is as important as knowing the material. Before you begin taking the test, read the instructions. Be sure you understand the instructions and do exactly what is directed. Listen to any verbal instructions your instructor gives before the test begins. Sometimes these instructions are different from the written ones. If you don't understand the directions, ask the professor for an explanation.

Look over the entire test. Find out if different parts of the test are worth different points. Allocate your time so that you can complete questions that will give you the greatest number of points possible. For example, don't make the mistake of spending too much time on an essay question that is worth only a few points and not having time to complete the entire test.

As you take the test, first answer all the questions you know. Put a check mark beside the ones you don't know. You can come back to them later. As you answer other questions, you may find a clue that will help you with one of these questions. When you have gone through the entire test, return to these questions. If you are not penalized for wrong answers, make logical guesses.

Use all the time you are given to complete the test. If you have additional time, recheck your answers. Change any answers that need correcting. Before making corrections, consider how sure you are about the change you are making. Usually, your first response is more accurate. Unless you make a blatant error or have misinterpreted the question, it is often better to stick with your original answer. Make sure you have not skipped any questions.

Answering Objective Tests

Objective tests include multiple choice, true-false, matching, and listing questions. Reading carefully is important when you take this type of test. Normally, multiple choice questions have one correct answer, several almost correct answers, and one totally incorrect answer. However, sometimes more than one answer is needed. Giving attention to plural verbs and nouns in the question can be a clue to the need for more than one answer. For example, "The names of some U.S. presidents are . . . "

a. Adams

b. Washington

c. Lincoln

d. Roosevelt

e. All of the above

The noun "names" and the verb "are" indicate that more than one choice is needed to answer this question.

If you are unsure of a multiple-choice answer, make a logical guess by the process of elimination. First eliminate all the answers that are totally wrong. Look at the answers that are left. Look for context clues in the question, such as singular or plural nouns or verbs. Eliminate any answers that can't be used correctly with the question. Now make a logical choice from the remaining options.

Objective tests often are graded by a computer. When a scantron card is used, only one answer is used for each question. If you use a scantron card for testing, you might want to use a straight edge, ruler, or note card to avoid marking the wrong box on the card. Scantron cards usually require that you use a number 2 pencil to mark answers, the box or circle must be completely filled, and you must completely erase any incorrect answers.

Recalling Facts

Short-answer questions, such as lists or definitions and fill-in-the-blank questions, are one way of testing for facts. The answers are not always complete sentences but, rather, brief phrases or words. This type of question often requires memorization of facts.

Essay questions require more organization and writing skills. Professors often use a bluebook to record essay tests. A bluebook is an inexpensive booklet filled with white, lined paper bound in a blue paper cover. Find out if the instructor provides the bluebooks or if you have to purchase them from the bookstore. You may need extra paper, pens or pencils, and a watch to help you know how much time you have to work on the test.

Before you begin answering an essay question, be sure you understand what is being asked. Look for key words like *summarize*, *list*, or *give examples*. Be sure you do what is asked. Instructors sometimes list several questions and allow students to choose a certain number to answer.

Before writing, you can make a quick list of all you know about the topic: dates, names, places, facts. This short time of brainstorming will help your memory as you write. An essay answer should have an introduction, middle, and a summary. The introduction and summary should be short. The middle section of the essay should state facts and be supported by details. Present your answer in a logical manner. Explain the assumptions used and the logic that was applied to answer essay questions that require you to arrive at a personal analysis. Padding the answer is not usually wise; instead, include information that is pertinent and shows that you understand the subject.

While the professor may not say so, neatness probably will count. A neatly written essay answer is simply easier to grade. You may lose points if your answer can't be read. As you are writing, double-spacing is wise. Then if you want to add more information when you recheck your essay, there is room for additions. Use good grammar and spelling because they also affect readability and understanding as the instructor checks the answer.

If you have time, reread your answer. Check to make sure you have answered each part of the question. If there is a question you cannot answer, write what you do know about it. You may not get all of the points for the question, but you might get some.

Using the Returned Test as a Learning Tool

When the test is returned to you, study the questions you missed. If you don't understand the answers, ask your instructor to explain them. If you missed something because you misinterpreted the test instructions, make sure you understand what you did incorrectly. Use the test as another way to learn. By studying your mistakes, you will be prepared for the next test.

Snatching Time for Studies

As you look at your daily schedule, do you see activities you could shorten to find time for studying? For example, if you are allowed an hour for lunch at your workplace, you might consider a 50/50 split. Pack your lunch but spend only a half hour eating it. Use the remaining half hour to read for class. Don't skip eating to make time for reading. Instead, shorten one activity to free up time for the other.

Getting up an hour earlier or going to bed an hour later than your family can give you some extra study time. Try to do this without neglecting sleep. Your body and mind need sleep to keep functioning.

Commuting time is often wasted time. If you use public transportation or belong to a car pool, study during travel time. If you drive, record class notes or lectures. Play the recording while you are driving.

If you have time between classes, use it for studying. Think about all the time you waste while you wait for appointments, to pick up children from activities, or to meet a friend. Get into the habit of always keeping something with you to read or study while you are waiting.

Class Participation

Interaction with the instructor and other students during class is important for a number of reasons. You learn more by participating in a discussion because you become a more active listener. You also are likely to be more prepared for a class when you know that active participation will be taking place and you plan to be a part of it. In addition, many instructors make classroom participation a part of each student's grade. Participation in classroom discussions demonstrates the student's knowledge of the subject and motivation to learn.

Some students are reserved and hesitate to say anything in class. Others fear being wrong or looking stupid. Preparation for a class—reading textbooks and articles, completing all assignments, and reviewing notes from past classes—increases your level of comfort in participating in classroom discussions. If you are reluctant to participate in discussions, begin with simple statements until you feel more comfortable. You can relate issues and points in the discussion to personal experiences. Providing illustrations from personal experience is often more comfortable than discussing abstract concepts. It takes effort to participate in class discussions, but it is worthwhile because of improved learning and usually better grades.

Responding to an instructor's questions is also important. Some instructors will call on specific students to answer questions, but more often the question is addressed to the class in general, and any student can respond. In both situations, it is important to respond with well-thought-out ideas. Use the same strategies for improving participation in class discussions to develop effective responses to an instructor's questions.

Putting It All Together

The experience of millions of adult students attending college each year demonstrates that it is possible for you to do the same. Challenges and problems will occur, but you can overcome them. Most adults who experienced problems with high school or previous college work are reluctant to go back to college. However, a large number of such students find that maturity, experience, and learning skills acquired on the job contribute to a successful educational experience the second time around.

In Chapter 1, we examined several doubts that adults have about going back to school. After reading this book, you should find many of your doubts dispelled.

Your chances of succeeding in college are quite good. You won't know whether you can succeed until you try. Begin making plans today, because procrastination is a trap that can keep you from achieving your dreams. The next section of this book is a guide to 240 colleges that offer you the potential to fulfill you dream. Good luck!

Introduction to the College and University Guide

This College Guide contains descriptions for 240 colleges and universities that provide nontraditional degree programs for adults. A survey was sent to more than 525 institutions of higher education. These institutions were identified from a variety of sources as potential providers of nontraditional degree programs. There were three criteria an institution was required to meet for inclusion in the guide.

1. **All colleges and universities listed are accredited.** An institution must be accredited by an agency recognized by the U.S. Department of Education. This means that all colleges and universities included in this guide are accredited and qualify for federal financial aid programs. It also ensures that the quality of education at these institutions is recognized by other universities and colleges. This can be particularly important if you decide to pursue a graduate degree at some point.

2. **You can get a bachelor's degree or graduate degree from these institutions.** All of the schools are either four-year colleges or universities with

graduate degree programs as well as undergraduate degrees. This limitation is not meant to ignore community and junior colleges—particularly as most of these institutions work hard to accommodate the needs of adult students. Rather, it is an effort to identify institutions that provide adults with bachelor's, master's, or doctoral degrees. Thus, students who already have associate degrees or credits earned at a community or junior college can use this guide to identify institutions where they can complete a bachelor's degree. It should be noted that several of the institutions listed also offer associate degrees.

3. **Every institution has nontraditional degree programs for adult students.** Some colleges and universities that responded to the survey did not offer nontraditional programs, or they offered nontraditional courses that did not lead to a degree. These institutions were not included in the guide. All institutions included in this guide provide a degree or degrees in a nontraditional program designed for adult students. There are almost 1,000 nontraditional degree programs provided by the institutions listed here.

This College and University Guide contains two parts. The first presents a list of all institutions organized by state. Forty-five states and the District of Columbia are represented. However, you should review programs from several states—not just the one in which you reside—because many colleges offer degrees that do not require you to attend courses on the campus. In addition, some campus residency requirements have flexible designs to accommodate the needs of working adults.

The second part of the guide lists the colleges and universities in alphabetical order and provides detailed information about each institution. The information on each institution was provided by a representative of that institution. We used the institution's own words to describe each degree program and the appeal of those programs to adult students. If information is missing, it wasn't provided by the institution on the survey. The information in this guide has been carefully checked; however, it is always possible to make mistakes. Every attempt has been made to provide accurate and useful information. We apologize to any college or university that has not been fairly represented.

You should use this information as the first step in collecting data about potential colleges where you can earn a degree. Verify the information with the institutions in which you are interested. Realize that all institutions in the guide are interested in recruiting college students or they would not have responded to the survey. This means that, as a consumer, you have a strong base of potential providers and are likely to find many excellent schools that can meet your educational needs.

A consistent pattern of information is provided for each school. Immediately following the institution's name are the name and address of a person who can be contacted for information, such as a college catalog and application form. Phone and fax numbers have also been provided so you can communicate with the contact person. You will notice that many of the colleges provide toll-free telephone numbers. The year in which the institution was founded provides some guidance on the institution's stability. The accrediting agency data assures you that the institution is accredited and furnishes information that might be needed by an employer providing tuition reimbursement.

The number of students gives you an idea of the size of the institution. The number of adult students helps you identify institutions that are currently serving adults. In reviewing this number, be aware that some colleges have been offering adult degree programs for a short time and have not yet developed a large adult student population. The figure therefore may not reflect accurately an institution's level of commitment to adult degree programs or effort to serve the adult population.

Representative degrees are listed for each college. Some colleges only offer one or two degree programs. Others listed dozens, but there is a limit to the number that can be included in the guide. In cases where the university offers degrees at several levels—associate, bachelor's, master's, and doctoral—an attempt was made to list at least one degree program at each level. Listed to the right of the degree is the major or concentration that students can obtain in conjunction with the degree. In addition, many colleges provided additional information to describe a degree and the major or concentration. This information is displayed immediately below the identifying information about the major or concentration.

The final piece of information included about each college is the special appeal the institution has for adult students. The survey question specifically asked, "What characteristics of your adult degree programs are most appealing to students?" In almost all cases, the response to this question is quoted verbatim from the answer written on the survey. However, in some cases we added additional information we thought would be useful to readers of the guide. When a college left this blank—but provided a catalog or promotional literature—a statement was selected from this material that seemed to be an appropriate answer to this question.

If you read this book and decide that you should complete a college degree, this guide can be a valuable resource. Read through the descriptions and locate institutions that seem to satisfy most of your needs. Contact several institutions and ask for complete information about their degree programs for adults. Compare the detailed information from each college with the data that you completed about your career in Chapter 2. Good luck in making your final decision.

College and University Guide

List of Colleges by State

State	College	City
Alabama	Judson College	Marion
	United States Sports Academy	Daphne
	University of Alabama	Tuscaloosa
Arkansas	John Brown University	Siloam Springs
Arizona	Grand Canyon University	Phoenix
	University of Phoenix	Phoenix
California	California Baptist College	Riverside
	California State University, Chico	Chico
	California State University, Dominguez Hills	Carson
	California State University, Sacramento	Sacramento
	The Fielding Institute	Santa Barbara
	Fresno Pacific College	Fresno
	John F. Kennedy University	Orinda
	The Master's College	Santa Clarita
	New College of California	San Francisco
	Saint Mary's College, School of Extended Education	Moraga
	Saybrook Institute	San Francisco
	Simpson College	Redding
	Southern California College	Costa Mesa
	University of California, Santa Barbara	Ventura
	University of San Francisco	San Francisco
	University of West Los Angeles	Inglewood
	West Coast University	Los Angeles

State	College	City
Colorado	Colorado State University	Ft. Collins
	Mind Extension University	Englewood
	The Naropa Institute	Boulder
	National Technological University	Fort Collins
	Regis University	Denver
	University of Denver	Denver
Connecticut	Charter Oak State College	Newington
	Sacred Heart University	Fairfield
	University of Bridgeport	Bridgeport
	University of Connecticut	Storrs
	University of New Haven	West Haven
Delaware	University of Delaware	Newark
District of Columbia	The American University	Washington
Florida	Barry University	Miami
	Embry-Riddle Aeronautical University	Daytona Beach
	Palm Beach Atlantic College	West Palm Beach
	Rollins College	Winter Park
	Southeastern College of the Assemblies of God	Lakeland
	St. Leo College	St. Leo
	University of Miami	Coral Gables
	University of Sarasota	Sarasota
	University of South Florida	Tampa
	Warner Southern College	Lake Wales
Georgia	Shorter College	Marietta
Hawaii	Chaminade University	Honolulu
Idaho	Boise State University	Boise
Illinois	American Schools of Professional Psychology	Chicago
	Barat College	Lake Forest
	Chicago State University	Chicago
	College of St. Francis	Joliet
	DePaul University	Chicago
	Eastern Illinois University	Charleston
	Governors State University	University Park
	Greenville College	Greenville
	Judson College	Elgin
	Moody Bible Institute	Chicago
	North Park College	Chicago
	Northeastern Illinois University	Chicago
	Olivet Nazarene University	Schaumburg
	Sangamon State University	Springfield
	Shimer College	Waukegan
	Western Illinois University	Macomb
Indiana	Ball State University	Muncie
	Ball State University Teachers College	Muncie
	Bethel College	Mishawaka
	Calumet College of St. Joseph	Whiting
	Concordia University Wisconsin	Indianapolis
	Goshen College	Goshen

State	College	City
Indiana (*Continued*)	Huntington College	Huntington
	Indiana Institute of Technology	Ft. Wayne
	Indiana University	Bloomington
	Indiana Wesleyan University	Marion
	St. Mary-of-the-Woods College	St. Mary-of-the-Woods
	University of Evansville	Evansville
Iowa	Briar Cliff College	Sioux City
	Dordt College	Sioux Center
	St. Ambrose University	Davenport
	Teikyo Marycrest University	Davenport
	The University of Iowa	Iowa City
	Upper Iowa University	Fayette
Kansas	Baker University	Overland Park
	Bethel College	N. Newton
	Kansas State University	Manhattan
	Saint Mary College	Shawnee-Mission
	Saint Mary College	Leavenworth
	Tabor College, Wichita	Wichita
Kentucky	Bellarmine College	Louisville
	Campbellsville College	Campbellsville
	Thomas More College	Crestview Hills
	University of Louisville	Louisville
Louisiana	Loyola University for Ministry	New Orleans
	Grantham College of Engineering	Slidell
Maine	Saint Joseph's College	Windham
	University of Maine	Orono
Maryland	College of Notre Dame of Maryland	Baltimore
	College of Notre Dame—Weekend Classes	Baltimore
	Towson State University	Towson
	University of Baltimore	Baltimore
Massachusetts	Atlantic Union College	South Lancaster
	Boston College	Chestnut Hill
	Cambridge College	Cambridge
	Eastern Nazarene College	Quincy
	Hebrew College	Brookline
	Lesley College	Cambridge
	Metropolitan College	Boston
	North Adams State College	North Adams
	Northeastern University, University College	Boston
	Suffolk University	Boston
	University of Massachusetts—Amherst	Amherst
	University of Massachusetts—North Dartmouth	Dartmouth
	Wentworth Institute of Technology	Boston
Michigan	Calvin College	Grand Rapids
	Central Michigan University	Mt. Pleasant
	Cornerstone College	Grand Rapids
	Ferris State University	Big Rapids

State	College	City
Michigan (*Continued*)	Northwood University	Midland
	Spring Arbor College	Spring Arbor
	Wayne State University	Detroit
Minnesota	College of St. Scholastica	Duluth
	Hamline University	St. Paul
	Metropolitan State University	St. Paul
	Winona State University	Winona
Missouri	Berean College	Springfield
	Columbia Union College Adult Evening Program	Tukana Park
	Drury College	Springfield
	Fontbonne College	St. Louis
	Lindenwood College	St. Charles
	Maryville University of Saint Louis	St. Louis
	Stephens College	Columbia
Nebraska	College of Saint Mary	Omaha
New Hampshire	Franklin Pierce College	Nashua
	University of New Hampshire	Durham
New Jersey	Caldwell College	Caldwell
	Centenary College	Hackettstown
	Fairleigh Dickinson University	Teaneck
	Ramapo College of New Jersey	Mahwah
	Rider University	Lawrenceville
	Rutgers University College	Camden
	Saint Peter's College	Jersey City
	Thomas Edison State College	Trenton
New Mexico	St. John's College	Santa Fe
New York	Audrey Cohen College	New York
	Bard College	Annandale-on-Hudson
	College of Mount Saint Vincent	Riverdale
	College of New Rochelle	New Rochelle
	Empire State College, SUNY	Saratoga Springs
	Fordham University—Ignatius College	Bronx
	Hofstra Univeristy	Hempstead
	Houghton College	West Seneca
	Mount Saint Mary College	Newburgh
	New School for Social Research	New York
	Nyack College	Nyack
	Queens College	Flushing
	Regents College	Albany
	Rochester Institute of Technology	Rochester
	Sage Evening College of the Sage Colleges	Albany
	Sarah Lawrence College	Bronxville
	Skidmore College, University Without Walls	Saratoga Springs
	State University at Buffalo— Millard Fillmore College	Buffalo
North Carolina	Campbell University	Buies Creek
	Mars Hill College	Mars Hill
	Montreat-Anderson College	Montreat

State	College	City
North Caroline (*Cont.*)	North Carolina Wesleyan College	Rocky Mount
North Dakota	University of Mary	Bismarck
Ohio	Bluffton College	Bluffton
	Lake Erie College	Painesville
	Malone College	Canton
	Malone College Graduate School	Canton
	Marietta College	Marietta
	Mount Vernon Nazarene College	Mount Vernon
	Ohio University's External Student Program	Athens
	The Union Institute	Cincinnati
	Wittenberg University	Springfield
	Xavier University	Cincinnati
Oklahoma	Bartlesville Wesleyan College	Bartlesville
	Oral Roberts University	Tulsa
	Southern Nazarene University	Bethany
	University of Oklahoma	Norman
Oregon	Eastern Oregon State College	La Grande
	George Fox College	Newberg
	Linfield College	McMinnville
	Marylhurst College	Marylhurst
	Northwest Christian College	Eugene
	Warner Pacific College	Portland
	Western Baptist College	Salem
	Western Oregon State College	Monmouth
Pennsylvania	Cedar Crest College	Allentown
	Drexel University	Philadelphia
	Eastern College	St. Davids
	Edinboro University of Pennsylvania	Edinboro
	King's College	Wilkes-Barre
	Marywood College	Scranton
	Messiah College	Grantham
	Millersville University	Millersville
	Philadelphia College of Bible	Langhorne
	Philadelphia College of Textiles and Science	Philadelphia
	University of Pennsylvania	Philadelphia
	Westminster College	New Wilmington
Rhode Island	Roger Williams University	Bristol
	The University of Rhode Island	Kingston
South Carolina	Southern Wesleyan University	Central
South Dakota	University of Sioux Falls	Sioux Falls
Tennessee	Covenant College, Quest Program	Chattanooga
	Lee College	Cleveland
	Milligan College	Milligan College
	Tennessee Wesleyan College	Athens
	University of Memphis	Memphis
	Vanderbilt University	Nashville
Texas	Dallas Baptist University	Dallas
	Lamar University	Beaumont

State	College	City
Texas *(Continued)*	LeTourneau University	Longview
	Southwestern Adventist College	Keene
	Trinity University	San Antonio
	University of Central Texas	Killeen
	Wayland Baptist University	Plainview
Utah	University of Utah	Salt Lake City
	Westminster College of Salt Lake City	Salt Lake City
Vermont	Burlington College	Burlington
	Goddard College	Plainfield
	Southern Vermont College	Bennington
	Trinity College of Vermont	Burlington
Virginia	Eastern Mennonite University	Harrisonburg
	Mary Baldwin College	Staunton
	Regent University	Virginia Beach
	University of Richmond	Richmond
	Virginia Commonwealth University	Richmond
Washington	Eastern Washington University	Cheney
	Seattle Pacific University	Seattle
	Seattle University	Seattle
West Virginia	West Virginia University	Morgantown
Wisconsin	Cardinal Stritch College	Milwaukee
	Marquette University	Milwaukcc
	Milwaukee School of Engineering	Milwaukee
	University of Wisconsin—Madison	Madison
	University of Wisconsin—Platteville	Platteville
	University of Wisconsin—River Falls	River Falls
	University of Wisconsin—Superior	Superior

Guide to Colleges and Universities with Nontraditional Degree Programs for Adults

American Schools of Professional Psychology

Coordinator of Admissions and Financial Aid
220 South State Street
Chicago, IL 60604
Phone: (312) 922-1025
Toll free: (800) 742-0743
Fax: (312) 922-1730
Founded: 1976
Accrediting agency: North Central Association
Number of students: 848
Number of adult students:

Representative Degrees

Psy.D.	Doctorate—Clinical Psychology
M.A.	Clinical Psychology
M.A.	Professional Counseling

The American University

Dr. Morris Jackson, Director, Return-to-School
  Programs
The American University, Nebraska Hall
4400 Massachusetts Ave., NW
Washington, DC 20016
Phone: (202) 885-3964
Toll free:
Fax: (202) 885-3991
Founded: 1893
Accrediting agency: Middle States Association
Number of students: 11,708
Number of adult students: 3,860

Representative Degrees

B.A.	Liberal Studies
Bachelor's	Assessment of Prior Experiential Learning
M.A.	Communication: Public Communication
M.A.	Communication: Journalism and Publications

Appeal of Program

Ability to earn credit for experiential learning; weekend master's programs; ability to enter any traditional major in addition to special programs.

Atlantic Union College

Dr. Ian Bothwell, Director, Adult Degree
  Program
P.O. Box 1000
South Lancaster, MA 01561
Phone: (508) 368-2304
Toll free: (800) 282-2030
Fax: (508) 368-2015
Founded: 1882
Accrediting agency: New England Association
Number of students: 700
Number of adult students: 105

Representative Degrees

M.Ed.	Special Education Independent study at home between annual seminars on campus.
B.A.	Art Independent study at home between seminars on campus every six months.
B.S.	Art Independent study at home between seminars on campus every six months.
B.S.	Behavioral Science Independent study at home between seminars on campus every six months.
B.A.	Business Administration Independent study at home between seminars on campus every six months.

Appeal of Program

Flexibility; compatibility with full-time employment and family responsibilities; on-campus seminars at six-month intervals.

Audrey Cohen College

Steven Lenhart, Admissions Director
345 Hudson Street
New York, NY 10014
Phone: (212) 989-2002
Toll free: 800-33-THINK
Fax: (212) 924-4396
Founded: 1964
Accrediting Agency: Middle States Association
Number of students: 1,150
Number of adult students: 1,150

Representative Degrees

Bachelor's	Human Services
	Bachelor's can be completed in two years and eight months while working full-time.
Bachelor's	Business Management
Master's	Administration
	Master's can be completed in one year while working full-time.

Appeal of Program

Day, evening, and evening weekend classes; individualized learning; accelerated degree programs. Students apply classroom theory to internships or their place of employment.

Baker University

Ms. Royce Collins, Director of Academic Records and Student Services
6600 College Blvd., Suite 340
Overland Park, KS 66211
Phone: (913) 491-4432
Toll free: (800) 955-7747
Fax: (913) 491-0470
Founded: 1858
Accrediting Agency: North Central Association
Number of students: 1,800
Number of adult students: 1,008

Representative Degrees

B.B.A.	Business Administration
	Classes meet one night a week; students also meet in study groups to complete team projects.
B.S.M.	Science in Management
M.S.M.	Science in Management
M.B.A.	Business Administration
M.L.A.	Liberal Arts
	Classes offered on a semester basis.

Appeal of Program

Class meetings one night a week; lock-step program; study groups.

Ball State University

Dr. Judith Roepke, Dean for Continuing Education
CA 200 Ball State University
Muncie, IN 47306
Phone: (317) 285-1582
Toll Free: (800) 872-0369
Fax: (317) 285-5795
Founded: 1918
Accrediting Agency: North Central Association
Number of students: 19,500
Number of adult students: NA

Representative Degrees

A.A.	General Studies
	Distance Education
M.B.A.	Business Administration
A.A.	General Arts

Appeal of Program

Undergraduate classes can be taken by correspondence or through a statewide televised network. Through a partnership with other state institutions, a wider selection of courses are available and easily articulated.

Ball State University Teachers College

Dr. James McElhinney, Director of Adult Degree Programs
Educational Leadership T.C.

2000 University Avenue
Muncie, IN 47306
Phone: (317) 285-5348
Toll free:
Fax:
Founded: 1921
Accrediting Agency: North Central Association
Number of students: 19,000
Number of adult students: 150
Representative Degrees

M.A.	Adult Education
Ed.D.	Adult and Community Education

Appeal of Program
Concern for student learning.

Barat College
Mr. Horace Staples, Director of Adult Admission
700 East Westleigh Road
Office of Adult Admission
Lake Forest, IL 60045
Phone: (708) 295-4260
Toll free:
Fax: (708) 615-5000
Founded: 1858
Accrediting Agency: North Central Association
Number of students: 730
Number of adult students: 329
Representative Degrees

B.A.	Management and Business Department Accounting, Marketing, and Management
B.A.	Computer Information Systems
B.A.	Communication Arts
B.A.	Elementary, Learning Disabilities, Secondary, Dance

Bard College
Ms. Karen Becker, Program Administrator
Bard College
Annandale-on-Hudson, NY 12504
Phone: (914) 758-7508
Toll free:
Fax: (914) 758-5801

Founded: 1860
Accrediting Agency: Middle States Association
Number of students: 1,000
Number of adult students: 75
Representative Degrees

B.A.
B.S.
B.P.S.

Appeal of Program
Small classes; more personalized curriculum.

Barry University
Mrs. Joanne Suarez, Coordinator of Admissions
11425 NE 2nd Avenue
Miami Shores, FL 33161
Phone: (305) 899-3318
Toll free: (800) 945-2279
Fax: (305) 899-3346
Founded: 1940
Accrediting Agency: Southern Association
Number of students: 7,500
Number of adult students: 2,000
Representative Degrees

B.P.S.	Business
B.P.S.	Personal Financial Planning
B.P.S.	Health Services Administration
B.P.S.	Human Resource Management
B.P.S.	Management Information Systems

Appeal of Program
Credit awarded for college-level learning from work experience (portfolio); four 10-week terms per year.

Bartlesville Wesleyan College
Mr. Paul Likens, Marketer
2201 Silver Lake Road
Bartlesville, OK 74006
Phone: (918) 335-6259
Toll free: (800) 375-4647
Fax: (918) 335-6244
Founded: 1910
Accrediting Agency: North Central Association
Number of students: 508
Number of adult students: 95

Representative Degrees

B.S. Management of Human Resources

Appeal of Program

Shortened time; convenient location; one night a week.

Bellarmine College

Mrs. Kendra Chancellor, Director of Nontraditional Student Recruitment
Office of Continuing Studies
2001 Newburg Road
Louisville, KY 40205
Phone: (502) 452-8155
Toll free: (800) 274-4723
Fax: (502) 452-8203
Founded: 1950
Accrediting Agency: Southern Association
Number of students: 2,414
Number of adult students: 1,150

Representative Degrees

B.S. Nursing
Weekend format available only to RNs who want to complete the BSN.

B.S. Computer Information Systems

B.S. Management Information Systems
Accelerated courses offered in summer.

B.S. Computer Engineering
Accelerated courses offered in summer

B.A. Communications

Appeal of Program

Phone registration; evening and weekend courses; small class size; deferred payment options for college credit.

Berean College

Dr. Joe Nicholson, Academic Dean
1445 Boonville Avenue
Springfield, MO 65802
Phone: (417) 862-2781
Toll free: (800) 443-1083

Fax: (417) 862-1447
Founded: 1948
Accrediting Agency: Distance Education & Training Council
Number of students: 6,000
Number of adult students: 6,000

Representative Degrees

B.A. Bible and Theology
Students proceed at their own pace.

B.A. Ministerial Studies

B.A. Christian Education
Students proceed at their own pace.

B.A. Christian Counseling
Students proceed at their own pace.

B.A. Religious Studies
Students proceed at their own pace.

Appeal of Program

Student proceed at their own pace and study during the hours of their choice. Berean College is a distance education college with rolling enrollment—no beginning or ending terms. Students can begin or graduate at any time.

Bethel College

Mr. Wayne Gerber, Assistant Dean, Adult Programs
1001 W. McKinley Avenue
Mishawaka, IN 46545
Phone: (219) 257-3353
Toll free: (800) 422-4251
Fax: (219) 257-3357
Founded: 1947
Accrediting Agency: North Central Association
Number of students: 1,200
Number of adult students: 500

Representative Degrees

B.A. Bible and Ministry

B.S./B.A. Organizational Management

B.S. Computer Information Systems Management
62 semester hours required for admission to this degree-completion program.

A.A.　　　Early Childhood Education
A.A.　　　Writing

Appeal of Program

Accelerated courses; simplified admissions and registration; and personal attention.

Bethel College

Mr. Michael Lamb, Director of Admissions
300 E. 27th St.
N. Newton, KS 67117
Phone: (316) 283-2500
Toll free: (800) 522-1887
Fax: (316) 284-5286
Founded: 1887
Accrediting Agency: North Central Association
Number of students: 645
Number of adult students:

Representative Degrees

B.A.　　　Nursing
　　　　　62 semester hours required for
　　　　　admission to this degree-
　　　　　completion program.

Appeal of Program

Small classes.

Bluffton College

Betty Kurtz, Assistant Dean for Continuing
　Studies
Office of Continuing Studies
280 W. College Avenue
Bluffton, OH 45817
Phone: (419) 358-3311
Toll free:
Fax: (419) 358-3232
Founded: 1899
Accrediting Agency: North Central Association
Number of students: 900
Number of adult students:

Representative Degrees

B.A.　　　Organizational Management
　　　　　Degree-completion program for
　　　　　students with 60 semester hours
　　　　　or more.
B.A.　　　Business Administration
B.A.　　　Accounting

　　　　　2+2 degree-completion program
　　　　　for those who have associate
　　　　　degree.
B.A.　　　Early Childhood Education
　　　　　2+2 degree-completion program
　　　　　for those who have associate
　　　　　degree.
B.A.　　　Social Work
　　　　　2+2 degree-completion program
　　　　　for those who have associate
　　　　　degree.

Appeal of Program

Accelerated schedule; classes one night a week; mixture of full-time faculty and academically qualified practitioners teaching in the program; responsive to student input; delivery of textbooks and business office correspondence to classroom.

Boise State University

Ms. JoAnn Fenner, Program Developer
Division of Continuing Studies
1910 University Drive
Boise, ID 83725
Phone: (208) 385-4457
Toll free: (800) 824-7017
Fax: (208) 385-3346
Founded: 1932
Accrediting Agency: Northwest Association
Number of students: 15,000
Number of adult students: 13,500

Representative Degrees

M.S.　　　Instructional and Performance
　　　　　Technology
　　　　　This is a fully accredited, totally
　　　　　nonresident master's degree
　　　　　program.

Appeal of Program

Diverse group of students from all professions and geographic regions enrich the interaction. Convenience. Can interact 24 hours a day.

Boston College

James Woods, SJ
Evening College
Chestnut Hill, MA 02167

Phone: (617) 552-3900
Toll free:
Fax: (617) 552-3199
Founded: 1863
Accrediting Agency: New England Association
Number of students: 14,500
Number of adult students: 1,500
Representative Degrees
    A.B.   Liberal Arts (all majors)
Appeal of Program
Atmosphere.

Briar Cliff College

Dr. Sean Warner, Associate Dean
3303 Rebecca Street
Sioux City, IA 51104
Phone: (712) 279-1629
Toll free: (800) 662-3303
Fax: (712) 279-1698
Founded: 1930
Accrediting Agency: North Central Association
Number of students: 1,158
Number of adult students: 380
Representative Degrees
    B.A.   Business Administration
    B.A.   Human Resource Management
    B.A.   Accounting
    B.S.N.   Nursing
Appeal of Program
Flexibility; location; cost.

Burlington College

David Zoy, Director of Independent Degree
   Program
Burlington College
95 North Avenue
Burlington, VT 05401
Phone: (802) 862-9616
Toll free: (800) 862-9616
Fax: (802) 658-007
Founded: 1972
Accrediting Agency: New England Association
Number of students: 200
Number of adult students: 25

Representative Degrees
    B.A.   Psychology
                  Four-day residential retreat
                  followed by a semester of work
                  study.
    B.A.   Transpersonal Psychology
    B.A.   Humanities
                  Four-day residential retreat
                  followed by a semester of study.
    B.A.   Writing and Literature
                  Four-day residential retreat
                  followed by a semester of study.
    B.A.   Human Services
Appeal of Program
Flexible; challenging; individualized; low
residency; frequent contact; independent study.

Caldwell College

Ms. Lisa DiBisceglie, Director of Continuing
   Education
9 Ryerson Avenue
Caldwell, NJ 07006
Phone: (201) 228-4424
Toll free:
Fax: (201) 403-8042
Founded: 1939
Accrediting Agency: Middle States Association
Number of students: 1,620
Number of adult students: 900
Representative Degrees
    B.A.   Psychology
    B.A.   Religious Studies
    B.A.   Sociology
    M.A.   Curriculum Instruction
    B.S.   Business Administration
Appeal of Program
Flexibility; accessibility; safety; cost.

California Baptist College

Mr. Brian Carroll, Director/Professor
Evening College
8432 Magnolia Avenue
Riverside, CA 92504
Phone: (909) 689-5771
Toll free: (800) 782-3382

Fax: (909) 351-1808
Founded: 1950
Accrediting Agency: Western Association
Number of students: 875
Number of adult students: 147
Representative Degrees
B.S./B.B.A. Business Administration
B.S. Political Science
B.S. Psychology
M.S. Counseling Psychology
Appeal of Program
Degree-completion programs are structured and delivered in 16 months.

California State University, Chico
Ms. Leslie Wright, Associate Dean
Center for Regional and Continuing Education
California State University, Chico
Chico, CA 95929
Phone: (916) 898-6105
Toll free:
Fax: (916) 898-4020
Founded: 1887
Accrediting Agency: Western Association
Number of students: 12,000
Number of adult students: NA
Representative Degrees
B.S. Social Science
B.S. Sociology
B.S. Liberal Studies
Appeal of Program
Students attending off-campus learning centers can use a credit card to order books by phone. Courses broadcast to regional learning centers in Northern California.

California State University, Dominguez Hills
Dr. Arthur Harshman, HUX Coordinator
190 E. Victoria St.
HUX Program SACII 2126
Carson, CA 90747
Phone: (310) 516-3743
Toll free:
Fax: (310) 516-4399

Founded:
Accrediting Agency: Western Association
Number of students: 5,000
Number of adult students: 800
Representative Degrees
M.A. Humanities

California State University, Sacramento
Nancy Lewis, Director of Re-Entry Services
6000 J Street
Sacramento, CA 95819
Phone: (916) 278-6750
Toll free:
Fax:
Founded: 1947
Accrediting Agency: Western Association
Number of students: 23,000
Number of adult students:
Representative Degrees
PACE program currently under development. The Re-Entry Services department provides assistance and advocacy for adult students. Experiential learning portfolio for credit.

Calumet College of St. Joseph
Mr. Roy Scheive, Admissions Counselor
2400 New York Avenue
Whiting, IN 46394
Phone: (219) 473-4226
Toll free:
Fax: (219) 473-4259
Founded:
Accrediting Agency: North Central Association
Number of students: 1,100
Number of adult students: 120
Representative Degrees
B.S. Organization Management
Students meet one night a week for four hours for 57 weeks.
Appeal of Program
Students get their degree in 15 months and can get college credit for life experience.

Calvin College

Dr. Shirley Roels, Director of Degree Completion
  Programs
Calvin College
1801 E. Beltline, S.E.
Grand Rapids, MI 49546
Phone: (616) 957-6555
Toll free:
Fax: (616) 957-8551
Founded: 1876
Accrediting Agency: North Central Association
Number of students: 3,793
Number of adult students: 49

Representative Degrees

B.A.	Organizational Leadership Required courses can be supplemented with graduation credits by correspondence courses and life-experience portfolio.

Appeal of Program

Strong coverage of many management functions.
Integration of an applied research project into
the program. Strong emphasis on applied
computer and statistical information skills.
Distinctly Christian value-based teaching.

Cambridge College

Mr. Bruce Grigsby, Director of Enrollment
  Services
1000 Massachusetts Ave.
Cambridge, MA 02138
Phone: (617) 868-1000
Toll free: (800) 877-GRAD
Fax: (617) 349-3545
Founded:
Accrediting Agency: New England Association
Number of students: 1,600
Number of adult students: 1,600

Representative Degrees

B.A.	Counseling
M.Ed.	Education or Counseling
M.M.O.	Management

Appeal of Program

Some off-campus sites. Average age of graduate
students is 39; average age of undergraduate
students is 33.

Campbell University

Mr. David Heinzman, Director of Continuing
  Education
P.O. Box 1135
Buies Creek, NC 27506
Phone: (910) 893-1200
Toll free: (800) 334-4111
Fax:
Founded: 1887
Accrediting Agency: Southern Association
Number of students: 6,650
Number of adult students: 1,650

Representative Degrees

B.A.S.	Bachelor of Applied Science
B.H.S.	Bachelor of Health Science
B.B.A.	Business, Accounting, Computer
B.S.	Social Sciences

Appeal of Program

Credit for nontraditional education; evening
classes; accelerated terms.

Campbellsville College

Dr. Robert Clark, Vice President for Academic
  Affairs
200 West College Street
Campbellsville, KY 42718
Phone: (502) 465-8158
Toll free:
Fax: (502) 789-5020
Founded: 1906
Accrediting Agency: Southern Association
Number of students: 1,260
Number of adult students: 100

Representative Degrees

A.S.	Business Administration
B.S.	Organizational Administration
M.A.Ed.	Education Curriculum and Instruction Nights and Saturday.
B.S./B.A.	Christian Ministries During the day in Louisville, Kentucky.

Appeal of Program

Only 25% of the classes must be taken on the
campus.

Cardinal Stritch College

Dr. Arthur Wasserman, Associate Dean
6801 N. Yates Road
Milwaukee, WI 53217
Phone: (414) 352-5400
Toll free: (800) 347-8822
Fax: (414) 351-0257
Founded:
Accrediting Agency: North Central Association
Number of students: 5,100
Number of adult students: 2,250
Representative Degrees

Associate	Business
Bachelor's	Business Management
Bachelor's	Business Administration
Master's	Business Administration
Master's	Management

Appeal of Program
Accelerated format. Most major courses are completed on same night of the week with same group of students, with instructor changing every five to six weeks.

Cedar Crest College

Ms. Ann DeLazard, Director of Center for
    Lifelong Learning
100 College Dr.
Allentown, PA 18104
Phone: (610) 437-4471
Toll free: (800) 360-1222
Fax: (610) 740-3786
Founded: 1867
Accrediting Agency: Middle States Association
Number of students: 1,765
Number of adult students: 900
Representative Degrees
All degrees are open to adults.
Appeal of Program
User-friendly staff and faculty.

Centenary College

Dr. Tom Brunner, Associate V.P. Academic Affairs
400 Jefferson Street
Hackettstown, NJ 07840
Phone: (908) 852-1400

Toll free:
Fax: (908) 852-3454
Founded: 1867
Accrediting Agency: Middle States Association
Number of students: 1,000
Number of adult students: 950
Representative Degrees

| B.S./B.A. | Various programs available through night courses. |

Central Michigan University

College of Extended Learning
128 Rowe Hall
Mt. Pleasant, MI 48859
Phone: (517) 774-3865
Toll free: (800) 950-1144
Fax: (517) 774-3542
Founded: 1892
Accrediting Agency: North Central Association
Number of students: 17,000
Number of adult students: 10,000
Representative Degrees

M.S.A.	General Administration
M.S.A.	Human Resources Administration
M.S.A.	Health Services Administration
M.S.A.	International Administration
B.S.	Community Development Correspondence courses available to Michigan residents only.

Appeal of Program
Entire program offered; convenient weekend format, toll-free library services; affordable tuition; prior learning assessment; relevant transfer credit; distinguished faculty.

Chaminade University

Mr. Skip Lee, Director of OCEP
3140 Waialae Avenue
Chaminade University
Honolulu, HI 96816
Phone: (808) 735-4851
Toll free: (800) 735-3733
Fax: (808) 739-4647

Founded: 1955
Accrediting Agency: Western Association
Number of students: 2,350
Number of adult students: 1,650
Representative Degrees

B.A.	Psychology
B.B.A.	Accounting, Management, Marketing
B.A.	Biology
B.S.	Biology
B.S.	Education

Appeal of Program
Flexibility; accelerated sessions; number of
degrees available.

Charter Oak State College

Mr. Paul Morganti, Director of Admissions
Charter Oak State College
66 Cedar Street
Newington, CT 06111
Phone: (203) 666-4595
Toll free:
Fax: (203) 666-4852
Founded: 1973
Accrediting Agency: New England Association
Number of students: 1,215
Number of adult students: 1,215
Representative Degrees
The college awards a variety of individually
designed degrees.
Appeal of Program
COSC does not limit the number of credits that
can be transferred from other regionally accred-
ited institutions. Students often can complete a
degree faster at COSC than elsewhere. Flexibility
on choice of credit-earning options. Cost is less.

Chicago State University

Mr. Humberto Rivera, Director of Nontraditional
    Programs
9501 South King Dr., Library 326
Chicago, IL 60628
Phone: (312) 995-2457
Toll free:
Fax: (312) 995-2457

Founded: 1867
Accrediting Agency: North Central Association
Number of students: 10,000
Number of adult students: 600
Representative Degrees

B.A.	Board of Governors Degree Program provides life experience credit opportunities.
Bachelor's	University Without Walls provides individualized degree programs through a variety of traditional and nontraditional methods.

Appeal of Program
The prior learning option.

College of Mount Saint Vincent

Ms. Lisa Fermicola, Director of Adult Education
6301 Riverdale Avenue
Riverdale, NY 10471
Phone: (718) 405-3322
Toll free:
Fax: (718) 601-6392
Founded: 1847
Accrediting Agency: Middle States Association
Number of students: 1,300
Number of adult students: 580
Representative Degrees

B.A.	Economics
B.A.	Communications
B.S.	Nursing
	For registered nurses.
B.A.	Humanities majors
B.A.	Business

Appeal of Program
Adults can take courses days, evenings, Saturdays; transfer credit policies; location of campus
(proximity to New York City, Westchester,
Northern New Jersey); credit for life experience.

College of New Rochelle Graduate School

Dr. Laura Ellis, Graduate Dean
29 Castle Place
New Rochelle, NY 10805

Phone: (914) 654-5320
Toll free:
Fax: (914) 654-5554
Founded: 1904
Accrediting Agency: Middle States Association
Number of students: 1,000
Number of adult students: 1,000

Representative Degrees

M.S.	Education-Elementary; Reading; Gifted; TESL; Special Education
M.S.	Studio Art; Art Therapy
M.A.	Art Education
M.S.	Career Development; Guidance & Counseling; Gerontology; School Psychology

Appeal of Program

Small class size; attention to individuals; strong academic programs.

College of Notre Dame of Maryland

Mr. Harold Jopp, Jr., Director, Graduate Studies
4701 North Charles Street
Baltimore, MD 21210
Phone: (410) 532-5316
Toll free:
Fax: (410) 435-5937
Founded: 1896
Accrediting Agency: Middle States Association
Number of students: 3,000
Number of adult students: 2,200

Representative Degrees

M.A.	Leadership in Teaching Concentrations: TESOL, Mathematics, English, History, Latin. Some evening courses available.
M.A.	Adulthood and Aging
M.A.	Liberal Studies
M.A.	Management Concentrations: Communications, Health Care Admin., Human Resource Mgt., Corporate Mgt., Educational Admin. Some evening courses available.
M.A.	Teaching MAT certification: Secondary Ed., Elementary Ed., Early

Childhood. Some evening courses available.

Appeal of Program

Flexible schedule on weekends and evenings; classes meet ten times a semester.

College of Notre Dame—Weekend Classes

Ms. Bernadette Brenner, Acting Director
Weekend College
4701 North Charles Street
Baltimore, MD 21210
Phone: (410) 532-5500
Toll free:
Fax: (410) 435-5937
Founded: 1896
Accrediting Agency: Middle States Association
Number of students: 3,000
Number of adult students: 2,200

Representative Degrees

B.A.	Human Services Specialty areas: Administration, Direct Service.
B.A.	Liberal Arts
B.A.	Elementary Education Final semester of student teaching done on weekdays.
B.A.	Religious Studies
B.A.	Business Emphasis in Management, Finance, Accounting, Marketing, Human Resource Management.

Appeal of Program

Flexible schedule on weekends. Classes meet five or ten times a semester; adults do guided independent study.

College of Saint Mary

Mrs. Sheila Haggas, Vice President, Enrollment
   Services
1901 S. 72 Street
Omaha, NE 68124
Phone: (402) 399-2407
Toll free: (800) 926-5534
Fax: (402) 399-2341

Founded: 1923
Accrediting Agency: North Central Association
Number of students: 1,168
Number of adult students: 500
Representative Degrees

B.S.	Accounting
	Associate degree also available in this area.
B.S.	Business
B.A.	Communications
	Associate degree also available in this area.
B.S.	Computer Information Management
B.A.	Computer Graphics

Appeal of Program
Flexibility for scheduling (three formats: day, evening, and weekend); ample free parking; convenient hours.

College of St. Francis

Dr. Lyle Hicks, Director, Adult and Continuing
  Education
500 N. Wilcox Street
Joliet, IL 60435
Phone: (815) 740-3600
Toll free:
Fax: (815) 740-4285
Founded: 1920
Accrediting Agency: North Central Association
Number of students:
Number of adult students:
Representative Degrees

| B.S. | Professional Arts |
| | Specializations: Applied Organizational Management, Human Resource Management. |

Appeal of Program
Adult student services; convenience of class schedule; modular format.

College of St. Scholastica

Ms. Becky Urbanski-Junkert, V.P. Admissions and
  Financial Aid
1200 Kenwood Ave.

Duluth, MN 55811
Phone: (218) 723-6046
Toll free: (800) 447-5444
Fax: (218) 723-6290
Founded: 1912
Accrediting Agency: North Central Association
Number of students: 1,849
Number of adult students:
Representative Degrees

B.A.	All
	At night, primarily Management, Behavioral Arts and Sciences, Nursing, and Media Generalist.
M.A.	All

Colorado State University

Mr. Armando Pares, Assistant Director
Continuing Education—Spruce Hall
Colorado State University
Ft. Collins, CO 80523
Phone: (303) 491-5288
Toll free:
Fax: (303) 491-7885
Founded: 1865
Accrediting Agency: North Central Association
Number of students: 21,000
Number of adult students: 500
Representative Degrees

M.B.A.	Business Administration
	Executive M.B.A. in Denver.
M.B.A.	Business Administration
M.S.	Engineering, Computer Science SURGE.
M.S.	Human Resource Development SURGE.

Appeal of Program
SURGE is a video-based program delivered to 200 class sites nationwide. Convenience of videotape delivery; EMBA-downtown Denver location; intensive format.

Columbia Union College Adult Evening Program

Dr. Don Vanoman, Director
7600 Flower Ave.

Tukana Park, MO 20912
Phone: (301) 891-4138
Toll free:
Fax: (301) 891-4023
Founded: 1983
Accrediting Agency: Middle States Association
Number of students: 900
Number of adult students: 350

Representative Degrees

B.S.	Business Administration
B.S.O.M.	Organizational Management
B.S.H.C.	Health Care Administration
B.S.I.S.	Information Systems Management

Appeal of Program
Eighteen months to complete B.S. degree; guaranteed classes; individual counseling/ advising. Friendly, caring environment; one night per week, same night, same group during 18 months.

Concordia University Wisconsin

Harold Wolf, Adult Learning Center
8465 Keystone Crossing, Suite 195
Indianapolis, IN 46240
Phone: (317) 259-5090
Toll free:
Fax: (317) 259-5095
Founded: 1881
Accrediting Agency: North Central Association
Number of students: 3,149
Number of adult students: 1,521

Representative Degrees

B.A.	Management/Communication Emphasis: Liberal Arts Pending.
M.A.	Individualized Masters
A.A.	Management/Communication Telecourses available (VCR/ correspondence) for additional credits.
B.A.	Management/Communication Telecourses available for additional credits.
B.A.	Management/Communication Emphasis: Health Care Pending.

Appeal of Program
Accelerated; one night a week; one subject at a time; small classes (20 or fewer); and instructors who work full-time and teach in their area of expertise.

Cornerstone College

Dr. John Lillis, Dean of Adult and Continuing Education
1001 East Beltline NE
Grand Rapids, MI 49505
Phone: (616) 285-9448
Toll free: (800) 968-4722
Fax: (616) 285-1528
Founded: 1941
Accrediting Agency: North Central Association
Number of students: 800
Number of adult students: 100

Representative Degrees

B.A.	Organizational Leadership

Appeal of Program
Accelerated; experiential learning; convenience; adult-oriented curriculum.

Covenant College

Mr. Dino Smith, Associate Director of Quest
Quest Program
409 Chestnut Street
Suite A-110
Chattanooga, TN 37402
Phone: (615) 265-7784
Toll free:
Fax: (615) 265-2703
Founded: 1955
Accrediting Agency: Southern Association
Number of students: 720
Number of adult students: 150

Representative Degrees

B.S.	Organizational Management 32-semester-hour accelerated senior year. We offer an experiential learning component that allows job training and life experience to count as credit.

Appeal of Program
Classes meet one night a week for four hours; program is designed to take 14 months.

Dallas Baptist University

Dr. Mike Rosato, Associate Dean
College of Adult Education
3000 Mountain Creek Parkway
Dallas, TX 75211
Phone: (214) 333-5337
Toll free: (800) 460-8188
Fax: (214) 333-5558
Founded: 1965
Accrediting Agency: Southern Association
Number of students: 2,989
Number of adult students: 1,455

Representative Degrees

B.A.B.A.*	Accounting
B.A.B.A.	Aviation Management
B.A.B.A.	Business Administration
B.A.B.A.	Finance
B.A.B.A.	Fire Management

*Bachelor of Applied Business Administration

Appeal of Program

Students can receive up to 30 hours of college credit for knowledge and skills obtained through life and work experience.

DePaul University

Mr. Joseph Regan,
1 East Jackson
Chicago, IL 60604
Phone:
Toll free: (800) 4-DEPAUL
Fax: (800) 362-5745
Founded: 1898
Accrediting Agency: North Central Association
Number of students: 16,747
Number of adult students: 1,981

Representative Degrees

B.S.	Accounting
B.S.	Computer Science
B.A.	Various—through School for New Learning
M.B.A.	Accounting
M.S.	Computer Science

Appeal of Program

DePaul's academic standing; multicampus locations (five campuses); evening and weekend class availability; and small class size.

Dordt College

Dr. Jack Fennema, Director of Graduate Education
498 Fourth Avenue, NE
Sioux Center, IA 51250
Phone: (712) 722-6236
Toll free: 800-34-DORDT
Fax: (712) 722-1198
Founded: 1955
Accrediting Agency: North Central Association
Number of students: 1,100
Number of adult students: 20

Representative Degrees

M.Ed.	Curriculum and Instruction Summer courses available.

Appeal of Program

Completion in three summers; minimum time on campus.

Drexel University

Dr. Rose Ketterer, Associate Dean for Evening Programs
4020 MacAlister Hall
33rd and Chestnut Street
Philadelphia, PA 19104
Phone: (215) 895-2159
Toll free: 800-2-DREXEL
Fax: (215) 895-4988
Founded: 1891
Accrediting Agency: Middle States Association
Number of students: 10,000
Number of adult students: 2,000

Representative Degrees

B.S.	Chemistry
B.S.	Computer Science
B.S.	Mathematics
B.S.	Physics and Atmospheric Science
B.S.	Chemical Engineering Fully accredited by the accrediting board for engineering and technology (ABET).

Appeal of Program

The variety of programs offered; the completion of programs entirely in the evening; and adjunct faculty who bring vast and varied experience from industry to the classroom.

Drury College

Dr. Sue Rollins, Assoc. Dean of the College/
   Director of Continuing Education
900 N. Benton
Springfield, MO 65802
Phone: (417) 873-7301
Toll free:
Fax: (417) 873-7529
Founded: 1873
Accrediting Agency: North Central Association
Number of students: 3,800
Number of adult students: 2,000
Representative Degrees

B.S.	History
B.S.	Psychology
B.S.	Sociology
B.S./A.S.	Accounting

Appeal of Program
Quality; rigor; personalized approach.

Eastern College

Mr. Shawn Wolf, Director of Marketing
10 Fairview Drive
St. Davids, PA 19087
Phone: (610) 341-1398
Toll free: (800) 732-7669
Fax: (610) 341-1468
Founded: 1952
Accrediting Agency: Middle States Association
Number of students: 2,000
Number of adult students: 550
Representative Degrees

B.A.	Organization Management
M.B.A.	Business Administration
B.S.	Nursing

Appeal of Program
15-month completion format; cohort learning
model.

Eastern Illinois University

Dr. Kaye Woodward, Director
Board of Governors Degree Program
205 Blair Hall
Charleston, IL 61920
Phone: (217) 581-5618

Toll free:
Fax: (217) 581-6697
Founded: 1895
Accrediting Agency: North Central Association
Number of students: 11,000
Number of adult students: 1,200
Representative Degrees
   B.A.
Appeal of Program
Flexibility; assessment of prior learning;
availability of classes.

Eastern Mennonite University

Mr. Daryl Peifer, Director
1200 Park Road
Harrisonburg, VA 22801
Phone: (703) 432-4150
Toll free:
Fax: (703) 432-4444
Founded: 1917
Accrediting Agency: Southern Association
Number of students: 1,000
Number of adult students: 45
Representative Degrees

B.S.	Management and Organizational Development
	Lock-step curriculum/cohort groups.

Appeal of Program
Cohort group; accelerated.

Eastern Nazarene College

Ms. Cheryl Anderson, Marketing Manager
LEAD Program
2 Adams Place
Quincy, MA 02169
Phone: (617) 849-0225
Toll free: 800-439-LEAD
Fax: (617) 849-2911
Founded: 1910
Accrediting Agency: New England Association
Number of students: 1,300
Number of adult students: 600
Representative Degrees

B.S.B.A.*	Business Administration

*Bachelor of Science in Business Administration
Appeal of Program
Accessibility; convenience; structure; adult-learner-oriented; accelerated.

Eastern Oregon State College
Dr. Joseph Hart, Director,
Distance Learning/External Degree
Division of Extended Programs
1410 L Avenue
La Grande, OR 97850
Phone: (503) 962-3378
Toll free: (800) 547-8887
Fax: (503) 962-3627
Founded: 1929
Accrediting Agency: Northwest Association
Number of students: 1,800
Number of adult students: 600
Representative Degrees

B.A.	Liberal Studies Requires some on-campus attendance.
B.S.	Liberal Studies
M.A.	Master's in Teacher Education Requires internship placement.

Appeal of Program
High-quality instruction.

Eastern Washington University
John Neace, Director, Center for Liberal Studies
209 Har Hall, Mail Stop 14
Cheney, WA 99004
Phone: (509) 359-2402
Toll free:
Fax:
Founded: 1882
Accrediting Agency: Northwest Association
Number of students: 8,500
Number of adult students: 400
Representative Degrees

B.A.	Liberal Studies Prior learning assessment program.
B.A.	Communication Studies
M.A.	Public Administration

Appeal of Program
Night and weekend courses; prior learning credit.

Edinboro University of Pennsylvania
Ms. Jane Springer, Coordinator
Office of Adult Information Services (OASIS)
Advising and Career Services
Edinboro, PA 16444
Phone: (814) 732-2701
Toll free:
Fax:
Founded: 1857
Accrediting Agency: Middle States Association
Number of students: 7,484
Number of adult students: 1,391
Representative Degrees

B.S.	Business Administration/ Accounting Many adult students can attend day classes only.
B.S. A.S.	Elementary Education Computer Science Many adult students can attend day classes only.
B.A.	Sociology Many adult students can attend day classes only.
B.S.	Mentally Physically Handi-capped Many adult students can attend day classes only.

Appeal of Program
Priority prescheduling; life-experience credit; CLEP examinations; special weekend courses for adults (bowling, golf, marketing).

Embry-Riddle Aeronautical University
Mr. Thomas Pettit, Director, Department of
  Independent Studies
600 South Clyde Morris Boulevard
Daytona Beach, FL 32114
Phone: (904) 226-6397
Toll free: (800) 866-6271

Fax: (904) 226-6949
Founded: 1926
Accrediting Agency: Southern Association
Number of students: 19,000
Number of adult students: 3,000
Representative Degrees

B.S.	Bachelor of Science in Professional Aeronautics
B.S.	Bachelor of Science in Aviation Business Administration
A.S.	Associate of Science in Professional Aeronautics
A.S.	Associate of Science in Aviation Business Administration

Appeal of Program
No on-campus time requirement.

Empire State College, SUNY
Mr. Martin Thorsland, Director of Admissions
2 Union Avenue
Saratoga Springs, NY 12866
Phone: (518) 587-2100
Toll free:
Fax:
Founded: 1971
Accrediting Agency: Middle States Association
Number of students: 6,500
Number of adult students: 6,500
Representative Degrees

A.A.	Business, Community & Human Services, and Interdisciplinary Degrees are available through correspondence (mail and phone) from the Center for Distance Learning.
B.A.	Business, Community & Human Services, and Interdisciplinary
B.A.	Several areas of liberal arts and sciences Available in mentor-guided independent study program at many learning centers throughout the state.
M.A.	Liberal Studies, Business & Policy Studies, Labor & Policy Studies

Available involving courses
through residency-based,
directed independent study.
Appeal of Program
Flexibility; individualized degree program.

Fairleigh Dickinson University
Dr. Bill Clutter, Dean of Continuing Education
1000 River Road
Dickinson Hall (H311)
Teaneck, NJ 07666
Phone: (201) 692-6500
Toll free: (800) 338-3887
Fax: (201) 692-6505
Founded: 1942
Accrediting Agency: Middle States Association
Number of students: 11,000
Number of adult students:
Representative Degrees

B.A.	General Studies New program: student designs the major.

Appeal of Program
Flexibility to design the program; minimum of 120 credits for degree; a variety of delivery formats on and off campus.

Ferris State University
Mr. Nick Coso, Acting Director of Continuing Education
410 Oak Street
113 Alumni Building
Big Rapids, MI 49307
Phone: (616) 592-3809
Toll free: (800) 562-9130
Fax: (616) 592-3539
Founded: 1884
Accrediting Agency: North Central Association
Number of students: 9,100
Number of adult students: 1,050
Representative Degrees

A.A.S.	Health Information Technology
B.S.	Nursing
B.S.	Accountancy
B.S.	Business Administration

M.S.   Occupational Education

Appeal of Program
Location and time of classes.

The Fielding Institute
Mrs. Sylvia Williams, Director of Admissions
2112 Santa Barbara St.
Santa Barbara, CA 93105
Phone: (805) 687-1099
Toll free:
Fax: (805) 687-9793
Founded: 1974
Accrediting Agency: Western Association
Number of students: 850
Number of adult students:
Representative Degrees

Ph.D.	Psychology Combination of residential events and distance learning format.
Ph.D.	Human Organization and Development Combination of residential events and distance learning format.

Appeal of Program
Students do not have to leave their communities and personal and professional responsibilities.

Fontbonne College
Dr. Robert Ratcliffe, Dean
6800 Wydonn Boulevard
St. Louis, MO 63105
Phone: (314) 889-4587
Toll free:
Fax: (314) 863-0917
Founded: 1923
Accrediting Agency: North Central Association
Number of students: 1,900
Number of adult students: 900
Representative Degrees

M.B.A.	Business Administration
B.B.A.	Business Administration
M.A.Ed.	Reading
M.A.Ed.	Early Childhood Administration

Appeal of Program
Less than two-year guaranteed degree sequence on same nights/weekly. Guaranteed tuition and fee level for entire two-year sequence. Approximately eight degree program start dates per calendar year. Faculty are full-time professionals in areas they teach.

Fordham University—Ignatius College
Ms. Kathleen Caltagirone, Associate Director of Admissions
Dealy Hall, Room 101
Fordham University
Bronx, NY 10458
Phone: (718) 817-3720
Toll free: (800) FORDHAM
Fax: (718) 367-9404
Founded: 1966
Accrediting Agency: Middle States Association
Number of students: 15,000
Number of adult students: 500
Representative Degrees

B.A.	Economics
B.A.	English
B.A.	Fine Arts
B.A.	History
B.A.	Political Science

Appeal of Program
Strong Jesuit tradition; program designed to "service" evening students (scheduling, advisement availability, support services); association with the Fordham reputation.

Franklin Pierce College
Lou D'Allesandro, Vice President for Continuing Education
20 Cotton Road
Nashua, NH 03063
Phone: (603) 889-6146
Toll free: (800) 325-1090
Fax: (603) 889-3795
Founded: 1962
Accrediting Agency: New England Association
Number of students: 4,250

Number of adult students: 3,000
Representative Degrees

B.S.	Accounting
B.S./A.A.	Management
B.S./A.A.	General Studies

Fresno Pacific College

Mr. Dennis Langhofer, Director
Center for Degree Completion
1717 South Chestnut Avenue
Fresno, CA 93702
Phone: (209) 453-2288
Toll free: (800) 660-6089
Fax: (209) 453-2003
Founded: 1944
Accrediting Agency: Western Association
Number of students: 1,500
Number of adult students: 125
Representative Degrees

B.A.   Management and Organizational
Development
Classes meet one night per week,
four hours per night, for 13
months.

Appeal of Program
Working adults can complete their bachelor of
arts degree in 13 months. Credit is given for prior
learning. Curriculum is interesting and
challenging. Classes focus on the skills that
employers prefer: management, leadership, and
communication.

George Fox College

Director of Admissions
414 North Meridian, Box #6099
Newberg, OR 97132
Phone: (503) 538-8383
Toll free: (800) 632-0921
Fax: (503) 537-3834
Founded: 1891
Accrediting Agency: Northwest Association
Number of students: 1,650
Number of adult students: 300
Representative Degrees

B.A.   Management of Human Resources

15 months (Junior or Senior
year); 30 semester hours of life
experience credit can be granted
toward bachelor's degree.

M.B.A.   Business Administration

Appeal of Program
Graduate: 24-month format; cohort model, with
work teams; full-time faculty; convenience of
location; and M.B.A. with a management focus.

Goddard College

Ellen Codling, Associate Director of Admissions
Goddard College
Rt. 2
Plainfield, VT 05667
Phone: (802) 454-8311
Toll free: (800) 468-4888
Fax: (802) 454-8017
Founded: 1938
Accrediting Agency: New England Association
Number of students: 500
Number of adult students: 350
Representative Degrees

B.A.   Self-designed major
One-week residency required
each semester.

M.A.   Self-designed major

M.A.   Education
One-week residency required
each semester.

M.A.   Psychology and Counseling
One-week residency required
each semester.

M.A.   Social Ecology
One-week residency required
each semester.

Appeal of Program
All programs individually designed by student.

Goshen College

Dr. Jon Swanson, Director of Degree Completion
Programs
1700 South Main Street
Goshen, IN 46526
Phone: (219) 535-7464
Toll free:

Fax: (219) 535-7293
Founded: 1894
Accrediting Agency: North Central Association
Number of students: 1,000
Number of adult students: 100
Representative Degrees
  B.S.   Organizational Management
  B.S.   Nursing
Appeal of Program
Institutional quality; location; faculty.

Governors State University

Mr. William Craig, Admissions Officer
University Park, IL 60466
Phone: (708) 534-4490
Toll free:
Fax: (708) 534-8951
Founded: 1969
Accrediting Agency: North Central Association
Number of students: 5,700
Number of adult students: 500
Representative Degrees
  B.A.   The Board of Governors Bach-
           elor of Arts
           A nontraditional degree program
           without a set curriculum.
Appeal of Program
Ability to match present interests with previous
academic work.

Grand Canyon University

Dr. Charles Maxson, Vice President for Academic
  Affairs
3300 W. Camelback Road
Phoenix, AZ 85017
Phone: (602) 589-2531
Toll free: (800) 800-9776
Fax: (602) 589-2534
Founded: 1949
Accrediting Agency: North Central Association
Number of students: 2,100
Number of adult students: 300
Representative Degrees
  B.S.   Organizational Management
           Pending North Central Associa-
           tion approval.

  M.A.T.   Teaching
Appeal of Program
(As proposed to North Central Association)
Evening/weekend hours; location near central
business district.

Grantham College of Engineering

Mr. Philip Grantham, Vice President/Director of
  Student Services
Grantham College Road
Slidell, LA 70469
Phone: (504) 649-4191
Toll free: (800) 955-2527
Fax: (504) 649-4183
Founded: 1951
Accrediting Agency: Distance Education and
  Training Council
Number of students: 811
Number of adult students: 811
Representative Degrees
  B.S.   Electronics Engineering
           Technology
           Self-paced independent study; no
           residency required.
  B.S.   Computer Engineering Technol-
           ogy
           Self-paced independent study; no
           residency required.
  B.S.   Computer Science
           Self-paced independent study; no
           residency required.
Appeal of Program
Consistent with traditional colleges; education
that students can complete at home or work at
their own pace.

Greenville College

Dr. James Plett, Dean of Academic
  Administration
315 East College Avenue
Greenville, IL 62246
Phone: (618) 664-1840
Toll free:
Fax:
Founded: 1892

Accrediting Agency: North Central Association
Number of students: 850
Number of adult students:
Representative Degrees
B.A. Business Leadership
      Adult degree-completion
      program.

Hamline University
Barbara Coleman, Assistant Dean
Graduate School
1536 Hewitt Avenue
St. Paul, MN 55104
Phone: (612) 641-2900
Toll free: (800) 888-2182
Fax: (612) 641-2987
Founded: 1854
Accrediting Agency: North Central Association
Number of students: 2,500
Number of adult students: 900
Representative Degrees
M.A.L.S. Liberal Arts
M.F.A.   Fine Arts in Writing
M.A.P.A. Public Administration
M.A.Ed.   Education
B.A.   Variety
Appeal of Program
Quality programs aimed at the working adult;
practitioner-based programs; no standardized
testing required for admission.

Hebrew College
Ms. Norma Frankel, Registrar
43 Hawes Street
Brookline, MA 02146
Phone: (617) 232-8710
Toll free:
Fax: (617) 734-9769
Founded: 1921
Accrediting Agency: New England Association
Number of students: 150
Number of adult students: 80
Representative Degrees
M.A.   Judaic Studies
M.J.Ed. Jewish Education

B.J.Ed.   Jewish Education
B.Heb.Lit. Hebrew Literature-Judaic
           Studies
Appeal of Program
Flexible hours; programs tailored to needs of
individual students.

Hofstra University
Ms. Elaine Anton, Senior Assistant Dean
New College
130 Hofstra University
Hempstead, NY 11550
Phone: (516) 463-5820
Toll free: (800) HOFSTRA
Fax: (516) 463-4832
Founded: 1935
Accrediting Agency: Middle States Association
Number of students: 12,000
Number of adult students: 12
Representative Degrees
B.A. Various
B.S. Various
M.A. Interdisciplinary Studies
Appeal of Program
Flexibility; individualized mode of study; limited
residency requirement.

Houghton College
Dr. V. James Mannoia, Jr., Academic Vice
    President
PACE Program
910 Union Road
West Seneca, NY 14224
Phone: (716) 674-6363
Toll free: (800) 777-2556
Fax: (716) 674-6363
Founded: 1883
Accrediting Agency: Middle States Association
Number of students: 1,300
Number of adult students: 150
Representative Degrees
B.S. Organizational Management
      Experiential learning credits,
      military credit, professional
      development, CLEP/DANTES
      testing for credit.

Appeal of Program

Time-shortened (one night per week for 15 months); no examinations (continual assessment); faculty and staff support; predetermined major and minor courses.

Huntington College

Mr. Jeffrey Sherlock, Director, EXCEL Program
2303 College Avenue
Huntington, IN 46750
Phone: (219) 356-7920
Toll free: (800) 600-4888
Fax: (219) 356-9448
Founded: 1897
Accrediting Agency: North Central Association
Number of students:
Number of adult students: 50+

Representative Degrees

B.S.	Organizational Management The EXCEL program is 45 semester hours. With previous college credit, credit for prior learning, and other credits, a student can complete a degree in 18 months.
M.C.M.	Christian Ministry Two-by-three classes meet for two days each month for three consecutive months.
M.E.M.	Educational Ministries Two-by-three classes meet for two days each month for three consecutive months.

Appeal of Program

Study with same adult students in mutually supportive environment throughout 18-month program; once-per-week classes; collaborative seminar format.

Indiana Institute of Technology

Marion Wixted, Associate Director
1600 East Washington Boulevard
Ft Wayne, IN 46803
Phone: (219) 422-5561
Toll free: (800) 937-2IIT

Fax: (219) 422-1518
Founded: 1930
Accrediting Agency: North Central Association
Number of students: 1,450
Number of adult students: 1,000

Representative Degrees

A.S.	Business Administration Finance/Management
B.S.	Business Administration (Variety)

Appeal of Program

Defined tuition payments; books and materials included in tuition; books mailed directly to students at home.

Indiana University

Dr. Lawrence Keller, Director, Division of Extended Studies
Owen Hall, Indiana University
Bloomington, IN 47405
Phone: (812) 855-5792
Toll free: (800) 334-1011
Fax: (812) 855-8680
Founded:
Accrediting Agency: North Central Association
Number of students: 86,000
Number of adult students: 11,000

Representative Degrees

Associate	General Studies
Bachelor	General Studies

Appeal of Program

Flexible; accessible degree.

Indiana Wesleyan University

Mr. Jerry Shepherd, Director of Student Recruitment
211 E. 45th Street
Marion, IN 46953
Phone: (317) 677-2362
Toll free: (800) 234-327
Fax: (317) 674-8028
Founded: 1920
Accrediting Agency: North Central Association
Number of students: 4,754
Number of adult students: 3,001

Representative Degrees

A.S.	Business	
	$135 per credit hour.	
B.S.	Management	
	$172 per credit hour.	
B.S.	Business Administration	
	$172 per credit hour.	
B.S.	Nursing	
	$180 per credit hour.	
M.B.A.	Business Administration	
	Accelerated program.	

Appeal of Program

Statewide class locations are close to students. Classes are discussion-oriented, designed for adults, and meet one night per week. Accelerated, lock-step class schedules.

John Brown University

Dr. Richard Ellis, Chair, Division of Adult
  Education
2000 West University
Siloam Springs, AR 72761
Phone: (501) 524-7100
Toll free: (800) JBU-GRAD
Fax: (501) 524-9458
Founded: 1919
Accrediting Agency: North Central Association
Number of students: 1,211
Number of adult students: 100

Representative Degrees

B.S.	Organizational Management

Appeal of Program

Classes are small; students stay together as a group throughout the program. Studies are practical and applied. Locations in Springdale, Bentonville, and Fort Smith areas of Arkansas.

John F. Kennedy University

Ellena Bloedorn, Director of Admissions and
  Records
12 Altarinda Road
Orinda, CA 94563
Phone: (510) 253-2212
Toll free:
Fax: (510) 254-6964

Founded: 1964
Accrediting Agency: Western Association
Number of students: 1,850
Number of adult students: 1,850

Representative Degrees

M.A.	Variety	
	Combination of evening and weekend courses.	
M.A.	Management	
M.A.	Career Development-Field Studies Program	
	Combination of correspondence, summer two-week residency, and internships in student's locale.	

Appeal of Program

Programs geared toward working adults; evening and weekend classes; small classes. Faculty are practitioners in the fields in which they teach. Average age of students is 37.

Judson College

Dr. Christine Henson, Director of External
  Studies
Judson College
Marion, AL 36756
Phone: (205) 683-5123
Toll free:
Fax:
Founded: 1837
Accrediting Agency: Southern Association
Number of students: 400
Number of adult students: 40

Representative Degrees

B.A.	Business, English, History Also ministry studies, psychology, and religious studies.
B.S.	Business, Psychology
B.M.	Ministry Studies

Judson College

Dr. Dennis Jameson, Director of Adult Education
1151 North State Street
Elgin, IL 60123
Phone: (708) 695-2500
Toll free:

Fax: (708) 695-2500
Founded: 1964
Accrediting Agency: North Central Association
Number of students: 706
Number of adult students: 90
Representative Degrees
  B.A.   Management and Leadership
                16 months, one evening per
                week; talent development
                approach.

Appeal of Program
Customized educational plan using a talent
development instructional design. Convenience
and individualized attention.

Kansas State University

Ms. Cynthia Trent, Coordinator, Nontraditional
  Study
Division of Continuing Education
225 College Court
Manhattan, KS 66506
Phone: (913) 532-5687
Toll free: (800) 622-2KSU
Fax: (913) 532-5637
Founded: 1863
Accrediting Agency: North Central Association
Number of students: 20,000
Number of adult students: 130
Representative Degrees
  B.S.   Interdisciplinary Social Science
                We offer video, audio, indepen-
                dent study, broadcast TV, CLEP,
                and much more. Students use a
                combination of methods to earn
                a degree.
  B.S.   Agriculture, Animal Sciences
                and Industry

Appeal of Program
Degree can be completed entirely off-campus.

King's College

Mrs. Sally McGuire, Director, Lifelong Learning
133 North River Street
Wilkes-Barre, PA 18711
Phone: (717) 826-5865

Toll free:
Fax: (717) 825-9049
Founded: 1946
Accrediting Agency: Middle States Association
Number of students: 2,200
Number of adult students: 450
Representative Degrees
  B.S.   Business Administration
  M.S.   Accounting
  M.S.   Finance
  M.S.   Health Care Administration
  M.S.   Taxation

Lake Erie College

Ms. Mary Ann Kalbaugh, Director of Admissions
391 West Washington Street
Painesville, OH 44077
Phone: 216-639-7879
Toll free: 800-533-4996
Fax: 216-352-3533
Founded: 1856
Accrediting Agency: North Central Association
Number of students: 700
Number of adult students:
Representative Degrees
  B.S.   Business Administration
                Classes are offered Friday nights
                and Saturdays. Students need
                strong English and math skills.
  B.A. or B.S. All majors
                Independent study program.

Appeal of Program
Small classes; flexibility.

Lamar University

Ms. Janice Trammel, Director, Center for Adult
  Studies
P.O. Box 10008
Beaumont, TX 77710
Phone: (409) 880-8431
Toll free: (800) 458-558
Fax: (409) 880-8683
Founded: 1923
Accrediting Agency: Southern Association
Number of students: 9,000

Number of adult students: 500

Representative Degrees

B.A.	General Studies-Liberal Arts
B.A.	Applied Arts & Sciences

Awards up to 24 semester hours of experiential credit.

Appeal of Program

Off-campus courses; evening courses; and self-designed degree program.

LeTourneau University

Ms. Linda Fitzhugh, Assistant Dean, LEAP
P.O. Box 7668
Longview, TX 75607
Phone: (903) 237-2780
Toll free: (800) 388-5327
Fax:
Founded:
Accrediting Agency: Southern Association
Number of students: 1,930
Number of adult students: 1,130

Representative Degrees

B.S.	Business Management
M.B.A.	Business

Appeal of Program

Classroom book delivery; instructors academically qualified and practitioners in their fields. We strive to remove as many barriers as possible for our students. Sequential programs and open enrollment fit adult needs.

Lee College

Dr. Ray Hughes, Jr., Director of External Studies
100 8th Street
Cleveland, TN 37311
Phone: (615) 478-7456
Toll free:
Fax: (615) 478-7928
Founded: 1976
Accrediting Agency: Southern Association
Number of students: 1,000
Number of adult students: 1,000

Representative Degrees

B.S.	Christian Ministries
B.A.	Christian Ministries

Appeal of Program

Distance learning.

Lesley College

Dr. Bard Hamlen, Director, Adult Bachelor's
Degree Program
29 Everett Street
Cambridge, MA 02138
Phone: (617) 349-8482
Toll free: (800) 999-1959
Fax:
Founded: 1930
Accrediting Agency: New England Association
Number of students: 5,600
Number of adult students: 700

Representative Degrees

B.A.L.*	Intensive residency option.
	Use of life experience portfolio.
B.A.L.	American Studies
B.A.L.	Human Development
B.A.L.	Individualized

*Bachelor of Arts and Liberal Studies

Appeal of Program

Small classes; individualized programs; caring, excellent teaching faculty; faculty advising.

Lindenwood College

Jerry Bladdick, Director
Graduate and Adult Professional Admissions
209 South Kingshighway
St. Charles, MO 63301
Phone: (314) 949-4933
Toll free:
Fax: (314) 949-4910
Founded: 1827
Accrediting Agency: North Central Association
Number of students: 4,500
Number of adult students: 2,300

Representative Degrees

B.A.	Business Administration
B.A.	Corporate Communication
B.A.	Gerontology
B.A.	Health Management
B.A.	Human Resource Management

Appeal of Program

Earning nine credits hours in 11 weeks while attending class only one night per week. Emphasis on written and oral presentations rather than exams.

Linfield College

Ms. Vicki Lind, Director, DCE; Adult Degree
  Program
Linfield College DCE
900 South Baker
McMinnville, OR 97128
Phone: (503) 434-2447
Toll free: (800) 452-4176
Fax: (503) 434-2215
Founded: 1849
Accrediting Agency: Northwest Association
Number of students: 2,000
Number of adult students: 900
Representative Degrees

B.A.	Management
	Formats we use: nights, weekends, computer-based, and telecommunications based.
B.A.	Arts and Humanities
B.A.	International Business
	Formats we use: nights, weekends, computer-based, and telecommunications based.
B.A.	Accounting
	Formats we use: nights, weekends, computer-based, and telecommunications based.
B.A.	Social and Behavior
	Formats we use: nights, weekends, computer-based, and telecommunications based.

Appeal of Program

Local advisors; evening and weekend classes; high educational quality.

Loyola University for Ministry

Ms. Cecelia Bennett, Assistant Director
6363 St. Charles Avenue
Campus Box 67

New Orleans, LA 70118
Phone: (504) 865-3728
Toll free: (800) 777-LIMX
Fax: (504) 865-3883
Founded: 1912
Accrediting Agency: Southern Association
Number of students: 5,400
Number of adult students: 900
Representative Degrees

Master's	Pastoral Studies
	Off-campus course; local learning group with on-site print and video.
Master's	Religious Education
Master's	Pastoral Studies
	Special on-campus summer sessions.
Master's	Religious Education
	Special on-campus summer sessions.

Appeal of Program

Intentional learning community in home location; flexible; center areas.

Malone College

Mr. Donald Murray, Dean of Academic Services
515 25th St. NW
Canton, OH 44709
Phone: (216) 471-8342
Toll free: (800) 867-6267
Fax: (216) 454-6977
Founded: 1892
Accrediting Agency: North Central Association
Number of students: 2,004
Number of adult students: 461
Representative Degrees

B.A.	Management
	Courses must be taken in a lock-step schedule.
B.S.N.	Nursing
M.A.	Christian Ministries
M.A.	Education

Appeal of Program

Delivery systems; nonacademic services provided; student interaction and camaraderie; relevance of applied curricula.

Malone College-Graduate School

Dr. Tom Rosebrough, Dean of Graduate School
515 25th St. NW
Canton, OH 44709
Phone: (216) 471-8210
Toll free: (800) 867-6267
Fax: (216) 454-6977
Founded: 1892
Accrediting Agency: North Central Association
Number of students: 2,004
Number of adult students: 461
Representative Degrees

B.A.	Management
	Courses must be taken in a lock-step schedule.
B.S.N.	Nursing
M.A.	Christian Ministries
M.A.	Education

Appeal of Program
Delivery systems; nonacademic services provided; student interaction and camaraderie; relevance of applied curricula.

Marietta College

Dr. Mark Bagshaw, Director of Continuing Education
Marietta College
Marietta, OH 45750
Phone: (614) 376-4723
Toll free:
Fax:
Founded: 1835
Accrediting Agency: North Central Association
Number of students: 1,050
Number of adult students: 250
Representative Degrees

Associate	Variety
Bachelor's	Variety
	Night classes Monday through Thursday.
M.A.	Education
	Night classes Monday through Thursday.
M.A.	Liberal Learning
	Night classes Monday through Thursday.

Appeal of Program
Small discussion classes; highly qualified faculty.

Marquette University

Dr. Robert DeRoche, Associate Director
Continuing Education
1212 West Wisconsin Ave., Rm. 103
Milwaukee, WI 53233
Phone: (414) 288-5318
Toll free:
Fax: (414) 288-3298
Founded: 1881
Accrediting Agency: North Central Association
Number of students: 10,780
Number of adult students: 844
Representative Degrees

B.S.	Organization and Leadership
B.A./B.S.	Various concentrations

Appeal of Program
Format: evenings and Saturdays; accelerated on Saturdays.

Mars Hill College

Dean Raymond Trapp, Dean of Continuing Education/Summer Session
Marshbanks Hall
Mars Hill College
Mars Hill, NC 28754
Phone: (704) 688-1166
Toll free: (800) 582-3047
Fax: (704) 688-1474
Founded: 1856
Accrediting Agency: Southern Association
Number of students: 1,350
Number of adult students: 300
Representative Degrees

B.S.W.	Social Work
	Accredited by American Council of Social Work Education
B.S.	Elementary Education
B.S.	Business Administration
B.A.	Religion
B.S.	Allied Health

Appeal of Program
Degrees available; cost; convenience of location in Asheville, Mars Hill, and Burnsville.

Mary Baldwin College

Ms. Sandra Sprouse, Secretary to the Associate
  Dean
Adult Degree Program
Mary Baldwin College
Staunton, VA 24401
Phone: (703) 887-7003
Toll free: (800) 822-2460
Fax: (703) 887-7265
Founded: 1842
Accrediting Agency: Southern Association
Number of students: 1,700
Number of adult students: 1,000
Representative Degrees

B.A.	Variety of 18 majors Flexible scheduling available through the use of independent tutorials in which a student works one on one with a faculty member.

Appeal of Program
Scheduling flexibility of independent tutorials; academic reputation of the school; the presence of full-time faculty advisors in four regional centers around the state; personal attention to each student; job search services.

Marylhurst College

Janet Cleveland, Admission Counselor
P.O. Box 261
Marylhurst, OR 97036
Phone: (503) 636-8141
Toll free: (800) 634-9982
Fax: (503) 636-9526
Founded: 1893
Accrediting Agency: Northwest Association
Number of students: 1,500
Number of adult students: 1,500
Representative Degrees
All majors are designed for adults.

Appeal of Program
Flexible hours of course scheduling; ability to design majors around areas of specific interest; credit for prior learning experiences.

Maryville University of Saint Louis

13550 Conway Road
St. Louis, MO 63141
School of Education:
Dr. Kathe Rasch, Director of Graduate Studies
Phone: (314) 529-9466
Toll free:
Fax: (314) 542-9918
John E. Simon, School of Business:
Ms. Jeri Mullins-Beggs, Director of Graduate Admissions and Enrollment
Phone: (314) 529-9418
Toll free:
Fax: (314) 9085
Weekend College
Mr. Michael Gillick, Director of Weekend College
Phone: (314) 343-0300
Toll free:
Fax: (314) 343-7557
Founded: 1872
Accrediting Agency: North Central Association
Number of students: 3,425
Number of adult students: 2,070
Representative Degrees

M.B.A.	Business Administration
M.A.	Education
B.A.	Communication
B.A.	Liberal Studies

Appeal of Program
Graduate courses offered at times convenient to students' professional schedule. Weekend college has alternate weekend option, plus desirable degree programs offered.

Marywood College

Ms. Peggi Munkittrick, Director of Distance
  Education
2300 Adams Avenue

Scranton, PA 18509
Phone: (717) 348-6235
Toll free: (800) 836-6940
Fax: (713) 343-5030
Founded: 1915
Accrediting Agency: Middle States Association
Number of students: 3,000
Number of adult students: 140
Representative Degrees
B.S.   Accounting, Business
Administration, Management
Appeal of Program
Individually paced to meet the needs of working professionals; advisement; faculty support; regionally accredited.

The Master's College

Robert Turner, Director, Center for Professional
Studies
21726 Placerita Canyon Rd.
Santa Clarita, CA 91321
Phone: (805) 259-3540
Toll free: (800) 229-XCEL
Fax: (805) 254-1998
Founded: 1927
Accrediting Agency: Western Association
Number of students: 914
Number of adult students: 64
Representative Degrees
B.A.   Organizational Leadership
Video courses offered to complete general educational requirements.
B.A.   Christian Ministries
Video courses offered to complete general educational requirements.
Appeal of Program
Discussion-oriented teaching format; application focused; equipping emphasis. Also, CLEP, testing center, and experiential learning accepted.

Messiah College

Dr. Rod Niner, Director of Adult Degree
Programs

Messiah College
Grantham, PA 17027
Phone: (717) 691-6054
Toll free:
Fax: (717) 691-6057
Founded: 1909
Accrediting Agency: Middle States Association
Number of students: 2,400
Number of adult students: 40
Representative Degrees
BACH. SCI. Nursing
BACH. SCI. Business Administration
Appeal of Program
Accelerated classes; reduced tuition rates; credit for life-learning.

Metropolitan State University

Ms. Janice Harring-Hendon, Director of
Admissions
700 E. Seventh St.
St. Paul, MN 55106
Phone: (612) 772-7600
Toll free:
Fax: (612) 772-7738
Founded: 1971
Accrediting Agency: North Central Association
Number of students: 4,982
Number of adult students: 4,484
Representative Degrees
B.A./B.S.   All programs can be completed at night.
M.B.A.   All programs can be completed at night.
M.M.A.   All programs can be completed at night.
Appeal of Program
Flexible.

Metropolitan College

Dr. Fred Yalolinis, Associate Dean
Metropolitan College Boston University
755 Commonwealth Ave.
Boston, MA 02215
Phone: (617) 353-6000
Toll free:

Fax: (617) 353-6633
Founded: 1965
Accrediting Agency: New England Association
Number of students: 29,000
Number of adult students: 3,500
Representative Degrees

A.S.	Accounting, Biomedical & Clinical, Computer Science, Criminal Justice
B.L.S.	Art History, English, History, Interdisciplinary Studies
B.S.	Biology, Biomedical & Clinical Sciences, Computer Science
B.S.	Hospitality, Administration, Management Studies, Mathematics
M.S.	Actuarial Science, Administrative Studies

Appeal of Program
Diversity of courses and programs. A flexible, part-time, evening college, providing adults with ongoing advising throughout their program.

Millersville University
Dr. Robert Labriola, Dean of Graduate Studies and Extended Programs
PO Box 1002
Dilworth Building
Millersville, PA 17551
Phone: (717) 872-3030
Toll free:
Fax: (717) 871-2022
Founded: 1860
Accrediting Agency: Middle States Association
Number of students: 7,500
Number of adult students: 2,500
Representative Degrees

B.A.	Accounting, Marketing, Management
B.A.	English
B.A.	History
B.S.	Computer Science

Appeal of Program
Student-oriented.

Milligan College
Ms. Paula Gentry, Director of Adult Degree Programs
P.O. Box 22
Milligan College, TN 37682
Phone: (615) 461-8782
Toll free: (800) 262-8337
Fax:
Founded: 1866
Accrediting Agency: Southern Association
Number of students: 850
Number of adult students: 80
Representative Degrees

B.S.	Business Administration Accelerated format is concentrated.

Appeal of Program
Accurate advising regarding: graduation requirements prior to admission; access to staff; quality of teaching.

Milwaukee School of Engineering
Deborah Utter, Counselor
1025 N. Broadway
Milwaukee, WI 53202
Phone: (414) 277-7282
Toll free:
Fax:
Founded: 1903
Accrediting Agency: North Central Association
Number of students: 3,027
Number of adult students: 600
Representative Degrees

A.S.	Electrical Engineering Technology
A.S.	Management Systems
A.S.	Mechanical Engineering Technology
B.S.	Business and Computer System
M.S.	Engineering Management

Appeal of Program
Evening class hours; parking; payment plans; tutoring.

Mind Extension University

Education Center
9697 East Mineral Ave.
P.O. Box 6612
Englewood, CO 80155
Phone:
Toll free: (800) 777-MIND
Fax:
Founded:
Accrediting Agency: Varies by cooperating
institution.
Number of students:
Number of adult students:

Representative Degrees

A.A.	General Studies Degree from Seattle Community College.
B.A.	Management or Business
B.A.	Social Science Degree from Washington State University or Kansas State University.
B.S.	Nursing Degree from California State University, Dominiguez Hills
M.A.	Education and Human Development From George Washington University.

Appeal of Program

Receive degrees from a regionally accredited
university through video-based programs offered
on some cable television systems or through
video tapes mailed to your home.

Montreat-Anderson College

Dr. Isaac Oinolabi, Associate Dean of Adult
Education
School of Professional and Adult Studies
P.O. Box 1267
Montreat, NC 28757
Phone: (704) 669-8011
Toll free: (800) 806-2777
Fax: Phone+Ext.3538
Founded: 1916
Accrediting Agency: Southern Association
Number of students: 500

Number of adult students: 100+
Representative Degrees

B.S.	Business Administration Students can earn the degree by attending classes one night a week.

Appeal of Program

Accelerated format and the use of laptop
computers throughout the entire degree program.

Moody Bible Institute

Dr. Brent Garrison, Vice President of External
Studies
820 N. LaSalle Blvd.
Chicago, IL 60610
Phone: (312) 329-4135
Toll free: (800) 955-1123
Fax: (312) 329-2081
Founded: 1886
Accrediting Agency: North Central Association
Number of students: 2,700
Number of adult students: 1,120
Representative Degrees

A.S.	Bible

Appeal of Program

Cost; available locations through extensions.

Mount Saint Mary College

Mrs. Jean Teske, Director of Continuing
Education Division
330 Powell Avenue
Newburgh, NY 12550
Phone: (914) 569-3187
Toll free:
Fax: (914) 562-MSMC
Founded: 1954
Accrediting Agency: Middle States Association
Number of students: 1,980
Number of adult students: 450
Representative Degrees

B.S.	Accounting
B.S.	Business Management and Administration
B.S.	Nursing
B.A.	Human Services

B.A.   Computer Science

Appeal of Program

Accelerated format; tuition deferment if employer reimbursed.

Mount Vernon Nazarene College

Mr. Doug Pillsbury, Director of Marketing
800 Martinsburg Road
Mount Vernon, OH 43050
Phone: (614) 397-1244
Toll free: (800) 839-2355
Fax: (614) 397-2769
Founded: 1968
Accrediting Agency: North Central Association
Number of students: 1,344
Number of adult students: 76

Representative Degrees

B.B.A.   Bachelor of Business
              Administration

Appeal of Program

Cohort design with books delivered to the classroom.

The Naropa Institute

Ms. Marta Shoman, Director of Admissions
2130 Arapahoe Avenue
Boulder, CO 80302
Phone: (303) 444-0202
Toll free:
Fax:
Founded: 1974
Accrediting Agency: North Central Association
Number of students: 750
Number of adult students: 631

Representative Degrees

B.A.   Contemplative Psychology
           This is an intense program
           designed for full-time study only.
B.A.   Early Childhood Education
B.A.   Environmental Studies
B.A.   Interarts Studies
M.A.   Buddhist Studies

Appeal of Program

Many weekend workshops that students can take for credit. At Naropa a strong emphasis is placed on life experience. Our students' personal experiences are held with high esteem. Many night classes. Classes held in 2- to 3-hour blocks.

National Technological University

Dr. Gearold Johnson, Academic Vice President
700 Centre Avenue
Fort Collins, CO 80526
Phone: (303) 495-6400
Toll free:
Fax: (303) 498-0601
Founded: 1984
Accrediting Agency: North Central Association
Number of students: 1,750
Number of adult students: 1,750

Representative Degrees

M.S.   Various engineering degrees
           Students must work for NTU-
           subscribing organizations.
M.S.   Engineering Management
M.S.   Health Physics Hazardous Waste
           Students must work for NTU-
           subscribing organizations.
M.S.   Management of Technology
           Students must work for NTU-
           subscribing organizations.

Appeal of Program

Flexibility of receiving high-quality graduate engineering courses from six leading engineering schools by telecommunications at the student's place of employment.

New College of California

Weekend College Program or Graduate
   Psychology
50 Fell St.
San Francisco, CA 94102
Phone: (415) 241-1364
Toll free: (800) 335-6262
Fax: (415) 626-5171
Founded: 1971
Accrediting Agency: Western Association
Number of students: 850
Number of adult students: 157

Representative Degrees

B.A.	Humanities
	Choose own emphasis. Degree-completion program—must be able to transfer at least 45 units.
M.A.	Psychology
	Emphasis in Social Work or Feminist Psychology. Classes start at 4:30 P.M. B.A. required. Leads to licensure for M.F.C.C.—Marriage, Family, Child Counselor.

Appeal of Program
Alternative; humanities-based; faculty/advisor and student relationships.

New School for Social Research
Ms. Gerianne Brusati, Director of Educational Advising and Admissions
66 West 12 Street
Room 401
New York, NY 10011
Phone: (212) 229-5630
Toll free:
Fax: (212) 989-3887d
Founded: 1919
Accrediting Agency: Middle States Association
Number of students: 20,000
Number of adult students: 7,000
Representative Degrees

B.A.	Humanities and Social Sciences

Appeal of Program
Flexibility of program; wide course selection; close advising through all course selection; other adult students; part-time nature of program.

North Adams State College
Ms. Denise Richardello, Director of Admissions
Church Street
North Adams, MA 01247
Phone: (413) 662-5410
Toll free: (800) 292-6632
Fax: (413) 662-5580
Founded:
Accrediting Agency: New England Association

Number of students: 1,638
Number of adult students: 220
Representative Degrees

B.S.	Business Administration
B.A.	Sociology
B.A.	Psychology

Appeal of Program
Affordability; scheduling flexibility; off-site courses; quality academic advising.

North Carolina Wesleyan College
Mrs. Frances Harrison, Associate Vice President for Adult Degree Programs
3400 N Wesleyan Blvd.
Rocky Mount, NC 27804
Phone: (919) 985-5129
Toll free:
Fax: (919) 917-3701
Founded: 1957
Accrediting Agency: Southern Association
Number of students: 1,900
Number of adult students: 1,200
Representative Degrees

B.S.	Business Administration
B.S.	Computer Information Systems
B.S.	Accounting
B.A.	Justice Studies

Appeal of Program
Convenience, quality, personal attention.
ADVANTAGE (one program in Raleigh) is accelerated.

North Park College
Dr. Pauline Coffman, Director of GOAL Program
3225 West Foster Avenue
Chicago, IL 60625
Phone: (312) 244-5770
Toll free: (800) 888-6728
Fax: (312) 244-4953
Founded: 1891
Accrediting Agency: North Central Association
Number of students: 1,400
Number of adult students: 110

Representative Degrees

B.A.	Organizational Management
B.A.	Human Development
M.B.A.	Two years to complete full-time
M.A.	Education
	Includes certification to teach in Illinois.
M.A.	Nursing
	Evenings.

Appeal of Program

Once-a-week classes, 4 hours at a time, one course at a time. We bring books and material to classes.

Northeastern Illinois University

Ms. Janet Sandoval, Director of Adult Degree
  Programs
5500 North St. Louis Avenue
Chicago, IL 60625
Phone: (312) 794-6684
Toll free:
Fax: (312) 794-6243
Founded: 1867
Accrediting Agency: North Central Association
Number of students: 11,000
Number of adult students: 2,400

Representative Degrees

B.A.	Liberal Arts
B.A.	University Without Walls

Appeal of Program

Special emphasis on individual academic advisement in degree programs designed especially for adult students.

Northeastern University-University College

180 Ryder Hall, 360 Huntington Avenue
Office of Academic and Student Affairs
Boston, MA 02115
Phone: (617) 373-2400
Toll free:
Fax:
Founded:
Accrediting Agency: New England Association
Number of students: 12,000

Number of adult students: 10,000

Representative Degrees

A.S.	Various Degrees
	16 degree programs.
B.A.	Various Degrees
	8 degree programs.
B.S.	Various Degrees
	20 degree programs.

Appeal of Program

Location (13 campus sites); flexibility of schedule; convenience. Courses all designed for part-time adult students.

Northwest Christian College

Dr. Allen Belcher, Director of Degree
  Completion Program
Northwest Christian College
828 E. 11th Ave.
Eugene, OR 97401
Phone: (503) 687-0397
Toll free: (800) 888-6927
Fax: (503) 343-9159
Founded: 1895
Accrediting Agency: Northwest Association
Number of students: 375
Number of adult students: 110

Representative Degrees

B.S.	Managerial Leadership
	16-month program.
M.A.	Marriage and Family Therapy
	2-year program.

Appeal of Program

Convenience of evening classes for working adults; modular, sequential classes; accelerated format.

Northwood University

Sheryl Beyer, Director, Michigan Outreach
  Center
3225 Cook Rd. University College
Midland, MI 48640
Phone: (517) 837-4411
Toll free: (800) 445-5873
Fax:
Founded: 1957

Accrediting Agency: North Central Association
Number of students: 1,500
Number of adult students: 6,000

Representative Degrees

A.A.	Management
	All formats.
B.B.A.	Management
	All formats.

Appeal of Program
Many course formats.

Nyack College

Mr. Charles Dresser, Director of Admissions
1 South Boulevard
Nyack, NY 10960
Phone: (914) 358-5360
Toll free: (800) 876-9225
Fax: (914) 358-4771
Founded: 1882
Accrediting Agency: Middle States Association
Number of students: 813
Number of adult students: 236

Representative Degrees

B.S.	Organizational Management

Appeal of Program
Length of program: 14 months when classes are offered evenings.

Ohio University's External Student Program

Ms. Barbra Frye, Educational Counselor
301 Tupper Hall
Athens, OH 45701
Phone: (614) 593-2150
Toll free: (800) 444-2420
Fax: (614) 593-2901
Founded: 1804
Accrediting Agency: North Central Association
Number of students: 17,000
Number of adult students: 1,100

Representative Degrees

A.S.	This degree focuses on Natural Sciences, Applied Sciences, and Quantitative Skills.
A.A.	Social Sciences or Arts and Humanities

Students may choose to focus their studies on either the social sciences or arts and humanities.

A.A.B.	Business Management Technology
A.S.	Varies
	Students design their own degree based on career goals and interests.
B.S.S.	Varies
	This degree provides students the opportunity to design an individualized four-year plan.

Appeal of Program
Flexible hours; affordable tuition; work basically at own pace; no on-campus attendance required; can enroll in Ohio University Independent Studies course work from anywhere in the country, or even out of the country.

Olivet Nazarene University

Mr. Mark Buck, Director of Marketing
1101 Perimeter Dr. #175
Schaumburg, IL 60173
Phone: (708) 240-6100
Toll free: (800) 765-4838
Fax: (708) 240-6109
Founded:
Accrediting Agency: North Central Association
Number of students: 2,200
Number of adult students: 500+

Representative Degrees

B.S.	Management
B.S.	Nursing
	Accredited by National League for Nursing.
M.B.A.	Computer Enhanced
M.A.	Education

Appeal of Program
Convenience; timeliness; effectiveness; professionalism.

Oral Roberts University

Mr. Jeff Ogle, Acting Dean, School of Lifelong Education
7777 South Lewis Ave.

Tulsa, OK 74171
Phone: (918) 495-6238
Toll free:
Fax: (918) 495-6033
Founded: 1965
Accrediting Agency: North Central Association
Number of students: 4,000
Number of adult students: 400+

Representative Degrees

B.S.	Business Administration 12-hour residency required— summer, short term.
B.S.	Christian Care and Counseling 12-hour residency required— summer, short term.
B.S.	Church Ministries 12-hour residency required— summer, short term.
B.S.	Elementary Christian School Education 12-hour residency required— summer, short term.

Appeal of Program
Can enroll any month of the year; rolling enrollment; semester starts when you do.

Palm Beach Atlantic College

Ms. Becky Hallden, Admissions Coordinator
Box 24708
West Palm Beach, FL 33416
Phone: (407) 835-4305
Toll free:
Fax: (407) 835-4341
Founded: 1968
Accrediting Agency: Southern Association
Number of students: 2,000
Number of adult students: 400

Representative Degrees

M.S.	Human Resource Development Classes meet either one night a week or one weekend a month. Both formats take 18 months to complete.
B.S.	Management of Human Resources Classes meet once a week for four hours. Degree-completion

program. Students who transfer 60 credits could possibly finish in one year. Includes credit for life experience and learning.

Appeal of Program
Convenient locations; accelerated classes.

Philadelphia College of Bible

Mr. Kevin Oessenich, Director of Degree Completion
200 Manor Ave.
Langhorne, PA 19047
Phone: (215) 752-5800
Toll free: 800-4-ADVANCE
Fax: (215) 752-5812
Founded: 1913
Accrediting Agency: Middle States Association
Number of students: 1,050
Number of adult students:

Representative Degrees

B.S.	Bible
M.S.	Bible
M.S.	Education
M.S.	Counseling

Appeal of Program
Undergraduate: module format; group structure; one session per week on campus; faculty skilled in adult learning. Graduate: practicality of curriculum; flexible scheduling; outstanding faculty.

Philadelphia College of Textiles and Science

Dr. Maxine Lentz, Dean of Continuing Education
Henry Ave. and School House Lane
Philadelphia, PA 19144
Phone: (215) 951-2902
Toll free:
Fax: (215) 951-2615
Founded: 1876
Accrediting Agency: Middle States Association
Number of students: 3,220
Number of adult students: 1,550

Representative Degrees

B.S.   All degrees offered by college

Appeal of Program

Three campuses allow 89 credits in transfer from a two-year school.

Queens College

Mr. Robert Weller, Director
Adult Collegiate Education Program
65-30 Kissena Blvd.
Flushing, NY 11355
Phone: (718) 997-5717
Toll free:
Fax:
Founded: 1937
Accrediting Agency: Middle States Association
Number of students: 20,000
Number of adult students: 1,500

Representative Degrees

B.A./B.S.   60 Liberal Arts Majors

Appeal of Program

Freshman year ACE classes meet once a week; only adults in classes; availability of counselors; evening and day classes and office hours; availability of prior learning credits; program is "user friendly."

Ramapo College of New Jersey

Ms. Katherine Talbird, Associate Vice President
  of Administration and Finance
505 Ramapo Valley Road
Mahwah, NJ 07430
Phone: (201) 529-7617
Toll free:
Fax: (201) 529-7685
Founded: 1971
Accrediting Agency: Middle States Association
Number of students: 4,674
Number of adult students: 98

Representative Degrees

B.S.   Biology
        Classes offered evenings and
        weekends.
B.S.   Business Administration
        Classes offered evenings and
        weekends.

B.S.   Chemistry
        Classes offered evenings and
        weekends.
B.S.   Computer Science
        Classes offered evenings and
        weekends.
B.A.   Economics
        Classes offered weekends and
        evenings.

Appeal of Program

Course availability for degree completion evening/weekend; small class sizes; enrollment with other returning adults.

Regent University

Dr. George Selig, Provost
1000 Regent University Drive
Virginia Beach, VA 23464
Phone: (804) 579-4320
Toll free:
Fax: (804) 424-7051
Founded: 1977
Accrediting Agency: Southern Association
Number of students: 1,316
Number of adult students: 171

Representative Degrees

M.B.A.   Business Administration
M.A.   Business Management
M.Ed.   Master Teacher (Elementary and
          Multiple Levels)
          Classes meet Thursday and
          Friday nights and all day
          Saturday 10 weekends per
          semester (Fall and Spring).

Appeal of Program

Business students may take classes without leaving jobs and uprooting family to another location. Education (primarily local) students can continue their current teaching positions while working on master's degree. Complete program in one year.

Regents College

Prospective Student Advisor
7 Columbia Circle
Albany, NY 12203

Phone: (518) 464-8500
Toll free:
Fax: (518) 464-8777
Founded: 1970
Accrediting Agency: Middle States Association
Number of students: 17,269
Number of adult students: 17,269

Representative Degrees

A.A.	Liberal Arts
	All degrees are based on work and credits from a variety of sources. Students do not attend any courses from the college.
A.S.	Liberal Arts
B.A.	Liberal Arts
B.S.	Liberal Arts
A.S.	Business

Appeal of Program

Flexibility of program: wide range of options for earning credit. Students accumulate hours from prior learning assessment, testing, correspondence, and transfer credits.

Regis University

Sharron Leonard, Admissions Representative
3333 Regis Blvd
Adult Learning Center RM. 305
Denver, CO 80221
Phone: (303) 458-4315
Toll free: (800) 967-3237
Fax: (303) 964-5539
Founded: 1877
Accrediting Agency: North Central Association
Number of students: 9,000
Number of adult students: 8,000

Representative Degrees

B.S.	Business Administration
	Areas of emphasis possible: marketing, finance, management, international business.
B.S.	Accounting
B.S.	Computer Information Systems
B.S. or B.A.	More than 40 different majors. Can also use accelerated or televised formats when appropriate for some classes.

M.B.A.   Business Administration

Appeal of Program

Flexibility; convenience; prestigious reputation; experience; service.

Rider University

Ms. Karen Crowell, Assistant Dean of the College of Continuing Studies
2083 Lawrenceville Road
Lawrenceville, NJ 08648
Phone: (609) 896-5033
Toll free:
Fax: (609) 896-5261
Founded: 1865
Accrediting Agency: Middle States Association
Number of students: 5,300
Number of adult students: 1,200

Representative Degrees

B.A.	Liberal Studies
	Concentrations in Social Sciences, Humanities, Natural Sciences, and Applied Social Sciences.
B.S.	Business Administration
B.S.	Chemistry
M.B.A.	

Appeal of Program

High level of service from Continuing Studies Office; excellent faculty; good location outside any city area. Midway between Philadelphia and New York City, near major highways.

Rochester Institute of Technology

Mr. Joseph Nairn, Director of Part Time Enrollment Services
Bausch and Lomb Center
58 Lomb Memorial Drive
Rochester, NY 14623
Phone: (716) 475-2229
Toll free: 800-CALL RIT
Fax: (716) 475-5476
Founded: 1829
Accrediting Agency: Middle States Association
Number of students: 13,000
Number of adult students: 4,400

Representative Degrees

B.S.	Applied Arts and Science
M.S.	Software Development and Management
B.S.	Polymer Chemistry/Chemistry upper division (Junior and Senior) program.
M.S.	Telecommunications Software Technology
B.S.	Electrical/Mechanical Technology Site-based program in partnership with community colleges or corporations.

Appeal of Program

Quarter calendar; evening scheduling; variety of evening offerings.

Roger Williams University

Mr. John Stout, Dean of University College
One Old Ferry Road
Bristol, RI 02809
Phone: (401) 254-3530
Toll free:
Fax: (401) 254-3560
Founded: 1956
Accrediting Agency: New England Association
Number of students: 3,900
Number of adult students: 1,500

Representative Degrees

B.S.	Accounting
B.S.	Administration of Justice Distance program option.
B.S.	Computer Information Systems
B.S.	Business Administration Distance program option.
B.S.	Computer Science

Appeal of Program

Nonclassroom courses; credit for prior learning and life experiences; credit for military training; distance and off-campus program options.

Rollins College

Ms. Sharon Lusk, Assistant Dean
1000 Holt Avenue Box 2725
Winter Park, FL 32789
Phone: (407) 646-2232
Toll free:
Fax: (407) 646-1551
Founded: 1885
Accrediting Agency: Southern Association
Number of students: 4,500
Number of adult students: 1,200

Representative Degrees

B.A.	Variety of 10 majors
M.L.S.	Master of Liberal Studies
M.A.	Human Resource Development
M.A.	Counseling

Appeal of Program

Performance-based admissions; mail-in registration; personal adviser; discussion-oriented small classes.

Rutgers University College

Ms. Nancy Gulick, Assistant Dean
Armitage Hall
5th and Penn Streets
Camden, NJ 08102
Phone: (609) 225-6060
Toll free:
Fax: (609) 225-6495
Founded: 1766
Accrediting Agency: Middle States Association
Number of students: 5,000
Number of adult students: 900

Representative Degrees

B.A.	Computer Science Information Systems Track.
B.A.	English
B.A.	History
B.A.	Physics Microelectronics track.
B.S.	Finance

Appeal of Program

Quality of faculty; requirements same for day and evening students; enabling flexible scheduling.

Sacred Heart University

Mr. Edward Donato, Jr., Associate Dean of
 Continuing Education
5151 Park Avenue
Fairfield, CT 06432
Phone: (203) 371-7830
Toll free: (800) 288-2498
Fax: (203) 365-7500
Founded: 1963
Accrediting Agency: New England Association
Number of students: 5,600
Number of adult students: 3,300
Representative Degrees

> Ahead Program—Business and
> Finance
> General Studies—Humanities,
> Science, Social Science
> Weekend UMV—Business of
> Finance

Appeal of Program
Accelerated models at convenient times; credit
for prior learning and CLEP exams.

Sage Evening College of the Sage Colleges

Neilia Campbell, Director of Advisement
Sage Evening College
140 New Scotland Ave.
Albany, NY 12110
Phone: (518) 445-1717
Toll free:
Fax: (518) 270-1728
Founded: 1916
Accrediting Agency: Middle States Association
Number of students: 4,000
Number of adult students: 800
Representative Degrees
A.S.	Variety of 13 degree programs
B.A.	Variety of 8 degree programs
B.S.	Variety of 15 degree programs

Appeal of Program
Flexibility; location; understanding of adult
needs.

Saint Joseph's College

Dr. Patricia Sparks, Dean of Distance Education
External Degree Programs
Windham, ME 04062
Phone: (207) 892-6766
Toll free: (800) 343-5498
Fax: (207) 892-7423
Founded: 1912
Accrediting Agency: New England Association
Number of students: 930
Number of adult students: 5,150
Representative Degrees
M.H.S.	Health Services Administration Independent study.
B.S.H.C.A.	Health Care Administration Independent study.
B.S.R.T.	Radiologic technology Degree-completion program for licensed health professional.
B.S.P.A.	Health Care Degree-completion program for licensed health professionals.

Appeal of Program
Strong student focus; beautiful campus.

Saint Mary College

Sr. Mary Fasenmyer, Director
10000 West 75th Street
Shawnee-Mission, KS 66204
Phone: (913) 384-6279
Toll free:
Fax: (913) 262-0405
Founded: 1923
Accrediting Agency: North Central Association
Number of students: 985
Number of adult students: 540
Representative Degrees
B.S.	Education
M.A.	Education
B.S.	Management
M.S.	Management
B.A.	Human Development

Appeal of Program
Accelerated schedule; faculty; convenience of
location.

Saint Mary College

Sr. Margaret Petty, Adult Student Coordinator
4100 S 4th St.
Leavenworth, KS 66048
Phone: (913) 758-6112
Toll free: (800) 752-7043
Fax: (913) 758-6140
Founded: 1859
Accrediting Agency: North Central Association
Number of students: 970
Number of adult students: 795

Representative Degrees

B.S.	Elementary Education
B.A.	Human Development
B.S.	Human Services
M.S.	Management
B.A.	Human Development

Appeal of Program

ELW format; services available; quality of installation; class size.

Saint Mary's College, School of Extended Education

Mr. Gary Murdough, Director of Program
   Counseling
PO Box 5219
1925 Saint Mary's Road
Moraga, CA 94575
Phone: (510) 631-4900
Toll free: (800) 538-9999
Fax: (510) 631-9869
Founded: 1863
Accrediting Agency: Western Association
Number of students: 4,000
Number of adult students: 750

Representative Degrees

B.A.	Management Primarily an off-campus program, one four-hour class meeting per week, offered at 20 locations in the Bay Area and Sacramento.
B.A.	Health Services Administration Primarily an off-campus program, one four-hour class meeting per week, offered at 6

locations in the Bay Area and Sacramento.

M.S.	Health Services Administration As above, but four locations, classes meet in two, three-hour sessions per week.

Appeal of Program

Opportunity to earn credit for prior learning (undergraduate only).

Saint Peter's College

Henry Shields, Jr., Academic Dean of Evening,
   Summer, and Continuing Education
2641 Kennedy Boulevard
Jersey City, NJ 07306
Phone: (201) 915-9009
Toll free:
Fax: (201) 451-0036
Founded: 1872
Accrediting Agency: Middle States Association
Number of students: 4,000
Number of adult students: 1,600

Representative Degrees

Associate	Marketing, Social Sciences, Banking, Management Trimester and/or summer schedule.
A.A.S.	Public Policy
B.S.	Accounting, Management, Computer Science, Economics Trimester and/or summer schedule.
B.A.	Elementary Education, English, History, Humanities, Philosophy Trimester and/or summer schedule.

Appeal of Program

Trimester; small class size; class hours; summer terms.

Sangamon State University

Dr. Ronald Ettinger, Director of the Individual
   Option Program
Sangamon State University
Springfield, IL 62794

Phone: (217) 786-7422
Toll free: (800) 252-8533
Fax:
Founded: 1969
Accrediting Agency: North Central Association
Number of students: 4,500
Number of adult students: 200
Representative Degrees

M.A.	Self-Designed Degrees; Self-Titled
	May mix traditional course work with independent study.
B.A.	Liberal Studies

Appeal of Program
Evening classes; self-designed degree; friendly atmosphere.

Sarah Lawrence College

Ms. Alice Olson, Director of Continuing
  Education
Sarah Lawrence College
One Mead Way
Bronxville, NY 10708
Phone: (914) 395-2205
Toll free:
Fax: (914) 395-2664
Founded: 1927
Accrediting Agency: Middle States Association
Number of students: 1,200
Number of adult students: 80
Representative Degrees

B.A.	Liberal Arts
M.A.	Dance, Theater, Child Development, Writing, Women's History
M.S.	Art of Teaching
M.S.	Human Genetics

Appeal of Program
Small classes (never more than 15 students); individual conferences with teachers biweekly throughout the term; high level of support and individual attention.

Saybrook Institute

Admissions Department
450 Pacific Ave., Third Floor

San Francisco, CA 94133
Phone: (415) 433-9200
Toll free: (800) 825-4480
Fax: (415) 433-9271
Founded: 1971
Accrediting Agency: Western Association
Number of students: 340
Number of adult students:
Representative Degrees

M.A.	Human Science, Psychology
	Two-week residency requirement per year.
Ph.D.	Human Science, Psychology
	Two-week residency requirement per year.

Appeal of Program
Saybrook is a regionally accredited, dispensed residency, at a distance graduate school.

Seattle Pacific University

Mr. David Kinard, Director of Marketing
Division of Continuing Studies
3307 Third Avenue West
Seattle, WA 98119
Phone: (206) 281-2450
Toll free: (800) 648-7898
Fax: (206) 281-2271
Founded: 1891
Accrediting Agency: Northwest Association
Number of students: 3,437
Number of adult students: 900
Representative Degrees

B.A.	Business Administration
B.A.	Science
B.S.	Arts
B.A.	General Studies

Seattle University

Dr. Carol Weaver, Program Coordinator, Adult
  Education and Training
School of Education
411 Loyola—Broadway and Madison
Seattle, WA 98501
Phone: (206) 296-5696
Toll free:

Fax: (206) 296-2053
Founded: 1891
Accrediting Agency: Northwest Association
Number of students: 6,000
Number of adult students: 100
Representative Degrees
M.A.   Adult Education and Training
        M.Ed. option also available.
Appeal of Program
Practical orientation; evening courses; Jesuit/
ethical focus. Internship required; provides work
experience.

Shimer College
David Buchanan, Director of Admissions
438 North Sheridan Road
P.O. Box A-500
Waukegan, IL 60079
Phone: (708) 623-8400
Toll free: (800) 215-7173
Fax: (708) 249-7171
Founded: 1853
Accrediting Agency: North Central Association
Number of students: 110
Number of adult students: 45
Representative Degrees
B.A.   Humanities
      All small discussion classes.
      Meets every third weekend.
B.A.   Social Science
B.A.   Natural Science
      All small discussion classes.
      Meets every third weekend.
B.A.   General Studies
      All small discussion classes.
      Meets every third weekend.
Appeal of Program
Every third weekend; classes of twelve or fewer;
all discussion classes; all reading in original
sources, not textbooks.

Shorter College
Dr. Phil Woolf, Dean, School of Professional
  Programs
1950 Spectrum Circle A-305

Marietta, GA 30067
Phone: (404) 980-3417
Toll free:
Fax: (404) 980-3413
Founded: 1873
Accrediting Agency: Southern Association
Number of students: 1,300
Number of adult students: 590
Representative Degrees
Bachelor's Business Administration
      Selected courses are computer
      based, but not entire program.
      Minor area offered in Leadership
      Studies.
Bachelor's Business Management
      Selected courses are computer
      based, but not entire program.
      Minor area offered in Leadership
      Studies.
Appeal of Program
Accelerated time for classes (five weeks); most
are taught by people who are actively in business;
classes meet one night per week; small study
groups required for collaborative learning and for
networking and support.

Simpson College
Dr. David Tarr, Executive Assistant to the
  President
2211 College View Drive
Redding, CA 96003
Phone: (916) 224-5600
Toll free: (800) 598-2493
Fax: (916) 224-5608
Founded: 1921
Accrediting Agency: Western Association
Number of students: 840
Number of adult students: 265
Representative Degrees
B.A.   Business and Human Resources
      Management
B.A.   Psychology
B.A.   Liberal Arts
Appeal of Program
Accelerated courses in established schedule
requirement match day-time regular.

Skidmore College-University Without Walls

Ms. Mary Cogan, Administrative Assistant
Skidmore College
Saratoga Springs, NY 12866
Phone: (518) 584-5000
Toll free:
Fax: (518) 581-7400
Founded: 1971
Accrediting Agency: Middle States Association
Number of students: 230
Number of adult students: 230

Representative Degrees

B.A.	Liberal Arts Field (Most) Includes many different formats in combination.
B.S.	Studio Art, Music, Theater Includes many different formats in combination.
B.S.	Business, Human Services Includes many different formats in combination.
B.A.	Self-Determined Includes many different formats in combination.
B.S.	Self-Determined Includes many different formats in combination.

Appeal of Program

Flexible degree plan; no residency; quality arts education. Adult degree programs are individually designed. Students communicate with independent study instructors through personal contact, phone, mail, Internet, audio tape, or a combination of these methods.

Southeastern College of the Assemblies of God

Dr. Charles Spong, Director for Distance
    Learning
1000 Longfellow Boulevard
Lakeland, FL 33801
Phone: (813) 665-4404
Toll free: (800) 854-7477
Fax: (813) 665-0486
Founded: 1935

Accrediting Agency: Southern Association
Number of students:
Number of adult students: 900

Representative Degrees

B.A.	Bible
B.A.	Christian Education
B.A.	Pastoral Studies
B.A.	Missions

Appeal of Program

No residency requirement; regional accreditation; exceptional staff/faculty support.

Southern California College

Ms. Kim Cross, Assistant Director
55 Fair Drive
Costa Mesa, CA 92626
Phone: (714) 668-6130
Toll free:
Fax: (714) 668-6194
Founded: 1920
Accrediting Agency: Western Association
Number of students: 1,100
Number of adult students: 60

Representative Degrees

B.A.	Organizational Management

Appeal of Program

One night per week; complete degree in 16 months; seminar style class meeting; experienced faculty; classmates are adults.

Southern Nazarene University

Dr. Wayne Murrow, Dean, Graduate and Adult
    Studies
6729 NW 39th Expressway
Bethany, OK 73008
Phone: (405) 491-6316
Toll free:
Fax: (405) 491-6302
Founded:
Accrediting Agency: North Central Association
Number of students: 1,737
Number of adult students: 320

Representative Degrees

B.S.	Management of Human Resources

B.S.	Family Studies and Gerontology
M.S.	Management
M.S.	Counseling Psychology

Appeal of Program
Service orientation geared to adult schedule.

Southern Vermont College

Ms. Bernyce Barnes, Continuing Education
   Coordinator
Office of Admissions
Southern Vermont College
Bennington, VT 05201
Phone: (802) 442-5427
Toll free: (800) 378-2782
Fax: (802) 442-5527
Founded:
Accrediting Agency: New England Association
Number of students: 750
Number of adult students: 325

Representative Degrees

B.S.	Accounting
A.S.	Accounting
A.S.	Business
B.S.	Business Management
A.A.	Child Development

Appeal of Program
Evening and Saturday classes; classes in session
from 4 to 8 P.M. Life experience for credit is a very
popular class for adults.

Southern Wesleyan University

Dr. James Rhoe, Jr., Vice President of Adult and
   Graduate Studies
P.O. Box 1020
Central, SC 29630
Phone: 803-639-2453
Toll free:
Fax: 803-639-1956
Founded: 1906
Accrediting Agency: Southern Association
Number of students: 1,100
Number of adult students: 700

Representative Degrees

| B.S. | Management of Human |
| | Resources |

Some general education and
electives on Saturday.

B.B.A.	Business
B.S.	Education
A.S.B.	Business
M.S.	Management

Appeal of Program
Lock step; one night per week (plus study group).

Southwestern Adventist College

Dr. Larry Philbeck, Director, Adult Degree
   Program
Keene, TX 76059
Phone: (817) 645-3921
Toll free: (800) 433-2240
Fax: (817) 556-4742
Founded: 1893
Accrediting Agency: Southern Association
Number of students: 970
Number of adult students: 220

Representative Degrees

B.B.A.	Business Administration
	Outline for the class, on-campus
	and off-campus classes, course by
	correspondence.
Bachelor's	Communication
	Outline for the class, on-campus
	and off-campus classes, course by
	correspondence.
Bachelor's	Education
	Outline for the class, on-campus
	and off-campus classes, course by
	correspondence.
Bachelor's	English
	Outline for the class, on-campus
	and off-campus classes, course by
	correspondence.

Appeal of Program
Flexibility of study/class time; no on-campus
class requirement; video tapes of classes.

Spring Arbor College

Ms. Natalie Gianetti, Dean for Alternative
   Education
Spring Arbor, MI 49283

Phone: (517) 750-6343
Toll free: (800) 968-9103
Fax: (517) 750-6602
Founded: 1873
Accrediting Agency: North Central Association
Number of students: 1,900
Number of adult students: 750
Representative Degrees

B.A.	Family Life Education
B.A.	Management and Organizational Development
B.A.	Management of Health Service
B.A.	Management of Health Promotion

Appeal of Program
Evening class meeting one night a week; convenience of location; format; registration.

St. Ambrose University

Dr. Fred Holman, Dean, Center for Graduate and Continuing Education
518 W. Locust Street
Cosgrove Hall
Davenport, IA 52803
Phone: (319) 383-8758
Toll free:
Fax: (319) 383-8791
Founded: 1882
Accrediting Agency: North Central Association
Number of students: 2,584
Number of adult students: 645
Representative Degrees

M.C.J.	Criminal Justice
M.H.C.A.	Health Care Administration
B.A.	Business Administration
B.A./B.S.	Computer Science
B.S.I.E.	Industrial Engineering

Appeal of Program
Flexibility; may attend days, evenings, and weekends to complete degree.

St. John's College

Mrs. Susan Friedman, Assistant to the Director
1160 Camino Cruz Blanca
Santa Fe, NM 87505

Phone: (505) 984-6082
Toll free:
Fax:
Founded:
Accrediting Agency: North Central Association
Number of students: 505
Number of adult students: 105
Representative Degrees

M.A.	Liberal Arts
M.A.	Eastern Classics

Appeal of Program
Can take classes two evenings a week and get master's degree.

St. Leo College

Dr. Robert Wilson, Academic Programs Administrator
Center for Distance Learning
St. Francis Hall
St. Leo, FL 33574
Phone: (904) 588-8084
Toll free:
Fax: (904) 588-8207
Founded: 1889
Accrediting Agency: Southern Association
Number of students: 8,000
Number of adult students: 7,000
Representative Degrees

B.A.	Business Administration Specializations in Accounting, Marketing, Management, and Health Care.
B.A.	Criminology Specializations in Human Services and Administration.
B.A.	Education Elementary, Secondary, and Re-certification programs.
B.S.	Health Care Administration

Appeal of Program
Excellent faculty and supportive administrators.

St. Mary-of-the-Woods College

Gwen Hagemeyer, Director of Admissions
Women's External Degree Program

St. Mary-of-the-Woods, IN 47876
Phone: (812) 535-5106
Toll free: (800) 926-SMWC
Fax:
Founded: 1840
Accrediting Agency: North Central Association
Number of students: 1,300
Number of adult students: 900
Representative Degrees

B.A.	Accounting
B.A.	Business Administration
B.A.	Humanities
B.A.	Education
B.A.	Marketing

Appeal of Program
We offer 15 majors. All include correspondence, weekends, accelerated format. Flexibility; individualized service.

State University at Buffalo— Millard Fillmore College

Dr. Walker Kunz, Interim Dean
128 Parker Hall
State University at Buffalo
Buffalo, NY 14221
Phone: (716) 829-3131
Toll free:
Fax: (716) 829-2475
Founded: 1846
Accrediting Agency: Middle States Association
Number of students: 30,000
Number of adult students: 4,000
Representative Degrees

B.A.	Arts and Sciences Majors 12 majors from African/ American studies to Psychology.
B.S.	Arts and Sciences Majors
B.S.	Management
B.S.	Engineering
B.P.S.	Architecture

Appeal of Program
Part-time opportunities; certificate programs; services designed for adults.

Stephens College

Karen Lafrenz, Director of Marketing
School of Continuing Education
Campus Box 2141
Columbia, MO 65215
Phone: (314) 876-7125
Toll free: (800) 388-7579
Fax: (314) 876-7237
Founded: 1833
Accrediting Agency: North Central Association
Number of students: 850
Number of adult students: 250
Representative Degrees

B.A.	Business Administration 6 months to complete each course.
B.A.	English
B.A.	Philosophy
B.S.	Early Childhood Education
B.S.	Health Information Management

Appeal of Program
Flexible; responsive to needs of adult student; individual attention. Courses available through correspondence format.

Suffolk University

Majorie Kelleher, Associate Director of
    Undergraduate Admissions
Adult and Evening Studies
8 Ashburton Place
Boston, MA 02108
Phone: (617) 573-8070
Toll free: (800) 6SUFFOLK
Fax: (617) 742-4291
Founded: 1906
Accrediting Agency: New England Association
Number of students: 6,600
Number of adult students: 6,600
Representative Degrees

M.B.A.	Business Administration
M.P.A.	Public Administration
M.S.F.	Finance
M.S.A.	Accounting
M.S.T.	Taxation

Appeal of Program

Convenience of location; cost; flexibility (can take courses day or evening); all classes taught by professors/faculty.

Tabor College-Wichita

Mrs. Jane Wallace, Director
8100 E 22nd W, Building 1400-1
Tallgrass Executive Park
Wichita, KS 67226
Phone: (316) 681-8616
Toll free:
Fax: (316) 689-0996
Founded: 1908
Accrediting Agency: North Central Association
Number of students: 500
Number of adult students: 28
Representative Degrees

B.A.	Management and Organizational Development

Appeal of Program

Christian emphasis; location; time; student services.

Teikyo Marycrest University

Dr. Marie Ven Horst, Director of Institutional Research
1607 West 12th Street
Davenport, IA 52804
Phone: (319) 326-9562
Toll free: (800) 728-9705
Fax: (319) 326-9250
Founded: 1939
Accrediting Agency: North Central Association
Number of students: 1,272
Number of adult students: 320
Representative Degrees

A.A./B.A.	Business Administration
M.A./M.S.	Education
M.A./M.S.	Computer Science
A.A./B.A.	Special Studies

Appeal of Program

Abbreviated class periods.

Tennessee Wesleyan College

Mr. Jay May, Director, Adult and Continuing Education
P.O. Box 40
Athens, TN 37303
Phone: (615) 745-7504
Toll free:
Fax: (615) 744-9968
Founded: 1857
Accrediting Agency: Southern Association
Number of students: 634
Number of adult students: 261
Representative Degrees

B.A.	Accounting
B.A.	General Management
B.A.	Human Resource Management
B.A.	Computer Information Systems

Appeal of Program

Convenience of branch campus location.

Thomas Edison State College

Ms. Janice Toliver, Director of Admissions Services
101 West State Street
Trenton, NJ 08608
Phone: (609) 984-1150
Toll free:
Fax: (609) 984-8447
Founded: 1972
Accrediting Agency: Middle States Association
Number of students: 8,619
Number of adult students: 8,619
Representative Degrees

B.A.	Accounting
B.A.	Management
B.A.	Humanities
B.A.	History

Appeal of Program

Variety of methods of earning credit at a distance; number of degree programs and specializations. Individualized degree programs—no residency required.

Thomas More College

Ms. Joyce Emery, Director, Continuing
  Education
333 Thomas More Parkway
Crestview Hills, KY 41017
Phone: (606) 344-3333
Toll free:
Fax: (606) 344-3345
Founded: 1921
Accrediting Agency: Southern Association
Number of students: 1,300
Number of adult students: 450
Representative Degrees

B.B.A.	Business Administration Accelerated degree program.
Associate	Eight majors available through night and weekend classes.
Bachelor's	Six majors available through night and weekend classes.

Towson State University

Mr. G. Franklin Mullen, Acting Dean
College of Continuing Studies
8000 York Road
Towson, MD 21204
Phone: (410) 830-2028
Toll free: (800) CALL-TSU
Fax: (410) 830-2006
Founded: 1866
Accrediting Agency: Middle States Association
Number of students: 14,551
Number of adult students:
Representative Degrees

Bachelor's	19 majors are available through the evening program.

Trinity College of Vermont

Ms. Kathleen Berard, Director of Programs for
  Adult Continuing Education
PACE Program
208 Colchester Avenue
Burlington, VT 05401
Phone: (802) 658-0337
Toll free:
Fax: (802) 658-5446

Founded: 1925
Accrediting Agency: New England Association
Number of students: 973
Number of adult students: 587
Representative Degrees

Bachelor's	Accounting
Bachelor's	Business Administration
Bachelor's	Human Services, Psychology
Bachelor's	Secondary Education
Bachelor's	Liberal Arts

Appeal of Program
Flexibility in scheduling and availability of
majors. For example, Business Administration or
Accounting degrees pursued entirely in the
evenings or on weekends.

Trinity University

Mr. Richard Elliot, Registrar
Trinity University
715 Stadium Drive
San Antonio, TX 78212
Phone: (210) 736-7206
Toll free:
Fax: (210) 736-7202
Founded: 1869
Accrediting Agency: Southern Association
Number of students: 2,479
Number of adult students: 46
Representative Degrees

M.S.	Health Care Administration Requires on-campus sessions at beginning and end of each term.

The Union Institute

Mr. Michael Robertson, Associate Registrar
Admissions
440 East McMillan Street
Cincinnati, OH 45206
Phone: (513) 861-6400
Toll free: (800) 486-3116
Fax: (513) 861-0779
Founded: 1964
Accrediting Agency: North Central Association
Number of students: 1,639
Number of adult students: 1,639

Representative Degrees

Ph.D.	Interdisciplinary: Liberal Arts and Sciences
	Individual, tutorial-based, non-residential.
Ph.D.	Professional Psychology
B.A./B.S.	Liberal Arts and Sciences
	Centers in Cincinnati, Ohio; Miami, Florida; and Los Angeles, Sacramento, and San Diego, California.
B.A./B.S.	Liberal Arts and Sciences
	Center for Distant Learning, requires modem-equipped computer.

Appeal of Program

Programs are individually designed. Flexible scheduling allows students to work while they learn. Geared to adult students.

United States Sports Academy

Director of Student Services
One Academy Drive
Daphne, AL 36526
Phone: (205) 626-3303
Toll free: (800) 223-2668
Fax: (205) 626-1149
Founded: 1972
Accrediting Agency: Southern Association
Number of students: 250
Number of adult students: 250

Representative Degrees

M.S.S.	Various
Ed.D.	Sport Management

Appeal of Program

Credit for hands-on experience; flexibility to earn degree with on-campus and off-campus course work.

University of Alabama

Nancy Stojkovic, Admission Coordinator
PO Box 870182
Tuscaloosa, AL 35487
Phone: (205) 348-6000
Toll free:

Fax:
Founded: 1970
Accrediting Agency: Southern Association
Number of students: 20,000
Number of adult students: 700

Representative Degrees

B.A.	Human Services
	Use out-of-class learning contracts, independent study, prior learning portfolios, CLEP exams, etc.
B.A.	Humanities
	Use out-of-class learning contracts, independent study, prior learning portfolios, CLEP exams, etc.
B.A.	Social Sciences
	Use out-of-class learning contracts, independent study, prior learning portfolios, CLEP exams, etc.
B.S.	Natural Sciences
	Use out-of-class learning contracts, independent study, prior learning portfolios, CLEP exams, etc.
B.S.	Applied Sciences
	Use out-of-class learning contracts, independent study, prior learning portfolios, CLEP exams, etc.

Appeal of Program

Prior learning credits; individualized curriculum.

University of Baltimore

Mr. Carlo Gizzi, Director of Adult Degree Programs
1420 N. Charles Street
Baltimore, MD 21201
Phone: (410) 837-4680
Toll free:
Fax: (410) 837-4860
Founded: 1925
Accrediting Agency: Middle States Association
Number of students: 5,000
Number of adult students: 50

Representative Degrees

B.A.	All majors
	All of our majors, both in College of Liberal Arts and the School of Business.
B.S.	All Majors
B.A.	Jurisprudence
	Can do this through either the College of Liberal Arts or the School of Business.
B.S.	Jurisprudence
	Can do this through either the College of Liberal Arts or the School of Business.

Appeal of Program

Extensive offering of evening classes. Evening classes meet one night per week.

University of Bridgeport

Mr. Andrew Nelson, Dean of Admissions and
  Financial Aid
380 University Avenue
Bridgeport, CT 06601
Phone: (203) 576-4552
Toll free: (800) 972-9488
Fax: (203) 576-4941
Founded: 1927
Accrediting Agency: New England Association
Number of students: 1,939
Number of adult students: 900

Representative Degrees

M.S.	Human Nutrition
	Classes meet each weekend for 18 months.
M.S.	Electrical Engineering
M.S.	Computer Engineering
M.S.	Computer Science
M.S.	Mechanical Engineering

Appeal of Program

Small class size; accelerated format; weekend format; specialized services.

University of California, Santa Barbara

Mrs. Susan Fauroat, Student Affairs Officer
UCSB Ventura Center
3585 Maple Street, Suite 112
Ventura, CA 93003
Phone: (805) 644-7261
Toll free:
Fax: (805) 644-7268
Founded:
Accrediting Agency: Western Association
Number of students: 18,120
Number of adult students: 120

Representative Degrees

B.A.	Anthropology
B.A.	English
B.A.	History
B.A.	Interdisciplinary Studies
	Live, in-person instruction at night; television of courses from main campus throughout the day.
M.A.	Computer Science

Appeal of Program

Time of offerings; flexibility or homework; convenience to home; quality education.

University of Central Texas

Dr. Kathy Snead, Director of Student Services
PO Box 1416
Killeen, TX 76540
Phone: (817) 526-8262
Toll free:
Fax: (817) 526-8403
Founded: 1973
Accrediting Agency: Southern Association
Number of students: 900
Number of adult students: 702

Representative Degrees

B.S.	Business Administration, Psychology, Interdisciplinary
	Night, weekend, and accelerated courses.
B.S.W.	Social Work
B.S.	Criminal Justice
	Some accelerated offerings.

M.S.   Management, Counseling
        Psychology, Educational
        Psychology

University of Connecticut

Priscilla Bakke, Statewide Program Coordinator
    for BGS
U-56C, One Bishop Circle
Storrs, CT 06269
Phone: (203) 486-3832
Toll free: (800) 622-9907
Fax: (203) 486-3845
Founded: 1881
Accrediting Agency: New England Association
Number of students: 25,000
Number of adult students: 900
Representative Degrees
    B.G.S.   Individualized
              Day and night classes during the
              week.
Appeal of Program
Flexible curriculum; individualized major; price;
convenience; liberal transfer policies.

University of Delaware

Ms. Anne Adkins, Credit Programs Manager
Room 205 John M. Clayton Hall
University of Delaware
Newark, DE 19716
Phone: (302) 831-1119
Toll free:
Fax: (302) 831-1077
Founded: 1743
Accrediting Agency: Middle States Association
Number of students: 21,700
Number of adult students: 300
Representative Degrees
    B.A.   English
    B.A.   History
    B.A.   Computer and Information
            Science
    B.S.   Accounting
    B.A.   Psychology

Appeal of Program
Evening format; disciplines.

University of Denver

Miss Gigi Camas, Executive Assistant
2211 S. Josephine Street
Denver, CO 80208
Phone: (303) 871-4594
Toll free:
Fax: (303) 871-3303
Founded: 1983
Accrediting Agency: North Central Association
Number of students: 1,700
Number of adult students: 850
Representative Degrees
    M.S.S.   Master of Special Studies
    M.C.I.   Master of Computer Information
    M.E.P.   Master of Environmental Policy
    M.H.S.   Master of Healthcare Systems
    M.L.S.   Master of Liberal Studies
Appeal of Program
Courses are at night and on weekends and are
very convenient for working adults.

University of Evansville

Dr. Lynn Penland, Program Director
Center for Continuing Education
1800 Lincoln Avenue
Evansville, IN 47722
Phone: (812) 479-2981
Toll free: (800) 423-8633
Fax: (812) 474-4079
Founded: 1854
Accrediting Agency: North Central Association
Number of students: 2,700
Number of adult students: 125
Representative Degrees
    B.A.   Liberal studies
    B.S.   External Studies-Organizational
            Studies

The University of Iowa

Mr. Scot Wilcox, Senior Educational Advisor
The University of Iowa
116 International Center
Iowa City, IA 52242
Phone: (319) 335-2575
Toll free: (800) 272-6430
Fax: (319) 335-2740
Founded: 1847
Accrediting Agency: North Central Association
Number of students: 29,000
Number of adult students: 436

Representative Degrees

B.L.S.   Bachelor of Liberal Studies
This is an external degree;
students need never come on
campus.

Appeal of Program

The BLS offers flexibility and convenience for those whose lifestyles or location prevent attending college full-time or on-campus. Educational advisors available through toll-free number to help students develop curriculum to fit personal needs.

University of Louisville

Ms. Lynn Bacon, Director of Admissions-School
    Relations
Admissions Office-Houchens Building
University of Louisville
Louisville, KY 40292
Phone: (502) 852-6168
Toll free:
Fax: (502) 852-0685
Founded: 1798
Accrediting Agency: Southern Association
Number of students: 21,826
Number of adult students: 9,685

Representative Degrees

Many degrees can be obtained through night or weekend courses.

Appeal of Program

Scheduling of courses; variety of course offerings.

University of Maine

Ms. Barbara Howard, Academic Advisor
Continuing Education Division
5713 Chadbourne Hall, Room 122
University of Maine
Orono, ME 04469
Phone: (207) 581-3142
Toll free:
Fax: (207) 581-3141
Founded: 1862
Accrediting Agency: New England Association
Number of students: 11,000
Number of adult students: 150

Representative Degrees

B.U.S.   University Studies

Appeal of Program

Evening classes and flexibility to self-design the degree to fit individual needs.

University of Mary

Sr. Gerard Wald, Coordinator of Adult Learning
7500 University Drive
Bismark, ND 58504
Phone: (701) 255-7500
Toll free:
Fax: (701) 255-7687
Founded: 1959
Accrediting Agency: North Central Association
Number of students: 1,850
Number of adult students: 650

Representative Degrees

B.S.   Business Administration
A combination of delivery
methods.

B.S.   Social and Behavioral Sciences
A combination of delivery
methods.

B.S.   Computer Information Systems
A combination of delivery
methods.

B.S.   Accounting
A combination of delivery
methods.

Appeal of Program

Convenience; quality; hospitality.

University of Massachusetts, Amherst

Elisabeth Bowman, Marketing Coordinator
Video Instructional Program
College of Engineering, Marcus Hall
University of Massachusetts, Box 35115
Amherst, MA 01003
Phone: (413) 545-0063
Toll free:
Fax: (413) 545-1227
Founded: 1974
Accrediting Agency: New England Association
Number of students: 1,110
Number of adult students: 220
Representative Degrees

M.S.	Electrical and Computer Engineering Complete master's program; same instruction as on-campus.
M.S.	Engineering Management

Appeal of Program
Convenience and flexibility of a video-based, distance-learning rogram that offers a university education to working professionals from across the country.

University of Massachusetts, Dartmouth

Ms. Barbara Brown, Staff Associate/Counselor
285 Old Westport Rd.
North Dartmouth, MA 02747
Phone: (508) 999-8041
Toll free:
Fax: (508) 999-8621
Founded: 1969
Accrediting Agency: New England Association
Number of students: 5,819
Number of adult students: 941
Representative Degrees

B.A.	English Literature option as well as writing communication option.
B.A.	Humanities/Social Science
B.A.	Psychology
B.A.	Sociology Criminal justice option as well as anthropology option (starting at junior standing.)
B.S.	Management, Accounting

University of Memphis

Ms. Claire Lowry, Advisor, University College
G1 Johnson Hall
University of Memphis
Memphis, TN 38152
Phone: (901) 678-2716
Toll free:
Fax: (901) 678-4913
Founded:
Accrediting Agency: Southern Association
Number of students: 20,000
Number of adult students: 10,000
Representative Degrees

B.P.S.	Individual Studies Self-designed degree programs, credit given for experiential learning.
B.L.S.	Individual Studies Self-designed degree programs, credit given for experiential learning.

Appeal of Program
Flexibility; ability to graduate in a shorter time.

University of Miami

Louise Sevilla, Director of Collegiate Studies
P.O. Box 248005
Coral Gables, FL 33124
Phone: (305) 284-4000
Toll free:
Fax: (305) 284-6279
Founded: 1926
Accrediting Agency: Southern Association
Number of students: 12,000
Number of adult students: 250
Representative Degrees

B.A.	Continuing Studies Students select area of concentration.

Appeal of Program
Area of concentration selected by student.

University of New Hampshire

Dr. William Murphy, Dean of Continuing
   Education
Varrette House
6 Garrison Avenue
Durham, NH 03824
Phone: (603) 862-1937
Toll free:
Fax: (603) 862-1113
Founded: 1866
Accrediting Agency: New England Association
Number of students: 12,500
Number of adult students: 233

Representative Degrees

   A.A.   General Studies

Appeal of Program
Quality of instruction.

University of New Haven

Dr. Dany Washington, Institutional Researcher
300 Orange Avenue
West Haven, CT 06516
Phone: (203) 932-7235
Toll free: (800) DIAL-UNH
Fax: (203) 933-5610
Founded: 1920
Accrediting Agency: New England Association
Number of students: 6,000
Number of adult students: 5,049

Representative Degrees

M.B.A.	Variety
M.P.A.	Variety
B.S.	Variety
Sc.D.	Variety
B.A.	Variety

Appeal of Program
Variety of program offerings.

University of Oklahoma

College of Liberal Studies
1700 Asp Avenue
Norman, OK 73072
Phone:
Toll free:

Fax:
Founded: 1890
Accrediting Agency: North Central Association
Number of students: 24,000
Number of adult students:

Representative Degrees

   M.A.   Liberal Studies
                    Combines on-campus seminars
                    with independent study.
   B.A.   Liberal Studies
                    Combines on-campus seminars
                    with independent study.

Appeal of Program
Independent study phases; accelerated completion; degree from OU.

University of Pennsylvania

College of General Studies
3440 Market Street, Suite 100
Philadelphia, PA 19104
Phone: (215) 898-7326
Toll free:
Fax: (215) 573-2053
Founded:
Accrediting Agency: Middle States Association
Number of students: 20,000
Number of adult students: 1,500

Representative Degrees

   A.A.   Full range of arts and sciences
                    majors
                    Students may take courses in the
                    day or evening, full- or part-time;
                    tuition is 1/3 cost of residential
                    day college.
   B.A.   Full range of arts and sciences
                    majors
   M.L.A.   Liberal arts—Individualized
                    Interdisciplinary
                    Students may take courses in the
                    day or evening, full- or part-time;
                    tuition is 1/2 cost of residential
                    day college.

Appeal of Program
Our students must meet the same requirements and earn exactly the same University of Pennsylvania degree as traditional students but at 1/3 of

the cost. No other Ivy League continuing education program offers this benefit.

University of Phoenix

Ms. Tandy Elisala, University Registrar
4615 East Elwood Street
Phoenix, AZ 85072
Phone: (602) 966-5050
Toll free:
Fax: (602) 894-1758
Founded: 1976
Accrediting Agency: North Central Association
Number of students: 19,700
Number of adult students: 18,000
Representative Degrees

B.S.B.	Administration
B.A.	Management
M.B.A.	
M.A.D.	Management

Appeal of Program
Flexible scheduling; classes at night.

The University of Rhode Island

Dr. John Boulmetis, Associate Professor
712 Chafee Social Science Building
Education Department, URI
Kingston, RI 02881
Phone: (401) 792-4159
Toll free:
Fax: (401) 792-5471
Founded: 1892
Accrediting Agency: New England Association
Number of students: 12,000
Number of adult students: 50
Representative Degrees

M.A.	Adult Education

Appeal of Program
Competency-based evening, adult-learner-oriented.

University of Richmond

Dr. James Narduzzi, Dean
School of Continuing Studies
Special Programs Building
Richmond, VA 23173
Phone: (804) 289-8133
Toll free:
Fax: (804) 289-8138
Founded: 1830
Accrediting Agency: Southern Association
Number of students: 4,315
Number of adult students: 558
Representative Degrees

B.A.S.	Humanities and Social Sciences Some Saturday classes; accept CLEP; limited Independent Study.
B.A.S.	Human Resource Management
B.A.S.	Information Processing Systems Some Saturday classes; accept CLEP; limited Independent Study.
B.A.S.	Paralegal Studies Some Saturday classes; accept CLEP; limited Independent Study.

Appeal of Program
Ease of entry and counseling one-step services. Programs developed for adults.

University of San Francisco

Ms. Jan Wilson, Assistant Dean
College of Professional Studies
2130 Fulton Street
San Francisco, CA 94117
Phone: (415) 666-2152
Toll free:
Fax: (415) 666-2793
Founded: 1855
Accrediting Agency: Western Association
Number of students: 7,000
Number of adult students: 1,400
Representative Degrees

M.H.R.O.D.	24-month program; master's project or thesis required; human resources and organization development.

M.P.A.	Master of Public Administration
M.P.A.	Master of Public Administration Concentration in health service administration; 27-month program; comprehensive examinations or thesis.
M.N.A.	Nonprofit Administration 27-month program; comprehensive examination or thesis required.
B.S.	Organizational Behavior Cohort model, adult learning portfolio for 21 months in length; experiential learning can give credit.

Appeal of Program
We offer five regional campuses in San Francisco, San Ramon, Cupertino, and Sacramento, as well as in Orange in Southern California. We have satellite offices in Oakland, Stockton, and Santa Rosa.

University of Sarasota
Ms. Linda Voles, Director of Enrollment
  Management
5250 17th Street
Sarasota, FL 34235
Phone: (813) 379-0404
Toll free: (800) 331-5995
Fax: (813) 379-9464
Founded: 1974
Accrediting Agency: Southern Association
Number of students: 650
Number of adult students: 650

Representative Degrees

D.A.B.	Marketing Eight one-week residencies.
Ed.D.	Educational Leadership Eight one-week residencies.
M.B.A.	Marketing, Management, Independent Studies Seven one-week residencies.
M.A.Ed.	Educational Leadership Seven one-week residencies.
B.A.	Marketing, Management, Independent Studies Eight one-week residencies.

Appeal of Program
Individualized programs of study.

University of Sioux Falls
Sioux Falls College
1101 West 22nd Street
Sioux Falls, SD 57105
Phone: (605) 331-5000
Toll free: (800) 888-1047
Fax: (605) 331-6615
Founded: 1883
Accrediting Agency: North Central Association
Number of students: 1,000
Number of adult students: 500

Representative Degrees

B.A.	Management (degree completion program) One evening a week for 17 months. For students with at least 64 transferable semester hours. Additional general courses may be necessary.
M.A.	Business Administration One evening a week, two-year program.
M.A.	Education Emphasis in reading education.

Appeal of Program
Modular courses; guaranteed courses; one night a week, accelerated; credit available for nontraditional options and life-long learning.

University of South Florida
Dr. James Bell, Interim Director
Bachelor of Independent Studies Program
University of South Florida
Tampa, FL 33620
Phone: (813) 974-4058
Toll free:
Fax: (813) 974-5101
Founded: 1956
Accrediting Agency: Southern Association
Number of students: 35,000
Number of adult students:

Representative Degrees

    B.S.I.   Interdisciplinary Liberal Arts
                      Summer seminars require
                      periodic short-term campus
                      residence.

Appeal of Program

Student proceeds at his or her own pace and for the most part in his or her own setting.

University of Utah

Dr. Marcia McClurg, Director
Center for Adult Development
1195 Annex Building, University of Utah
Salt Lake City, UT 84112
Phone: (801) 581-3228
Toll free:
Fax: (801) 585-5414
Founded: 1850
Accrediting Agency: Northwest Association
Number of students: 27,000
Number of adult students: 90

Representative Degrees

    B.A./B.S.   Business Administration
                  Three-year program.
    E.M.B.A.   Business Administration
                  Two-year program culminating
                  in seminar trip usually held
                  overseas.
    E.M.P.A.   Public Administration
                  Two-year program culminating
                  with a capstone held in Washington D.C.

Appeal of Program

Evening/weekend format; ease of registration; convenience of preparation, such as book buying.

University of West Los Angeles

Ms. Kathi Cervi, Director of Admissions
School of Law
1155 West Arbor Vitae Street
Ingelwood, CA 90301
Phone: (310) 215-4736
Toll free:
Fax: (310) 641-4736
Founded: 1966

Accrediting Agency: Commission of Bar Examiners
Number of students: 550
Number of adult students:

Representative Degrees

    J.D.   Law
                 Part-time: A.M. and P.M.; Full-time: A.M. only.

Appeal of Program

Flexible schedule; affordable tuition; intimate academic environment.

University of Wisconsin-Madison

Karen Al-Ashkar, Advisor, Professional
    Development Degree in Engineering
Engineering Professional Development
432 North Lake Street
Madison, WI 53706
Phone: (608) 262-0133
Toll free:
Fax: (608) 263-3160
Founded:
Accrediting Agency: North Central Association
Number of students: 40,000
Number of adult students:

Representative Degrees

    Graduate   Engineering
    Degrees   Candidate puts together program
                 to achieve degree goals. Uses
                 many media: correspondence,
                 seminars, video formats
                 (audiographic, satellite, traditional).

Appeal of Program

Self-planned program (within our guidelines and requirements) and no residency requirement.

University of Wisconsin-Platteville

Mr. John Adams, Director Extended Degree in
    Business Administration
506 Pioneer Tower, 1 University Plaza
University of Wisconsin Platteville
Platteville, WI 53818
Phone: (608) 342-1468
Toll free: (800) 362-5460

Fax: (608) 342-1460
Founded:
Accrediting Agency: North Central Association
Number of students: 4,500
Number of adult students: 200
Representative Degrees
  B.S.   Business Administration
                Available through correspon-
                dence courses. For Wisconsin
                residents.
Appeal of Program
Flexible; academically challenging; well-defined
goals; highly motivated student body.

University of Wisconsin-River Falls

Dr. Stephen Ridley, Associate Dean
College of Agriculture, UW-River Falls
410 South 3rd Street
River Falls, WI 54022
Phone: (715) 425-3239
Toll free: (800) 228-5421
Fax: (715) 425-3785
Founded: 1874
Accrediting Agency: North Central Associations
Number of students: 5,000
Number of adult students: 80
Representative Degrees
  B.S.   Broad Area Agriculture
                Extended Degree Program, self-
                paced, competency based.
  B.S.   Agricultural Business
                Extended Degree Program, self-
                paced, competency based.
Appeal of Program
Videotaped courses; self-paced.

University of Wisconsin-Superior

Ms. Carolyn Petroske, Director, Extended Degree
  Program
1800 Grand Avenue
Superior, WI 54880
Phone: (715) 394-8487
Toll free:
Fax:

Founded: 1893
Accrediting Agency: North Central Association
Number of students: 2,200
Number of adult students: 450
Representative Degrees
  B.S.   Individualized
                Distance learning program that
                incorporates print material with
                technology. For residents of
                Wisconsin.
Appeal of Program
Flexibility; opportunity to design own major.

Upper Iowa University

Ms. Kersten Shepard, Director of External
  Degree Program and IECL
P.O. Box 1861
605 Washington Street
Fayette, IA 52142
Phone: (319) 425-5283
Toll free: (800) 553-4150
Fax: (319) 425-5353
Founded: 1857
Accrediting Agency: North Central Association
Number of students: 3,175
Number of adult students: 2,634
Representative Degrees
  A.A.   General Business
  B.S.   Public Administration
  B.S.   Elementary Education
  B.S.   Human Resource Management
  B.S.   Public Administration-Law
                Enforcement Emphasis
Appeal of Program
Flexibility; options for degree completion;
reasonable tuition; provide for students needs;
qualified faculty.

Virginia Commonwealth University

Ms. Marcia Zwicker, Director
Office of Academic Advising
812 W. Franklin St.
P.O. Box 843028
Richmond, VA 23284

Phone: (804) 828-2333
Toll free:
Fax: (804) 828-2335
Founded:
Accrediting Agency: Southern Association
Number of students: 21,523
Number of adult students:
Representative Degrees

Various	The university does not have a separate university or college for adults. All of our traditional degree programs are available to adults full-time or part-time, with an integrated program of classes scheduled from 8:00 A.M. to 10:30 P.M. There is a large enrollment of adults in our evening classes.

Vanderbilt University

Mr. Thomas Hambury, Director Executive MBA
   Program
Owen Graduate School of Management
401 21st Avenue South
Nashville, TN 37203
Phone: (615) 322-2513
Toll free:
Fax: (615) 343-2293
Founded: 1873
Accrediting Agency: Southern Association
Number of students: 9,000
Number of adult students: 100
Representative Degrees

M.B.A.	Executive MBA Program Class begins in August with week in residence at conference center. Ongoing classes meet alternate weekends for two consecutive days (Friday and Saturday) for 22 months.

Appeal of Program
Top-quality national reputation of program; ability to work full-time while completing studies.

Warner Pacific College

Mr. David Matthews, Associate Director of
   Admissions
Degree Completion Program
2219 SE 68th Ave.
Portland, OR 97215
Phone: (503) 775-4366
Toll free: (800) 582-7885
Fax: (503) 775-8853
Founded:
Accrediting Agency: Northwest Association
Number of students: 700
Number of adult students: 233
Representative Degrees

B.S.	Business Administration
B.S.	Human Development

Appeal of Program
One evening per week class schedule; modular class design; PLE system.

Warner Southern College

Dr. Brian Satterlee, Dean, Adult and Continuing
   Education
5301 US Highway 27 South
Lake Wales, FL 33853
Phone: (813) 638-7240
Toll free:
Fax: (813) 638-1472
Founded: 1967
Accrediting Agency: Southern Association
Number of students: 593
Number of adult students: 248
Representative Degrees

B.A.	Organizational Management

Appeal of Program
Quality of curriculum and faculty; low cost; convenience; time frames.

Wayland Baptist University

Mr. Vernon Norris, Associate Registrar
1900 West 7th Street
Box 574-WBU
Plainview, TX 79072
Phone: (806) 296-5521
Toll free:

Fax:
Founded: 1908
Accrediting Agency: Southern Association
Number of students: 3,438
Number of adult students: 2,556
Representative Degrees

A.A.S.	Business Administration, Religion, Human Services, Occupational Education
B.S.O.E.	Business Administration, Religion, Human Services, Occupational Education, Vocational Education
Master's	Business Administration
Master's	Education
A.A.S.	Human Resources

Appeal of Program
Documented work-experience credit and prior-learning credit.

Wayne State University

Dr. Roslyn Schindler, Director
Interdisciplinary Studies Program, WSU
6001 Cass Avenue, Room 464
Detroit, MI 48202
Phone: (313) 577-4627
Toll free:
Fax: (313) 577-8585
Founded: 1973
Accrediting Agency: North Central Association
Number of students: 650
Number of adult students: 650
Representative Degrees

B.I.S.	Interdisciplinary Studies Mostly nights, some weekends, some video format, some computer-based, some audio format.
B.T.I.S.	Technical and Interdisciplinary Studies Mostly nights, some weekends, some video format, some computer-based, some audio format.
M.I.S.	Interdisciplinary Studies Some computer-based.

Appeal of Program
Flexible format designed for working adults; 23 full-time, resident, largely tenured faculty; interdisciplinary curriculum. Undergraduate program is excellent preparation for graduate school.

Wentworth Institute of Technology

Mr. Timothy McDonald, Marketing/Recruitment Manager
Office of Professional and Continuing Studies
550 Huntington Avenue
Boston, MA 02115
Phone: (617) 427-9010
Toll free: (800) 322-9481
Fax: (617) 427-2852
Founded: 1904
Accrediting Agency: New England Association
Number of students: 3,000
Number of adult students: 600
Representative Degrees

A.A.S.	Architectural Technology
A.A.S.	Biomedical Instrumentation
A.A.S.	Building Construction Technology
A.A.S.	Electromechanical Systems
B.S.	Architectural Systems Engineer

West Coast University

Mr. Roger Miller, Dean of Admissions and Registrar
Admission Office
440 Shatto Place
Los Angeles, CA 90020
Phone: (213) 427-4400
Toll free: (800) 2484-WCU
Fax: (213) 380-4362
Founded: 1909
Accrediting Agency: Western Association
Number of students: 1,500
Number of adult students: 1,500
Representative Degrees

M.B.A.	Various degrees in nine majors
M.S.	Engineering, concentration in 5 areas

M.I.B.A.	International Business
B.S.	Computer Science, Business Administration
A.A.	Business Administration, Engineering

Appeal of Program
Year-round classes after work and on weekends; practicing professional instructors in the classroom; small class size.

West Virginia University

Dr. Ann Paterson, Director, Regents B.A.
  Program
207 SSC West Virginia University
P.O. Box 6287
Morgantown, WV 26506
Phone: (304) 293-5441
Toll free:
Fax: (304) 293-7490
Founded: 1867
Accrediting Agency: North Central Association
Number of students: 23,000
Number of adult students: 212
Representative Degrees

B.A.	General Education

Appeal of Program
The absence of a major means that no single course is required. Great flexibility. The possibility of "course equivalent credit" for prior experience is also popular and accommodates most vocational training and associate programs.

Western Baptist College

Ms. Nancy Martyn, Director, Adult Studies
  Division
5000 Deer Park Drive S.E.
Salem, OR 97301
Phone: (503) 375-7590
Toll free: (800) 764-1383
Fax: (503) 375-7583
Founded: 1934
Accrediting Agency: Northwest Association
Number of students: 565
Number of adult students: 100

Representative Degrees

B.S.	Management and Communications One track utilizes the computer/modem and bulletin board service with periodic weekend visits to the campus.
B.S.	Family Studies

Appeal of Program
Convenient format; knowledge and experience of the instructors; caring, supportive staff and cohort groups.

Western Illinois University

Dr. Hans Moll, Director, Nontraditional
  Programs
5 Horrabin Hall
Macomb, IL 61455
Phone: (309) 298-1929
Toll free:
Fax: (309) 298-2226
Founded: 1898
Accrediting Agency: North Central Association
Number of students: 12,500
Number of adult students: 2,700
Representative Degrees

B.A.	Individually designed program through Board of Governors degree.

Appeal of Program
Flexible; Students are free to select their own courses based on the students' educational goals. Credits are earned in a variety of ways.

Western Oregon State College

Ms. Dori Beeks, Director, Continuing Education
345 North Monmouth Avenue
Western Oregon State College
Monmouth, OR 97364
Phone: (503) 838-8483
Toll free:
Fax: (503) 838-8473
Founded: 1856
Accrediting Agency: Northwest Association
Number of students: 3,900

Number of adult students: 300
Representative Degrees

B.A./B.S.	Fire Services Administration Student can complete the core of the major by correspondence. The rest may be done in the classroom and by videotape.

Westminster College

Carol Yova, Director, Lifelong Learning Program
South Market Street
New Wilmington, PA 16172
Phone: (412) 946-7353
Toll free: (800) 942-8033
Fax: (412) 946-7171
Founded: 1852
Accrediting Agency: Middle States Association
Number of students: 1,500
Number of adult students: 100
Representative Degrees

B.A.	Accounting Day courses also available.
B.A.	Business Administration
B.A.	English Day courses also available.
B.A.	History Day courses also available.

Appeal of Program
Accelerated format (nine weeks—one night a week per class); resident faculty; small and safe campus.

Westminster College of Salt Lake City

Beverly Levy, Associate Director of Admissions
1840 South 1300 East
Salt Lake City, UT
Phone:
Toll free:
Fax:
Founded: 1875
Accrediting Agency: New England Association
Number of students: 2,200
Number of adult students: 1,200

Representative Degrees

B.A.	Business, Accounting
B.A.	Communication
B.A.	Computer Science
M.B.A.	Accounting
Master's	Professional Communication

Appeal of Program
Flexibility; small class size.

Winona State University

James Erickson, Director, Continuing Education
Box 5838
Winona, MN 55987
Phone: (507) 457-5080
Toll free: (800) 342-5978
Fax: (507) 457-5571
Founded: 1868
Accrediting Agency: North Central Association
Number of students: 7,000
Number of adult students:
Representative Degrees

B.A.	Individualized Study The degree uses a combination of traditional classes, correspondence, video, computer, audio, and telecommunications methods for completing the degree.

Appeal of Program
Flexible design of degree courses.

Wittenberg University

Dr. Paul Parlato, Dean, School for Community Education
School of Continuing Education
P.O. Box 720
Springfield, OH 45501
Phone: (513) 327-7012
Toll free: (800) 677-7558
Fax: (513) 327-6340
Founded: 1845
Accrediting Agency: North Central Association
Number of students: 2,150
Number of adult students: 125

Representative Degrees

B.A.	Liberal Studies
	Choice of concentrations: Organization Studies, Human Services Administration, Culture and Technology
B.A.	All majors offered during the day.

Appeal of Program

Rigorous liberal arts experience; careful advising; strong faculty.

Xavier University

Ms. Susan Wideman, Dean
Center for Adult and Part-Time Students
3800 Victory Parkway
Cincinnati, OH 45207
Phone: (513) 745-3356
Toll free: (800) 344-4698
Fax: (513) 745-2969
Founded: 1831
Accrediting Agency: North Central Association
Number of students: 6,180
Number of adult students: 3,053

Representative Degrees

M.A.	Psychology Two-year, full-time program.
M.A.	Theology
M.H.A.	Hospital and Health Administration
M.B.A.	Human Resources
M.Ed.	Variety

Appeal of Program

Scheduling convenience; accelerated (in some cases).

Index